The Luberon Garden

The
Luberon Garden

A Provençal Story of Apricot Blossom, Truffles and Thyme

ALEX DINGWALL-MAIN

Illustrations by Don Grant

EBURY PRESS
LONDON

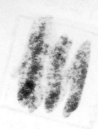

First published in Great Britain in 2001

3 5 7 9 10 8 6 4

Ebury Press
Random House · 20 Vauxhall Bridge Road · London SW1V 2SA

Random House Australia Pty Limited
20 Alfred Street · Milsons Point · Sydney · New South Wales 2061 · Australia

Random House New Zealand Limited
18 Poland Road · Glenfield · Auckland 10 · New Zealand

Random House (Pty) Limited
Endulini · 5A Jubilee Road · Parktown 2193 · South Africa

The Random House Group Limited Reg. No. 954009

www.randomhouse.co.uk

Papers used by Ebury Press are natural, recyclable products made from wood grown in sustainable forests.

A CIP catalogue record for this book is available from the British Library.

ISBN 0 09 187815 2

Designed by Lovelock & Co.

Printed and bound by Mackays of Chatham plc, Kent

Author photo by Laurence Cendrowicz

Illustrations © Don Grant

Contents

Acknowledgememts 6

Introduction 9

CHAPTER ONE In the Beginning 20

CHAPTER TWO Up and Walking 53

CHAPTER THREE Gloves in a Cold Climate 92

CHAPTER FOUR Be Prepared 123

CHAPTER FIVE Highly Sprung 166

CHAPTER SIX Going Swimmingly 201

CHAPTER SEVEN The Sinking Garden of Menerbylon 223

CHAPTER EIGHT Time Out 238

CHAPTER NINE Back to School 278

CHAPTER TEN The Home Run 309

Plant Lists 318

Thank You

R. Archer-Baronio, R. Baronio, G. Clark, T. Dingwall-Main
P. Eddy, D. Goodwin, F. Goodwin, D. Grant, H. MacDonald
P. Micou, A. Ravenscroft, V. Souffron, S. Waldon

Author's Note This is a true story. However, for the sake of a better narrative events have sometimes been relayed out of order. The names and identifying characteristics of many people and places have been changed to protect privacy.

To Nicky

For letting me be what I am when I am it

Introduction

There are enough books about Provence to make any self-respecting coffee table throw up its legs in submission. Quite apart from the library of travel books and best sellers, there are stacks of lavish photographic books loaded with sensational shots covering everything from the simple to the ornate. Large-format pages of medieval villages, lavender fields and olive orchards, of markets, churches and swooping countryside. There are books on interiors and books on cooking with local recipes, on truffles, and Provençal herbs, crafts and antiques, wines and wild boar. There are architectural books dissecting the vernacular of little cabins and chateaux, with farmhouses and manor houses in between, and there are, of course, gardening books. Lots of them. Usually accompanied by a barrow full of glossy pictures with quite-often questionable captions.

This particular gardening book is different. It has no photographs, and only a handful of drawings to help tell the tale. It is a story about how a wonderful little garden was restored and recreated, sometimes against the odds, on the slopes of the Luberon valley, in the village of Ménerbes, deep in the heart of Provence. It is also the story of a garden designer and his family taking up the challenge of moving from London and setting up tools in this much-loved corner of the Mediterranean.

Despite the threat of overexposure, it remains a region of rare beauty, seducing most that visit to return time and time again and occasionally to put down roots. It is quite different from all other parts of France and has always held a fascination for outsiders. History shows evidence that the Greeks and Romans, the Moors and marauders of the north have all left their stamp. It is also a country of climatic extremes; fiery summer temperatures climb to a neck-sweating 40°C and in winter can whack down to a finger-numbing -15°.

I had been running a landscaping practice for some twenty-five years, and although my work was widespread, I was based in London. I had recently been magnetised by a beautiful English girl called Nicky. She was hundreds of years younger, but none the less it easily led to marriage, and I immediately set about lobbying her to move out of London.

'We could find something not too far away,' I promised, knowing that she wasn't ready to drop the high-fashioned, high-powered overdrive life of a girl about town and turn into a green Land Rover driving, deep Dorset country lass.

'Perhaps St Albans?' I suggested, knowing nothing of the area, other than it was close to London. Being from Scotland anything south of the border was a bit of a tragedy.

'St Tropez, more like,' she replied.

Thus started a chain of discussions that moved us from a

possible near-suburban existence just outside London, to an old farmhouse in the South of France.

The reasoning behind moving to this part of Europe was two-fold. Firstly we would be going to an area where it was on the cards I would find work. There was a lot of development of old properties going on, carried out by a cosmopolitan crowd, many of whom had spectacularly successful careers. Secondly the weather was good. If you were going to move, why not move closer to the sun?

There was going to be a steep and slippery learning curve. Not only about language, culture and being without old friends, but about plants as well. It is a difficult and challenging place to get a hold on horticulture.

Gardening, generally speaking, tends to catch up with people a bit later in life. It struggles to fit into youth culture much beyond an occasional crop of marijuana being furtively grown in the allotments of leisure, unless of course it has been chosen as a profession. However, as first homes are acquired, and children born, the benefits of this pastime become increasingly apparent. Therapeutic and educational, gardening is deeply instilled into the human condition. There are people who, denied the luxury of space, will grow a runner bean plant out of an old baked bean tin just for the brilliant scarlet flower it brings to a window sill.

I believe that those who bemoan not having green fingers have simply not opened the doors of plant perception. Having green fingers, surely, is nothing more or less than a simple understanding that plants in all their manifestations are a living entity, and as such require care and attention in much the same way as humans and animals. By looking after them, giving what is needed, removing what is harmful, they respond and reward the gardener, amateur and professional alike. Speaking to plants, however dotty it may sound to the uninitiated, is good practice. Plants probably have some kind of nervous system that reacts to the ether of thought, perhaps more than the literal spoken word. So if you are shy of being heard discussing the traumas of young buds leaving home, go telepathic.

It was exciting when the first commission came through. It put the first bolt into place, and gave us a glimmer of hope that we might be on the right track.

That dull distillery, which bottles up insecurity and sells it wholesale to the self employed, lingers deep in one's psyche. In my time I've been sucked up by success, and spat out by failure. I have spent lots of money I had and even more I didn't have, I've surfed on the wave of recognition and slumped behind the soulless folds of obscurity. Now, more balanced in my middle age, I play the game a little more wisely, my judgements more considered and my awareness more consistent, but it never stops me from being flattered when someone invites me to step into the work arena with them.

New jobs or projects arrive by various channels: sometimes it might be a bit of editorial somebody has read, or a well-placed card in the palm of a conversation, but more probably it comes by word of mouth. Someone who knows what I do, or has heard about it, passes on the information to a friend who in turn calls the office, activating the first round of what might turn into a commission. The initial conversation is best kept to the point, a quick outline of requirements given, a time and date for the inaugural meeting, telephone and fax numbers exchanged and that's it. No need to discuss parenting problems or how unexpectedly small the world is or, come to that, money. It is ill advised to give a fee quote over the telephone having not even seen the site, and anyway the first meeting is free. Client and designer need to sniff each other out, need to find a common link in some way. If you're going to work together, develop ideas and cash cheques, it is important to like one another's attitudes at least, and if a mutual sense of humour emerges, so much the better. First impressions may count, but it's the portfolio that either inspires confidence or brings the meeting rather haltingly to a close.

Not all designer/client relationships are made in heaven and, despite reputations being intact, and character references as good as any dating agency could produce, things can still go wrong. I once met an Indian gentleman who asked me to help him with his garden. He lived in a part of north London where the streets are paved with gold Rolls Royces, where the architects manage to juggle Spanish Inquisition, Indian Empire and neo-Georgian influences with some success, and the planning departments have rubber-stamped the development of expensive lots of land with dubious global taste.

The first meeting was a little bizarre. I was ushered into the front of his brand new limousine, apparently to be taken round the corner to see another of his houses, or gardens. Unfortunately because I am very tall and the Indian's wife very small, I was caught by cramp as I tried to bend my legs into the foot well of the passenger side. Fumbling for the adjustment lever I quickly realised that everything was electrical and the pre-set positions of the seat were logged in with an unbreakable code. My prospective client, who had not yet fully acquainted himself with the upgrades and mechanical assets of his new machine, was equally busy. He was jiggling the master switches on the other side in the vain hope of helping me. In fact he was cancelling out all my promising work, pushing me inexorably towards the dashboard like the villain in a Bond movie. My mounting distress evidently changed his mind about going anywhere and, hauling me from the wreckage, blissfully releasing my legs back towards a more dignified position, he guided me through his palatial abode and out onto the terrace.

There, pressed up close to the industrial-sized sliding glass doors of his deep-piled sitting room, skulked a dying swimming pool. Like many old pools in Britain it had suffered badly from unkind winters and was in need of a total overhaul. 'As it obviously needs to be virtually rebuilt, why don't we relocate it further away from the house and perhaps screen it from view a bit?' I suggested.

'What!' he was incredulous. 'How will people know I have a swimming pool if they can't see it?'

His logic was faultless and my commission was rapidly heading down the malfunctioning filtering system. However with a little side-stepping, a few artful remarks about my fondness for alabaster and precious metal fountains, a leaning towards Buddhism and my absolute ease in the company of a briefcase full of cash, we progressed cautiously into a commission.

It was easier with The Owners in Ménerbes.

Richard Owner, an American Italian and his Scottish-born wife, Ros, live mostly in New York, but for some twelve years they have also owned a small house in the medieval town of Ménerbes, about 40 kilometres south-east of Avignon.

This ancient ridge-top, stone-built village with a population of a little over a thousand was first recorded as Menerba in 1081 and was named after the Roman goddess Minerva. It appears to be in the shape of a ship with a bow and stern, and has been inhabited by humans since prehistoric times. The only two dolmens in the Vaucluse (megalithic tombs with large flat slabs laid on upright stones, à la Stonehenge) are nearby. The Roman occupation ended with the Saxon invasions in the sixth century and it was here that Queen Joan (La Reine Jeanne) ruled during the fourteenth century. A period of religious wars ensued between Catholics and Protestants, only ceasing when Henri de Navarre, the future Henry IV, intervened in 1578.

With the end of the twentieth century came a storming of another sort: Peter Mayle. Now, it isn't because of him that we came to live here. Promise. Nicky had known and loved the region since childhood, but it is impossible to ignore his input into promoting the area into the conscience of several squillion people. For ages after we arrived, if we told anybody in Britain where we lived, there was this boringly predictable reaction and Mayle's name was inevitably trotted out. It was assumed we must have been seduced by his best seller *A Year in Provence.* There was a split between those 'old schoolers'; the ones who were P.M. (pre Mayle) and proud of it – some were even able to laugh publicly at the wit, and panache, of the writer's turn of phrase; and the poor old A.M. (after Mayle) who had to suffer the ignominy of their late arrival, pretending not to have read the book, but to have discovered the joys and jubilations of Provence entirely in their own right.

I was impressed by one confident and charming Englishman we met who, having retired early from a life of selling insurance,

decided to become a traveller with means. He bought a 13-metre Mercedes Benz chassis and had a house built on to the back. It was complete with double bedroom, en suite bathroom, dressing quarters, a fully equipped kitchen, and a drawing room that would have left most caravanners dribbling with envy and lust. The driving room, or captain's deck, ached with up-to-the-minute navigation equipment and digital communication systems. He had ventured forth.

He said that as he was rounding the cape-of-good-luck, he stumbled across a second-hand bookshop wherein he discovered a well-worn copy of *AYIP*. As he lay on his newly liberated hair, long and symbolic, blowing a spliff with a young Irish bride in his arms, reading the said literature, he had a smallish revelation and instantly became a zealous advocate. Next morning he programmed the Merc, headed south, and by the end of the week had bought a perfect little farmhouse with pool and desirable view. I thought it commendable the way he openly admitted that it was his dose of the Daily Mayle that was absolutely why he was here.

These days all is calm and the village gives shelter to, amongst others, a galaxy of painters, musicians and writers. I do feel a bit guilty writing about Ménerbes, and exposing it again, but things just worked out that way, and the garden that sits at the centre of this story just so happened to be in that village. Voilà!

The spectacular view that The Owners have of the Luberon valley, as it stretches out for miles beneath them, is more than a match for the vista of Central Park from their apartment on the Upper East Side of Manhattan.

I had met Richard and Ros before. But it wasn't until they rang me one day to say that they had bought this house in the same village, with a garden, or at least the space for a garden, that I had really had much chance to talk to them. Ros had worked as a painter and sculptor in the '70s, having had exhibitions at, amongst others, the Frank Marino Gallery in NY, The Royal Academy Summer Exhibition, and the Gulbenkian in London. She had then turned her hand to acting and singing, a part of her career that culminated with a successful one-woman show in NY. Now she was writing a book. A period of her life had been immortalised in a West End play, written and produced by her ex-lover. After a successful revival of the play, she was determined to tell the story from her point of view.

Richard is also an artist, having gained a degree in fine arts from Brown University, Rhode Island, and the University of New Mexico. He later founded the Pyxidium Press and set up the Yale Centre for British Art. He has also taught at the University of Illinois, Chicago, The College of Art, Sheffield, UK and Kenyan College, USA. Nowadays he concentrates on his business of interior design and contracting in Manhattan.

Between us we were going to tackle a project that would run the gamut of emotions. It would take us out on a limb and drop us into the quagmire. It would lift us up by the heart and fly us into the sun. We would ring our hands with despondency and clap them with appreciation.

And they weren't even here most of the time.

CHAPTER ONE

In the Beginning

It was a cold November night following a grey day with short horizons, the kind of day that limits your imagination. A stillness hung in the air and the stars were doing their shining somewhere else as I began to close the shutters and lock the back door. The two cats squinted at the kitchen light from under the stone table, like hobos watching a soup kitchen, willing me to dish out a nightcap in the form of a little warm milk. They know me to be an easy touch in the winter months.

We had inherited these two sisters when we arrived nearly six years ago. We were sitting in the notaire's office in Bonnieux, finalising the exchange of ownership with our vendors. We had just reached the critical moment when Le Maître leaves the room to find some paper clips, or iron his shoe laces in order to let the shady side of the dealings commence. It is that golden moment of farce, which anybody who has ever bought a property in France will know only too well. That little mellifluous moment during which there is a rather embarrassing, almost furtive and guilty exchange of cash, to supplement the official offer that the notaire has been completing on behalf of both parties. As the 'black' hung in the space between fingers giving and fingers taking, as the smiles of mutual pleasure were about to break and new lives begin, Mr Vendor, a small and somewhat hen-pecked chap whispered:

'We couldn't catch them.'

'Couldn't catch what?' asked our freelance estate agent who was brokering the deal, and clearly not looking for an interruption at this most critical moment.

'The kittens,' croaked the old boy, with watery eyes.

'I'll just be taking the cash then,' offered his large and determined wife.

With a mother hen countenance, she extended her hard-worked hand the last few inches towards the liquid asset, her fingers in pinching mode, her eyes busy checking over her ample shoulder to make sure that the great man was still outside. Any moment now he would reappear and no one wanted to be caught grappling with several hundred thousand francs in an undignified fashion. We withdrew the bundle of booty a little and enquired how many kittens, how old and what were they going to do about them.

'Two,' he trembled on. 'We couldn't catch them,' he said, ringing his cap and looking at Nicky imploringly. 'Perhaps *you* could look after them? They are *very* timid and won't go into the house.' He was practically blubbing by now. The tension was rising in the little room. It was like being in the Oval Office as Jack Kennedy worked out what to do with the Russians in Cuba.

'C'est un possibilité,' Nicky said falteringly. 'Depends if they hang around or not, they might be frightened off, they might ...'

'Good, that's settled then,' said the wife and she nearly fell off her undersized chair as she lurched forward in the general direction of her pension. And indeed it was. The kittens, one black and white, one tabby, became part of the deal and were duly christened Posy and Billy Tey. It was better than Purr Têtre.

I gave the outside world a last cursory glance and went indoors, patted the lights, turned off the dog, and went to bed thinking about what was needed for the meeting the following morning with The Owners, our new clients in Ménerbes. I awoke next morning to:

'Dada, you know somethin', the garden's turned into a cake.'

Theo, our son, who had recently pulled off becoming three with consummate ease, was standing beside the bed with a worried look on his face, urging me to get up and see for myself.

'You going to eat it?' I yawned, stirring slowly and sounding patronising. 'No no, you must look, it's having a birthday party.'

He was right, it had turned into cake. White as the icing he had helped his Mum make a few weeks previously for his birthday party. Incredibly, it had quietly snowed an enormous amount during the night. A deep luxuriant carpet of extra-virgin snow covered the garden and countryside with a pile that must have been at least 50cms deep, drifting up to more than a meter in places. Trees, shrubs and various garden miscellanies had all surrendered to a soft thick overcoat of white coldness. It all looked slightly sterilised, as if a team of medics had worked on it overtime. Not a sign of mud nor mishap anywhere to be seen.

It is perfectly normal to have snow in Provence. It had happened our first winter, and although we had not really realised such a thing went on in the South of France, we were happy to see it, because, for a few days it hid all the mess and rubble that the builders had spread around the place. It kind of cleaned everything up and helped us imagine what things might look like one day in the far distant future when the builders finally left, probably having died of old age. It is not, however, normal for it to fall so heavily in one night, and definitely not in November. We have all become accustomed to each year throwing up its new record breaker. Every July 'it has never been this dry or stormy'. Every autumn 'it has never been this hot, this low on water'. Memories are short, but here we had a unanimous verdict 'there had never been snow like this in November'. Ever. Well certainly not for thirty years.

Through the window I could see the little birds busy at work on the small string bags of seed that we had put up for them. Bearded reedlings, corn buntings, blue tits and of course the ubiquitous sparrows. Hopping nervously in and out, the black-eared wheater and, believe it or not, the Dartford warbler, who I thought had been locked up years ago. Up in the old almond tree, two pairs of unblinking eyes and chattering teeth, hung on every peck and watched the feathery activities with mounting optimism.

Naturally the great excitement and the promise of snow games, snow-men, skiing, tobogganing, tin-traying and Cresta Running, brought breakfast to a premature finish. 'I'm going swimming in it,' announced Theo, getting it all mixed up, but as he was poured into his coat and wellies, his determination was mounting. I wrapped myself up and ventured outside. Beautiful undoubtedly, doubly so now that the sun was announcing itself into a pink-blue sky, but oh Lord... what damage was I about to find? Gingerly I started spoiling the picture by shaking some branches, gently kicking some shrubs, and brushing plants with the back of my hand. The useful hedging plant, *Pittosporum tobira* had been badly smacked about. Split trunks and branches demanded to be bound up. Various standards had collapsed under the strain and broken their trunks, some phormiums were bent into deep shock, and the santolinas everywhere looked like they had been involved in a hit and run. And so it went on, but remarkably most things would recover, picking themselves up and dusting themselves down, showing a resilience that never ceases to amaze.

We were starting our fourth year of gardening in Provence. The first year had been mostly house stuff and some basic ground work, with a stiff, and at times, cruel learning curve. Winter temperatures can badly freeze your biscuits, much harder than Britain, sometimes sinking to a glacial −16°C. That's enough for many plants to fold up their stems and call it a day. Then, just when you've come to terms with, and recovered from, the ice age, in comes a blistering, searing, dry summer, wringing the sweat out of you as it climbs up into the 40s. In between you can have a bit of gardening fun, but you absolutely must check out plant performance figures before buying.

Provence is big. It runs from where we are in the Vaucluse, right up the coast towards St Tropez and beyond, in the Var. Up there the sea keeps the freezing temperatures minimal, with some areas experiencing virtually no frost at all. Of course this makes the selection of plants on the coast much more exotic than we can hope to enjoy. Our first year we tried a few things thinking that if they were well protected they might survive. In went, for example, a line of the beautiful *Dodonaea viscosa* 'Purpurea' with its long, delicate, stretching purple leaves planted thickly at the base of an allée of Florentine cyprus. As the autumn came on the colour darkened, and the effect strengthened. Also being evergreen, I looked forward to their winter input. Wrong. The first heavy frost in late November annihilated the poor darlings without mercy. They looked so sad and beaten up I felt ashamed by my casual approach, especially after being warned. I experimented with several others only to witness the same devastation. In the summer the sun reverses the story, burning leaves with its relentless heat if mistakenly planted in too open a spot. *Acer palmatum* complains in England, here it simply turns into a crisp bush. But at least you can fight the heat with water, giving everything a chance. That is if you have water. But more about that later.

My mind was hauled back into the now by Theo producing his best rendition of the breaststroke, little legs kicking up the snow whilst the flailing arms made waves of white powder. If this had been water he'd probably have been well on the way to Sardinia. He was as happy as Larry until it dawned on him: this stuff is cold, very cold. He suddenly realised that his hands were quietly getting frozen through his mittens, worse, they were hurting. The fun factor evaporated and, rather bewildered by the unkindness of this white matter, he quit. With a minimum exchange of words, a small indication of his contempt for winter sports, he hooked it inside. I went to look for the cars, which had virtually disappeared. I was trying to think about getting to the meeting with The Owners, but of course it was completely out of the question. The driveway was indistinguishable from the fields and impassable. A short phone call produced a mutual agreement: sitting back and doing nothing was the only way forward, for the moment. It's a difficult place this South of France.

That evening we ate a *daube* that Nicky had been cooking most of the day. This is a local meat or poultry dish, a kind of stew that gets adapted into an amazing number of variations according to the different village or towns. She had bought some lamb from the butcher in Bonnieux, and had been simmering it in red wine, seasoned with local herbs, for several hours. It was accompanied by some lightly buttered noodles, coated with the juices of the *daube* and sprinkled with a mixture of Emmenthal and Parmesan. I dug around the wine boxes and found a bottle of Côte Rôtie, one of the best of the Rhône wines, threw a few more logs on the huge open fire, and resigned for the evening.

The next morning I realised that had I been a bit more on the ball the day before, I would have shovelled all the snow off the side road that connects us to the main artery, as soon as I had gone outside. Instead I had wandered around the place like a poet without a cause. Our neighbours had started clearing just as soon as it had stopped snowing. They have 400 years more experience of this little slippery slope than me, and I had unwittingly left it without thinking it through. The net result being that it was frozen and ungrippable. I tried athletically, for a wreck of my age who had recently exacerbated his questionable fitness with a slipped disc, to clear it with pick and spade, but it was hopeless. Chinking and grinding away, I not only lost the battle but was also forced to surrender the war. I hoped there were plenty of rations in the larder.

This could be a long haul. 'I may be some time,' I bleated to anyone in the house that might be listening. It turned out to be four days.

Nicky had called the Mayor's office asking, or demanding that some machine should come and help. 'Ah les nouveaux! Vous avez un petit problème, n'est pas?' Six years and still 'les nouveaux.' I longed for somebody else to move into the commune and take this irritating mantle off our shoulders. Nicky mentioned lightly that we were dying. The central heating had gone off when the electricity failed to function, and the gas boiler needed a spark of some sort to fire it up. The plumber had tried courageously to reach us, but all we had seen was his little white jeep with a black roof getting so far up the hill, twisting slightly to one side, then pitiably disappearing down again. After that the fridge freaked and the freezer was a freeze-free zone – further, we couldn't even get out to the shops. About the only entertainment on hand was watching our two enormous ducks skating on the pond and Theo breaking the ice with a tree stake, whilst being held by a handful of coat from behind. After three days this amusement was beginning to run thinner than the ice. Possi and Billy had migrated up to the neighbour's cosy old barn for the duration, and I had yet to get to my meeting in Ménerbes. It is not easy to conduct garden speak when there's six feet of snow. I find clients' concentration tends to wander a little. I become a bit like a pedlar of fur coats on a beach in the Maldives, but The Owners were only here for a few more days, providing of course the airport was open, and things had to get sorted.

My first meeting with the garden and its owners had been towards the end of September, when the concluding days of summer still hung gently about us but the evenings were already beginning to draw in. It had been agreed that some preliminary drawings showing a few ideas would be in order. This involved photographing the site and giving some undetailed suggestions by making up half a dozen or so overlays, i.e. ideas that are sketched on tracing paper over a photograph, so that the picture is easily identifiable and concepts readable. They are then printed, coloured in and presented with comments, observations and suggestions. It normally works well and doesn't involve too much time or money at the early stages, giving everybody a bash at the project without too much commitment. Trouble here was that because the garden is on such a slope it was impossible to get far enough back to get a good snap. You needed an orang utan who's used to hanging out of a helicopter to take the shots.

The Owners and I had soon found we were happily discussing the world and his wife as well as the garden. What they had bought was two large village houses next door to each other. Entrance was from a narrow little street, either through a rather unprepossessing old garage door or, more poshly, a little further down, via an archetypal carved wooden portal. These two old houses, rather weakly joined at the hip and structurally relying on each other, groaned with age and legend, begging to be hauled into the twenty-first century. Perched as they are on the dramatic slopes of the ridge, with a dazzling view out across the plains below, I could see that the garden was going to have to be on several levels. There would be lots of steps — only useful to somebody who trusted their ticker to be in good working order. We stood high on the upper balcony looking northward and the mid-morning sun, already strong, threw its influence across the valley from the east, highlighting the village, a small chapel and several farmhouses.

A *mas*, the local word for an old farmhouse, tends to be a simple enough structure made of stone from the region and roofed with clay tiles. Indiscriminately added to over the years, the attachments and annexes often lend useful character and charm to the basic box shape. They are sturdily constructed using thick walls and incorporate small insignificant windows on the north side, to minimise intrusion by that bitter wind, the mistral, and have larger, shuttered windows on the south side. A *mas* seldom boasts much of a foundation but most have successfully stood the test of time. Many started life as homes for the hard-working farmers and have managed a metamorphosis from humble abode to chic and fashionable dwellings for the well-do-to. As the *mas* themselves have changed so too have the gardens. Farmers seldom had the money, time, energy or even the inclination to pretty up the areas around the home. A few annuals for a splash of colour and some creepers to give shade would do. Much the same story had been going on with the village houses albeit on a smaller scale. Whilst it is probably the amount of sunshine that makes life in Provence very seductive, it is also the charm of the countryside, the buildings and the villages that keep it so beguiling, but it didn't depend on gardens to create its allure.

It took a vantage point like this balcony to fully appreciate the skills the local farmers have for laying out their crops, be it vineyards, cherry orchards or even carrots, with the most perfect symmetrical lines. The geometry of this warm landscape exudes order and training. From a strict exercise in cultivation comes not only an organised beauty but also a singular sense of purpose. Straight lines demand less maintenance and avoid wastage of space, whilst this kind of regimentation spellbinds us with a sense of what's safe and proper. Even in gardening these disciplines apply to an extent. Should you stand on the great parterre at Versailles you will gaze across acres of tightly arranged planting set into mind-stretching patterns of low hedging with battalions of sober little plants not daring to nod for fear of punishment. Happily the great English landscape gardeners evolved the art. It was done by employing gracious curves and meandering lines, by hiding huge views behind screens of trees, tempting the visitor with a promise of something special, and by working with the given contours of the land, cajoling and extolling nature rather than adhering to a drill of linear regulations.

Clearly The Owners had some sort of terraced backyard down below their house, but at this first viewing it was hard to see or even imagine. An amorphous shape of attention-seeking brambles and convolvulus fought with miscellaneous squads of wild grasses, squabbling amongst themselves for space, light and domination, letting out only the smallest clues as to what lay beneath. We stood in silence for a while, contemplating the challenge.

'We would like to have the swimming pool just there,' said Ros after a while, pointing vaguely to a hovering space about 20 feet below us. 'I'd want to keep the quinces, cherries and roses but perhaps that old almond will have to go?'

'Good idea! Why not? Yes perhaps ...' And so we began, fuelled, as always by beautiful, vague dreams of future gardens.

We battled our way down the slope, occasionally being guided by a compliant step or threatened by a sinuous stretch of savage vine determined to take prisoners. The drop through what was calculated as six levels was dramatic but unrevealing. So close knit were the weeds and other intruders that it was with rash speculation that the briefing continued.

'We want the pool water to pour over the edge and to re-circulate,' called Richard from behind a little shed that had announced itself into the fray. 'And perhaps we can use this building as the pump and filtration room,' he advanced with mounting enthusiasm.

Just then two huge purple-black insects flew out of the hut like a pair of over-excited helicopters scrambling for air space. Seemingly attached to each other, they flew with such harmony and understanding you had to assume they were lovers and not two battling warlords. These are members of the hornet (*frelon*) family, and whilst enjoying a suitably fierce reputation, tend to pass us mortals up in favour of pollen pinching or ariel nooky. It is their yellow and black striped cousins that are more intimidating and more aggressive, and they nest prolifically around these parts. Sometimes so big they need runways to get airborne, they feast on fruit and sting like blunt needles. You'll need a doctor if you've been coerced into a couple of rounds with these guys, they tend to make your friendly little bumble bee sting something to positively relish.

Arriving on the final level, and still only about a third of the way down the side of the slope, brought no mean sense of achievement. The garden flattened out and a small orchard of elderly cherry and almond trees provided gentle, cool shade. The intense heat of August now over, they had already started to pull on an early autumn coat of fading colours. Pale green with a hint of dying yellow, the burnt edges of the leaves had begun to curl. The summer's parching heat had exhausted these old fellows – arriving early with their blossom in the spring, they were happy to be the first to retire in the fall. As we looked out once more across the valley from within the shadows of the trees, it was hard to imagine a much more spectacular rural backdrop anywhere, and what ever would be done to the garden, we had been given a starter for ten.

Nobody had said anything for a while, The Owners no doubt feeling content with their good fortune, and me just filling up with tranquillity.

Eventually, I said: 'I think the first thing we have got to do is clear it, get rid of the overgrowth and see what we have or haven't got. After that perhaps we can commission a surveyor to map it correctly if we think it necessary.'

A good survey carried out by a professional is a useful tool for any garden designer to have, doubly so if the site is on a slope, incorporating a load of levels. It speeds up the process and gives all the necessary information on which to build the plan.

As we started the haul back up to the house it gave me an opportunity to assess the neighbours. Anyone starting to make a garden with all that that implies: noisy machinery, general disruption, possible worries about privacy, etc., would be well advised to wag their tails at their neighbours. To have them on your side, even a bit involved, makes for a much easier passage through the whole exercise. By not accounting to them at all, you may find litigation raising its head because of ignorance or misunderstandings. In a town or city, planning permission is usually required if the blueprints involve permanent structures, high walls, new pathways and so on, thus protecting, we hope, the innocent from insensitive development.

So it is in the Luberon, only here it is quite on the cards to run up against another, altogether different type of adversary: The Mayor, the Pugwash of Le Paysan Provençal. On the surface, a fine figure of bureaucratic benevolence, host to a plethora of local anomalies. He smoothes rancour with a portfolio of platitudes, but underneath he plays the cards of his big brother close to his chest, swinging between the pragmatic duties of his office and the abstract wishes of his own commission. Arbitrating over marginal plunders with all the verve of a World Series umpire, he manages nonetheless to occasionally stupefy his constituency with a seemingly illogical granting of permission to build this, whilst denying the right to build that. His role is at times played out with a contortionist's ability to sit on the fence while keeping his ear to the ground. Of course each commune has its own head of council, the nominal subordinate to whom the power of his titular superior has passed. Some are more worthy than others. Ménerbes for example had, at the time, a successful film producer, who has to his credit, or debit as some might argue, the original film of *Emmanuelle*.

It would be a fool who underestimates how a small itch can be exacerbated into major rash by ignoring the *mairie*. In 749 Burchard, bishop of Wilrzburg, and Furad, priest and chaplain, were sent by Pepin, the mayor of the palace to see Pope Zacharias and to ask his advice in regard to the kings who were then ruling in France, who had the title of king but no real authority. The pope replied by these ambassadors that it would be better that he (the mayor), who actually had the power, should be king…

Armed with this wisdom, any plans for improvement should be run past the great office, and once in the bag you can cock a snook at any dissenting neighbour, sure in the knowledge that the *permis de construire* is bonafide. However, there is a 50cm band of 'no man's land' designated between properties. Resentment felt by some members of the community can be deeply rooted, their distaste for cosmopolitan intruders, *les nouveaux*, profound. It means that a small strip of neglected ground without title can be a dangerous battlefield. Best to slip in some orchestrated diplomacy mixed with a dollop of deferential grovelling, if it helps you get what you want, and have a relationship that is, if not harmonious, at least peaceful. If it's difficult at the beginning, it usually gets worse.

The west side of the garden seemed to suggest minimal aggravation: a ruin wheezed on the boundary, ensnared by a rancorous old orchard, but there was evidence of habitation on the east. A mental note was made to keep them informed of progress if the team agreed and we concluded the first meeting with the promise of a quote for the first stage of a design. We also agreed that straightaway it should be cleared of all weeds and pruned and cut back as necessary.

There was no doubt that this particular garden had every reason to be a nightmare. But then there was the location, the enormous potential of its staggering stages and ancient trees. But it was not going to be an easy project, the swimming pool alone was enough to send me off into a paroxysm of designer wobble.

And yet, niggling away in my imagination was the decrepit mystery of the overgrown enclosure. There was something intriguing about it. Like a well-kept secret.

Eventually the snow surrendered and started to withdraw its troops. It was a slow process, as if top-flight negotiations were taking place. Whilst the enemy may not have left land mines, it booby trapped the paths and terraces with black ice that clung on like Harold Lloyd to a seventieth floor window ledge.

One oddity of Provence is that it is made up of dozens of little climatic zones. This is due to the hills, the valleys and the mountains all creating their own particular weather pockets. In January, the difference between, say, Fontaine de Vaucluse and Lacoste can be quite a few degrees, although only a few kilometres apart. I slithered the senior Peugeot up the slope and out onto the main road. The change was weird. The tarmac was as shiny as a cadet's boots, the snow had become a memory and I motored over to Ménerbes as if on another continent. Actually we have two senior Peugeots. We bought one of them from Mr Actor, our friend and neighbour who is based here, when not filming in a distant part of the world. He had bought a plush high spec. 605 with a silky six cylinder automatic when he first arrived down here, and was waiting for a bunch of other cars to turn up from around the world. When eventually the fleet was in he decided to sell the Peugeot, and it became ours, or rather Nicky's. As she pointed out, she had to have something strong and solid to drive around in so that if anything untoward happened, Theo would at least be in with a chance. Could I disagree? I slipped off to promise undying allegiance to my beloved little Renault cinq.

One hot afternoon in May, the other half and a quarter went down to Marseille to do a little shopping, a little plastic card bending. She bought stuff here and she bought stuff there, bucketfuls of things we had surprised ourselves by being able to live without. The boot was full, the cabin was full and even the little spaces around the engine were numbered. She came out of the irritatingly named Toys R Us, staggering with parcels like some dysfunctional divorcée off a double-or-drop competition, towing a small boy and trying to find a car that was not there. It had gone. It absolutely was not there in any shape or form. It had been stolen, lock, stock and full boot.

The whole catastrophe proved to be a major upset, a shocking experience as is always the case. The police station was an eye opener in its own right. Filthy and depressing, it was staffed by bored guardians of order trying to deal with crummy creepos, distressed Latins and North Africans from the nether regions of Marseille. But beyond this we were surprised and concerned about how traumatised Theo seemed to be by it all.

'The trouble is, you see, they think it's all their fault,' somebody told us soon after it had happened.

'It's like when parents get divorced,' she went on with authority. 'They blame themselves.'

Oh dear, I thought quietly, oh dear, oh dear. The insurance company told us that they would not pay up until after 30 days had passed, giving time for the car to be found. Monsieur Neighbour told us that within a few hours it would have been shipped out to Morocco and would be in Tangier working as a taxi. Our garageiste thought it would probably have been stripped down and out in the back streets of Marseille and dumped ignominiously. Either way it didn't sound great. So I bought another one. I saw it on the Peugeot forecourt in Apt, went in and bought it, bang, just like that. It was exactly the same colour, slightly less leather but when I brought it home, it did the trick. Theo calmed down about the whole incident and carried on as if nothing had happened. Brilliant. I was very pleased with myself until the police rang that evening and said they had found the other one.

I arrived in Ménerbes on time and presented my first round of sketches to the clients. I had managed to take the photographs for the overlays soon after our last meeting, when everything was still overgrown and had yet to succumb to either the clearout or the withering and wilting of winter. But now as we looked down from the balcony that had become our resident spot for garden gazing, the scene had changed somewhat. In their absence we had, as promised, cleared it. Amar, an Algerian freelance garden blitzer who works with me from time to time, had unleashed himself on it, backed from time to time by a bit of directing. Not that Amar heard much of my directions, plugged into his Walkman as he was. You just pull the starter chord, engage gear and off he tears, stopping only for cigarettes, tape changes and a quick sandwich around mid-day.

Amar is a good-looking twenty-eight year old who has all the young mademoiselles hoping to take advantage of his pruning techniques and the older maidens gasping with rekindled fantasies. His repertoire of hair do's (and some don'ts) and beardy possibilities seem to have no boundaries. He arrives and leaves work looking as if he's about to flake into a night club, jet-black hair creamed to his skull, dark leather jacket and trousers, heavy dude boots and glasses so Cimmerian that he relies on knowing his route backwards to pull off his navigation. He is a veritable hell's angel, but instead of a blistering 1200cc Countcati he putt-putts along on a playful little mobilette called a Chappy. My French is never better than when I am talking to Amar, partly because he anticipates what I'm thinking and teaches me how to say what he imagines I mean, and partly because he is untainted by the local Provençal accent with its nangs and twangs. He hopped out of Algiers to avoid going into the army when he was seventeen and hot-footed it up to Paris, drifting down to the south some years later. Meanwhile he's waiting with trepidation for the Algerian army to terminate national service. It might mean he could go home and see his Mum, but he remains a little uncertain about his reception at Algiers passport control.

Now that the garden had been denuded of debris – mineral, animal and vegetable – it looked bleak and naked. The combination of late autumn winds tearing off the remaining leaves and the scraped surfaces of the ground left everything bland and characterless. The soil apologetically offered up a few saved roses whilst the fruit trees stabbed at the sky with threadbare limbs. The walls and steps, having shed their summer costumes, showed their true state of disrepair and vulnerability, and the boundary fences were now ready for inspection. But this is what we needed, it allowed a proper review to take place: it also helped the surveyor to take his measurements.

Our designated surveyor was a good-natured chap called Joel Bonjour. Apart from his name being a bit tricky to get hold of for a moment or two, he was a pleasure to work with. Inevitably the first meeting of the day sounded a bit officerish and commanding: 'Bonjour' I would call and before I could continue, he would give me a 'Oui, monsieur'. But it was no worse than a chap I met in Long Eaton called Mr Goodnight. Anyway Mr Bonjour was a small fellow who clearly enjoyed his tuck. He was dressed in an unexpected pair of moleskin plus fours, sensible walking shoes and an all-weather yellow plastic blouson specially designed for a gentleman of his profession. It had pockets for compasses and electronic measurers, slits for straps and belts, buckles to hang his level readers from and a pouch for the ubiquitous mobile telephone. I had arranged to meet Bonjour outside the house at nine, and I knew it was him because I saw a huge wooden tripod standing in the street. 'Bonjour!' I called and 'Oui, monsieur!' popped out sprightly from behind the three-legged implement like a jockey from the back of the weighing-in scales. He was pleased to see the site so naked and submissive, so I left him to it.

The drawings were, as always, presented to the client in book form. I mounted the photographs on the page with the sketch positioned just above it, so that comparisons of what it is, and what it could be, are easy to read. In this case there were about a dozen drawings including the placing of the swimming pool in different locations. On the left, more secluded but under a somewhat unsafe old ruin, on the right, easier to install but a bit overlooked. Some drawings showed lawn and others paving, there were railings and no railings, the steps going this way or that. The lower terraces deepened with new steps, or were left as was and used as planting beds for roses only. The bottom level was worked informally with various grasses, white and blue lavenders, grey and green santolinas with *Perovskia atriplicifolia*, various salvias and artemisias. More formal alternatives were offered, incorporating box hedging, *Teucrium 'en boule'*, standard *Photinias, Cupressus arizonica* and *Lotus hirsutus* for clipping to shape. The paths were laid geometrically and the sitting areas allocated in specific spots.

Plant schemes at this stage are always deliberately kept simple to suggest colours and textures, a type of structure. Here the choice was soft and free form against a harder, topiar-esque configuration, with strong year-round presence. The colours were greys and silvers, mixed with blues, pale pinks, and creams, against a wide selection of matt and glossy greens. (The sharp, clear light down here means that hard yellows and slashing reds fight and cause unease.) From this point, fine-tuning will follow, until we settle on an exact plant plan.

Questions were asked on both sides. I needed to know how they were scheduling their work, when the house would be started, at what stage the pool was likely to be installed, and what our budget was likely to run to. They wanted to know how long it would all take, what the order of events would be, what had to be done first and what could wait. They talked about the fact that their other house had not yet been sold, so the financing of this major project had to be extremely carefully mapped out. We talked about builders and contractors, planning permissions, who was doing what and for whom. Notes were taken, dates set for the next meeting and what was expected to be achieved between now and then.

Bidding my farewells I headed off for the carpark but somehow manage to slip on the icy road straight into the Café de France, landing head first into a bantam cup of coffee that by some twist of fate had had a small glass of cognac poured into it. I sat at the bar and allowed the cup of central heating to help me make sense of my notes. The Café de France is typical of small *tabac* bars found everywhere in France, and is a temperate spot to collect one's thoughts. The zinc-topped bar boasts a few ashtrays as a nod to gentility, but really all cigarette butts come to rest on the floor. A never-ending parade of locals popping in for their paper, cigarettes and quick fix of coffee runs like a video loop. On the wall, racks of magazines showing the prettiest bosoms vie for space with tourist guides showing the prettiest villages. In amongst the national and local papers will probably be a few copies of *The Herald Tribune* — the American newspaper popular with the English-reading community. It has a daily French edition produced in Marseille and means that yesterday's papers from the UK, invariably abridged of their supplements and additions, can be passed up.

Monsieur LaBour, the chosen builder, was a well-known local character of Spanish origin. I need hardly tell you that his first name was Manuel. He had an on-going quiescent reputation, and there are many who will swear by his abilities, but he also has a strong stable of detractors, who hiss at the very mention of his name. He keeps a fine line in dogtooth check jackets in his cupboard and a fine line of moustache on his upper lip. He may have a Spanish heart, he may like to play his guitar like a gypsy king, but he has French attitude. I have met him on several occasions, on projects and at parties. He is in a class of his own when it comes to talking. It seems that to enter into conversation with him, you must talk at the same time, then get louder, then start swearing. After a while you hope he will take a quick pause for breath, whereupon you will pounce. Best to be well rehearsed. You don't want to lose ground with any hesitations or repeats and you have to be ready to drive forward at breakneck speed. All your instructions will be ignored of course, as he only does things how he wants them done, which he assumes to be best. So why bother with drawings? Well, they give proof of what you were thinking and what was meant to be, they hearten the client, and stand testament to your intentions. And you never know – the builder might look at them.

I once told a particularly beefy maçon that I loved him, when what I meant was that I *liked it*. However, I am less intimidated these days by the likes of Manuel and, as my confidence with the language improves, I tend to get my own way, which is after all what the clients are paying for. But I still needed to watch Manuel like a hawk because old customs die hard and changes, especially in construction, especially from an outsider, are not usually welcomed. Still he's been a doddle compared to the workforce on a big project I had the year before last, near St.Tropez.

Monsieur Entrepreneur had owned a house in Port Grimoud for a generation, and being a gambler had nearly lost it on numerous occasions. Things being seriously on the up, he had cashed in his town house for a bit of grown-up playersville on the coast in Beauvallon, a stretch of coastland with its own private beach, across the bay from St Tropez. Of course you are not *allowed* to own a private beach in France. But you would have to be deeply committed to hurting the moneyed classes, or brass necked enough not to care about invading people's sanctuary, to land on a small slice of sandy strip at the bottom of someone's garden like this. The other side of the road, the north side, is where the Mediterranean South of France meets the Wentworth golf club. People sleep with their caddies just in case, and play by floodlight, have drinky parties at the exclusive and wallet-thinning club house, and employ private trainers and mechanics to keep the legs walking and the caddy carts working. It's a bit like posh skiing. You get out of bed, bypass your snuggy slippers and slide straight into your skiing boots, ready for action. Jack out the door straight on to the black run, putting your make-up on as you mogul down. Here it's from poolside to green side in one easy stroke.

The entrepreneur's house is so secluded that even the mayor had difficulty finding it. He had been invited to dinner to discuss the finer points of planning permission, but had found the place to be so concealed that he had to return to the local police station for help. I am happy to report that he got there in the end, but not without the help of a government-funded escort. It was an intriguing proposition that the entrepreneur was setting out. He had bought three houses, two on the sea front, and one just behind. The idea was to keep the big villa for him and his wife; the smaller, rather engagingly modern house behind, would be perfect for the children – it might need another swimming pool, a few more garages and a go-kart track, but basically it would do. The third property would have its land virtually removed from the deeds and sold on to a selected and screened punter. By decamping with the grounds from around this house, he could give himself guaranteed privacy, protection against development, and somewhere to put the tennis court that wasn't too close to his main hut. To make sure that all his plans would materialise he needed the authority of the main man of the commune behind him. Evidently, as he cajoled, flattered and flew the mayor through dinner, abetted by charismatic whites, upper house reds, sweet-natured pudding wines and brandies old enough to belong to somebody's ancestors, he managed to convince *Le Maire* that all was sound and sensible. That's where I came in. Not literally of course. I wasn't oiling my way around the passages of mini power, but I was a suitable candidate to help him reconcile the three gardens with some kind of cohesion, to make them run together as if they had been partners all their lives, and not a triad of opposing tabernacles.

I had been invited to spend a day with him and go through the possibilities. We sat down to lunch and were joined by his wife, Eva, a charming and elegantly pretty Swedish woman who had enjoyed an international life on the catwalk before retiring and having three children. The housekeeper, a smiley, laundered lady in her late fifties, served an unpretentious little mid-day snack. Fois gras, a 'home-bake' comprising fine products from the local charcuterie, a side salad with well-dressed rocket, accompanied by a display of cheeses the Red Arrows would have acknowledged as subtle, and capped by a tarte tatin to live for. We talked of living in the South of France, working in London. They had a house in Kensington. And of times spent in New York. I had recently completed the plans for a double brown-stone on 63rd and

Madison and reported on the foibles of gardening inside the big apple. We also talked of the different ways we all end up making our buck and what we considered to be the pecking order of expenditure. I, needless to say, lost the plot of our conversation somewhere around the second trillion, but our man was gracious enough to tell me how envious he was of my ability to design gardens and sketch a bit, and to think things through creatively. I parried with an admiration for the dextrous and cunning way in which he pulled off his venture capitalism, made all the more intoxicating by his reckless gambling. He is the only person I have met who has a swimming pool big enough to get lost in, yet hasn't actually swum in it.

'Why bother? I've got the sea right there with my own beach.'

Neither of us being drinkers at lunch time we agreed to call a halt to temptation after a scorchingly dry martini had been chased by twin grand cru '83's from St-Emilion. Madame Entrepreneur filled in details, generously lent wit and charm to the proceedings, and eventually pulled us to our senses. She reminded Ricard that he had a meeting with Global Conglomerates Inc. at 6.30 that evening in Paris, and that the Lear would be cleared for take-off from Nice by now, so he'd better get it together. Ricard dismissed himself, muttering about changing whilst I waddled out on to the lawn, a little the better for wear and tear, and took in the salty breezes. The rest of the briefing would come from Madame Eva.

The main house was some two hundred years old and had been built in the villa-esque style, not surprisingly. Approached down a cypress-lined and illegally extended driveway, the cars arrived and virtually parked on top of the front door. The first item on the agenda was to redirect traffic to a more discreet corner. A courtyard was to be constructed around four magnificent old olives that roosted in an off-set square some fifteen metres out from the house. They had probably been planted as big trees when the house had been built. Added to that was the landscaping around the tennis court, the reorganising of walks through the woods, and some bright ideas to make the front of the house, the sea side, a bit more interesting and dynamic. Sitting on a battered pallet near the front door, was an enormous stone basin with a grand and detailed font.

'I had this brought round on approval,' she said. 'I saw it the other day and thought it might work in our new courtyard. But if you don't think so I'll send it back.'

Assimilating proportions as quickly as I could I figured it might well look fine and should therefore be kept. 'Good,' she said happily. 'Ricard will have a fit at the price, but if I say you insisted, it should be all right.' Funny how much easier the mantle of responsibility is to wear after a light lunch.

It became clear as the project developed that the Entrepreneurs had a penchant for garden sculpture. For example, I was preparing the working drawings for the courtyard wall, when I had a phone call from Eva saying that I must include four niches, two on each of the side walls. She had just been to a country house sale held by Sotheby's, and had bought four sculptures representing the seasons, and would e-mail me the dimensions later that day. 'Fine,' I said, 'I'll pop in a Vivaldi CD and get to it.'

There was a lot of work going on in the other house in preparation for its sale. When you see a JCB fully deposited in a hallway poised for action, about to wreak havoc like Godzilla in Madison Square subway station, you *know* there's a lot of work going on and there was a glint in the operator's eye that told me he was really loving his work. Having all these architects, surveyors, engineers and construction crews on the doorstep, meant that I didn't have to look far to find someone to give me a quote for the courtyard wall. A few days later I arranged a meeting with the structural engineer, whose telephone manner was about as exciting as a talking clock. I sent the drawings on to him in advance, and arrived punctually, programmed with selected French sentences and well-known phrases, applicable to the job in hand. The surveyor arrived late, in a Tonka-toy jeep shod in don't-mess-with-me tyres, without apology and without my drawings. He had with him something that looked like a cross between a bulldozer and a drugged wrestler. And the closest thing to a smile came from the creases in his neck when he snorted. I introduced myself to them both, excused my shallow technical French, and set to discussing the intricacies of a scheme agreed between our clients and myself. At every turn they made me struggle, they left me hanging for words, they gazed hard and straight at me without the slightest offer of understanding, and terminated the meeting as if by some prearranged signal.

'Right ho then, chaps,' I called out sharply in English to their vanishing backs, 'I'll expect the quote by the end of the week, or you're both fired.'

All I could think about on the way home was that scene in *Spinal Tap*, the mad '70s movie lampoon of a rock band. The heavy metal boys arrive for their gig at some huge open-air concert, to discover that the full-size Stonehenge set they had ordered to lend a suitable *milieu*, had actually been built and delivered at $\frac{1}{12}^{th}$ scale. Not only could the audience hardly see the damned thing, it kept tripping the band up as they farcically tried to power drive their fenders into the ground. I just prayed that The Entrepreneurs weren't going to end up tripping over their courtyard wall.

Despite humourless construction engineers, virulent digger drivers, portentous and pestilent plantsmen, the job got done and, I dare say, with a degree of success. But each time I got back to the Luberon, I was reassured by how much more civil the workmen were here. The cut and thrust of the Côte d'Azur, the buck chasing and backstabbing competitiveness of the building and landscaping businesses were dreadful and anxious-making.

Water is a theme that one can't help returning to in Provence. It's not only necessary but primitively pleasurable. One day, I saw a bunch of children, under the supervision of an elderly couple, jumping in and out of an oversized paddling pool. Perhaps the most their grandparents could run to. They were bubbling with joy and over-excitement. It was just a few meters back from the roadside, but it could have been a secluded and heavily guarded compound on Cap Ferrat for all the kids cared. I watched them and wondered what deep yearning it was that lured us to frolic in the stuff.

There are thousands of swimming pools in the South of France. They range from fabulous extravaganzas on the coast, dripping with glitz and glamour, with their remote-controlled hard covers and see-through walls that any formation swimmer would be tickled to show off in; through to the humble plastic tubs that sit above ground, shawled in an arrogant panoply of blue skin. In between, an assembly of aluminium, pre-formed or liner pools take up the slack. By and large, the pools of the French Riviera are blue. The colour sympathises with the sea, it reflects the sunny skies and has an inviting and holidayish connotation. However the Luberon lies inland, between mountains and hills, and is a wholly different jug of Jacuzzis. No less hot in the summer months, and no less sunny, the concept of a blue pool is not so popular. Like all symbols of prestige, a swimming pool is a revealing asset and tells us as much about a person as a car or boat. It's not just money: this neck of Provence probably has a far more diverse bag of income returns than up the coast. It's also to do with style, hipness, discretion and keeping something that is essentially an agrarian misfit, as expedient as possible. Derigueur for the aged *mas* is the disguised *bassin*. This looks like a large, old-fashioned water cistern perhaps once used for animals, raised just slightly out of the ground, and surrounded by old stone capping that keeps the prairie grass back from the edges. Its inside will be dark in colour and slightly foreboding, but throbbing with modern technology. This doesn't mean that the region is without a fine range of razor-sharp numbers overlooking the views with seemingly no restraint on the water, slurping cheekily over a precipice. Why, there are even some that have beaches....

There are endless stories of woe about a pool's behaviour. The rip-offs from non-bonafide suppliers and installers, the crevices and cracks, the breakdowns of equipment, the cost of heating, the cost of maintenance, the algae, the dead animals, and the occasionally unexplainable disappearance of the damned water itself. But a new one threw up its head when Ros Owner wrote to me from NY saying that there was concern from the *mairie* about their application for a pool licence.

Apparently farmers are wary of village pools, especially villages that are built on the side of a hill like Menerbes. They claim that when the time comes to empty the pool in the autumn, the residual chemicals that have insinuated themselves into the water will damage their crops when it seeps into the farmland below. It's ironic really. Here we all are juggling our feelings about genetically modified carrots, when the panic should really be about a water disinfectant chucked out indiscriminately by a bunch of over-paid yahoos living the life of Riley. Chlorine is a non-metallic element, a heavy gas in fact with an irritating smell. It is not a particularly

Ménerbes

user-friendly additive but I hadn't considered it as an enemy of the farming fraternity. But you live and learn, and I thought I'd better look into this a bit further. Not wanting to start by trying to prove the crop kickers wrong, it seemed it would be more beneficial to look into alternatives, more comfortable solutions. So I climbed onto the internet. One of the problems with this device is that when you start the ball rolling by, say, keying in 'swimming pools', you find that you have fifteen hundred pages to look at. Pages that subdivide down into manufacturers, SPARTA salesmen conferences, cleaning equipment etc., etc. Then you fine tune it a bit more, until you have bought three hundred and sixty dollars worth of books on the best, most exotic pools in the world. Swimwear catalogues follow, and before you know it you're into Victoria's Secret, and it's only a shallow drop down from there to smutty leisure wear, and finally, a request for a credit card number if you want to continue webbing into something the police wouldn't approve of. Is there a subliminal signal being flashed, drawing us inexorably towards the sin pits of degradation? These naughty internet stations are, after all, the most visited web sites by far.

The second run of drawings had seen the pool moved over to the west side. It gave more size and, with a little adjustment to the existing steps, allowed for a more balanced and favourable setting all round. Now we had to decide on how it was to be built. It had always been agreed that I would provide ideas and concepts for the pool but not actually be responsible for its construction drawings. It is sensible to let specialists in the field take on the problems that can arise, besides which, they have infinitely more experience. They also have proper guarantees, insurance and presumably lawyers who are used to dealing with disgruntled clients. At this stage Manuel seemed quite jockeyish about taking it on himself. He didn't seem to be fazed by the special pack of tricks this site throws up, and whilst he had yet to really turn his mind to the project, everyone was quite happy to float on his confidence. There was still plenty to be sorted out in the house before work needed to begin on the exterior, and besides which it was winter.

Ros had also mentioned in her fax that she liked the idea of a black pool. Me too. It shimmers like silver when the water is flat, and is more reflective than a mirror. Ideal for ambushing the moon light. I sent a few catalogues for them to look at, a couple of web sites to check out and then I closed shop for Christmas.

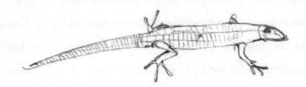

CHAPTER TWO

Up and Walking

A spruce Christmas tree bought from a local garden centre arrived in our little trailer. It had been lifted from the ground and potted up and we were duly promised that, given a good drink from time to time, it would live happily way beyond twelfth night. A certain amount of discussion had taken place about where it should go. Previously the tree had always been put against the wall in the sitting room where the ceiling manages double height, but this year was more difficult because a handsome piece of furniture, rather along the tall-boy principle, had arrived from a relative-in-law. It demanded to be well placed and scuppered the perfect spot for the tree. In the end it was decided that it could really only go in the middle of the room down at the far end. It would make it hopelessly difficult to draw the curtains, impossible to open the door into the garden, use up all the electric plugs and mean that there was nowhere to sit in that vicinity.

The next morning I flew to London to make a pilot for a TV quiz show, leaving Nicky and the Baby-Sitter to decorate. Once, years ago, I was spending a bit of Christmas time with a friend who played in a thinking-man's rock band called Soft Machine. Mike, who was the keyboard player with the 'Softs', as the university clique called them, said, looking at the tree I had proudly just rigged up, that he 'found the whole concept more a symbol of the bourgeoisie than of Christianity'. I never quite got over that, due in part I suppose because I thought his band was cool, his brightness dazzling and besides which, he had his own personal print of *Citizen Kane*. He wittered on about the dreadful predictableness of the middle-class propensity for masquerading, for hiding behind comfortable fantasies, that left me stamped with a lingering scepticism towards the whole festive goschmalocks. But nowadays, because of an over-excited pair of little feet in the house, it at least comes with the fun and promise of that fat old mercenary dressed in red, squeezing his corpulent figure down the chimney, and leaving what seems like half a toy shop under the tree.

Do you remember when a Christmas stocking was something that came out of your mother's top drawer and had a tangerine chased by a series of 'stocking fillers' that were really only posh cracker commodities? Not any more. In much the same way that department stores like to turn their gardening departments into 'Xmas Gift Wrap' around about the beginning of September, stockings have changed themselves into a kind of heavy duty, L-shaped sack, cavernous enough to hold the spending limit of half a dozen platinum cards.

Of course the trouble with going to London just before Christmas is that you overdose on the festival foible. Retailing the bank account out of its socket, hammering yourself with office parties and going quietly crackers trying to get a taxi, bus or train.

Hassled by crowds, soaked, dry of wit. I wished I had been hot footing it to the beaches of beyond.

Withdrawing from the UK the next day I reflected, as I always do, on my feelings about leaving the old country and living hand in pocket with the French. Of course Provence is and isn't French. It has a distinct heartbeat of its own, and many a native would argue that he was a Provençal rather than a Frenchman. I once asked my neighbour, whose family have been here for more than four centuries, what he felt about his neck of the woods being broken into by foreigners. He told me, revealingly, that he would rather have us lot than Parisians. Arrogant and demanding, insensitive and patronising, were the sympathetic observations.

Sometimes on a summer's evening, Monsieur Neighbour drops by in his large and worn-out van, maybe to help us pick the fruit, or to show us a goose that he has bought at market. Or perhaps to swap a few items of interest, like a recycled wine bottle full of lavender oil in exchange for some old flower pots, or a small wooden basket full of salad for a couple of glasses of pastis. The Provençal accent is as different from what we perceive as a French accent, as base line Glaswegian must be if you have only ever talked to a man from the ministry. It twangs and mings. Nicky seems to have got hold of it, but I am still perplexed over much of the conversation I hear when left alone. It doesn't stop us having lengthy dialogues about three of the Cs: Corruption, Communists, and Catholics. Naturally, Protestants, drugs and abuse of everything, also get a good look in. We tend to both talk at the same time, constantly nodding conspiratorially, winking and agreeing about everything.

Then, after chucking back another shot we tackle the next topic. Because we don't really understand each other, there is no chance of terminally upsetting the apple cart by our choice of delicate subjects. We are about the same age, and his feelings about whisky run pretty much parallel to mine about pastis. Besides which it gives me a chance to rib him about his dashing haircut, craftily executed by a style scholar in the local lady's hairdresser in Gordes, without him feeling offended. His face is crackled and brown, his voice raspy from Gitanes and his physique as wiry as a mountaineer. As we become more animated and the stories more hilarious and incomprehensible, we laugh and pat each other's backs, gesticulate wildly and when at last the time comes for him to depart, it's done on a note of bonhomie that belies our language barrier.

I never feel sad to be leaving Britain now. I have a different life, in most ways better than when I lived in the UK. I am, overall, happy that we unglued ourselves from England and struck out to try the game in a divergent reality. We miss friends, of course, but by the same token have found and made new ones. Provence has an eclectic bunch of wandering souls. Many are second homers, coming from all parts of Europe, North America and beyond; others are happy to set down roots and come and go as it pleases them. Tax situations dictate to a degree, with residents and non-residents alike generally abiding by the various rules laid down, and businesses are run in the most efficient ways that accountants can sanction. The other day I was talking to an American chum who has recently sold his house in Hollywood, and he got it about right when he said that Provence is a bit like Beverley Hills was sixty years ago.

We arrived, via Dover, five years ago, early one morning in September 1995, by train.

I had met Nicky three years earlier. A friend was having an exhibition of his photographs at the Hamilton Gallery in London, and after umming and erring, I decided to go along. I had hardly managed ten yards inside the showroom when I saw this destroyingly beautiful and sexy girl. When she caught my eye and smiled, I slipped and fell straight into a change of life. Later on, a friend's wife told me that I was looking slightly dazed and stupid, and asked if I was alright. I explained what had happened and she told me to behave myself, the girl was heavily involved with a crazy chef, and that she was far too young for me anyway. It all sounded consummately wonderful, so I bullied her for an introduction, and in order to get rid of this sick parrot she acquiesced. Following this orchestrated prologue I was placed opposite her at the dinner afterwards. Being deaf in my left ear it was difficult to hear what anyone was saying from across a large table, but add background noise of a restaurant and I was running on guesses. Therefore, I couldn't exactly work out what she was saying to the man on her right, a 'nice-looking boy', who was one of the partners in the gallery, but I already felt like charging him parking fees. When she got up to go, I nearly knocked the table over in my bid to secure a contract to drive her home. The journey didn't last long, but she did manage to mention that her waning boyfriend was a so-called celebrity cook who had an array of cleavers in his restaurant kitchen, so I rather succinctly dropped her about a hundred yards from her studio. I watched her walk down the street with bubbles in my blood.

We lay in each other's eyes for a few months, letting love play itself through wonderment until one morning I awoke with my bank manager trespassing on my mind. He had injected me with a cruel jab of despair about a recession that was grabbing the country by the throat and squeezing out its breath like an anaconda round an artless Sri Lankan umpire. I had bought a large old factory in Clapham, done it up with some of my own money, with some from one of my sisters, and a loan from Barclays, and they were getting jittery.

I had discovered Harper Banker, an American posted to the London Knightsbridge branch, when I was brokering around looking for the best borrowing rates. I had made an appointment to go in and meet the smooth Harvard man in his dying thirties, and, as luck would have it, I arrived at his office on the very morning that there was a double-page spread about my work in one of the national papers. His diligent secretary had spotted it and put it on his desk so that he might know a bit more about me before I arrived. Whilst the manager of small business developments was not overwhelmed by a slice of dubious editorial, it did ease my story into place, and after a visit to the ruin that would become our offices, the loan was secured.

I love commercial properties. Since my early twenties I had leased a studio in Fulham. It was above an old garage and was basically one huge room with a giant skylight and balcony doubling as a bedroom. The windows led out onto a terrace, with a rather nifty set of steps that took you up and over the ridge of the roof and down to the other side, to another enclosure. It was wrapped up with solid, painted, fencing panels and was completely private and pretty. Downstairs a kitchen and bathroom completed the particulars. I had found it when I was twenty-three by asking around warehouses and depots of various descriptions. The complex it was part of belonged to a very proper old building firm that had come to prominence in the Victorian terrace house building boom. The developer was a kindly old boy who liked the idea of helping a struggling gardener and organised the rent at an appropriate level. I moved out a few times during the following fifteen years, to get married twice, to sub-let it when I went up town with the posh parkers, to live in the country, but I always came back and was very settled there. Omelette, my old white labradorable of the time, bit a few people in the vicinity, but no one held it against her, she was just being a bit of a show off. No one, that is, apart from the gas meter man who sued me for a new pair of trousers.

Now I was about to start on another commercial property venture. It had been a factory that utilised very oily machines, and the realisation that it had actually been a working workshop up until just a few weeks before it became ours, was astonishing. Everything about it was Dickensian, the working conditions hard to stomach and the sanitation virtually non existent. We set to with a tight budget and a tight builder whom we had to sack. However with considerable tenacity and the banker's help, we pulled it together. For a couple of years all went smoothly, work was piling in and property prices rising. Then suddenly one day we all realised that the recession the moneymen had been talking about had come home to roost. Work slackened. Gardening is after all a luxury item, and even if people had the money they were shy of being conspicuous spenders in a time of hardship. Property prices started to slump.

Thatcher was thrown off her throne, and before you could say 'Maggie's your Man', we were jumping into the ring with the banker.

We had sub-let part of the space to a mixed bag of artists, including a chap who made waxworks for Madame Tussaud's. Coming in late one night I noticed that the reception area, which had an enormous table in it, was lit by a dimmed light. I opened the door cautiously and was surprised to see two smartly dressed old gentlemen sitting deep in discussion. I moved further into the room and was about to introduce myself when I realised it was Edison talking to Teddy Roosevelt.

The rest of the team of tenants were made up of a painter, a hat maker and a furniture restorer. My sister was making curtains in another room and a compact apartment took up the top floor, which again led out onto a roof terrace. As the financial climate worsened, visits to Barclays Knightsbridge became real in the day and virtual in my sleep. Their endless threats of calling in the loans and guarantees, their caveats on closure and exhortations of repossession all wore me down to a despondent wreck. The worry soon became unbearable, and after yet another sleepless night under that black blanket of despair that smothers you without remorse while your blood pressure's down, I threw the flag in. I called the powers that be and said: 'Have it. You can take the expletive building and stick it up your auction.'

An emergency meeting was held with all interested parties who did nothing to make life easier. They were in fact wonderfully imaginative about how to make things worse. The bank were compounding matters from the base line by saying that they didn't want the building after all, that they would fix interest at a choking eighteen percent and expect me to make my own arrangements for selling the place. They would say that, as they knew the building was unsellable in red times. The commercial market was weeping with wounded proprietors. Covered in stings I announced to the bank that if they didn't take the building back and terminate the rolling interest charges, if they wouldn't wave a pair of crutches in my direction, I would deliver myself to the bankruptcy court and leave them to eat cake. The bank tasted blood and they moved in like hungry jackals. They changed the keys whilst I was out buying some milk, they moved the liquidators on to the site and heaved to with all barrels firing. The tenants were granted a temporary lease, but my sister was forced to move herself out, pronto. There were no smiling faces and malice spread itself around like a tumour. Even if work had been offered at that point I wouldn't have known which end of the pencil to pick up to execute it.

Outside the building a human misfit, a gorilla mutant, was easing himself into my expensive motor car and repossessing it for the leasing company. He was dripping with hostility and practically tore the door off its hinges. I smiled at him genially, gave him a tenner for petrol and explained how the CD player worked. The freezing rivers of despair suddenly started to thaw. For some inexplicable reason at that moment, looking at the repo man muscling my car away from me, the sky opened a big window and a warm sun poured in and stoked up my soul. It pulled me up to my full height, pushed back my shoulders and filled me to brimming with optimism. A confidence was rekindled that just a few hours earlier I would never have thought possible. I was ready for anything and felt free to start again. I carried this redemption back home and it was infectious.

Soon we were making plans to move. It would take a lot of organising, some calculated risks, a deep intake of breath and a firm holding of hands, but we were ready to try. We were about to leap out of Britain, land in the Mediterranean, start house hunting and find some decent work.

We looked at something between fifty and sixty houses over the following three months, some achingly lovely but too expensive, some fine but over done up, which meant we would have to spend money un-doing them, others too far away from villages or towns. Nicky had been living in London for a long time and whilst being the motivator behind the move to the South of France, she had no intentions of becoming a fully fledged paysanne overnight. If she had to wear gum boots she wanted them made by Manolo.

We found a beautiful old farmhouse in-land from StTropez. It was relatively inexpensive and as irony would have it, it turned out to be a 'forced sale'. It was being dumped on the market with a knock-down price just to unload it from the bank's portfolio of unwanted property. The agent, having extolled the virtues of the house, walked us over to the swimming pool, fully aware of our mounting interest, probably thinking he had a sale on his hands, when to his and our horror we saw a dead dog floating in the water. It had blown up like a balloon and looked as if it might explode at any minute. The poor creature had probably been wounded by a car, had limped to find water to drink, and being weak, had slipped into the pool. It cast an immediate and total blanket over the whole thing. An appalling omen and an irremovable image. We turned and left with the agent hissing vehemently into his mobile phone at the *gardien*, something about him joining the dog if he didn't make it disappear pronto. As we drove out of the gates we felt a general doubt about the area. Sure there were plenty of big houses with big spenders, which we needed if I was to find work, but somehow it was amiss.

We belted down the autoroute through the Luberon and out at Montpellier, we looked at *manoirs* in the Ardeche, gawped at chateaux in the Gar, we drove through the Drome. We crawled over and under, backwards and forwards through houses everywhere. We met a roll-call of agents, and a business of vendors. We developed a professional friendliness and learned to move around a home quickly and efficiently. We were no longer seduced by the smell of coffee or burning fires on hot days, and we got our questions sharpened and fettled for the failures without embarrassment. Nothing ever quite fitted the bill. Occasionally we would lose sight of what we wanted, but we always maintained a keen sense of what we didn't want. After most of our forays into the various provinces, we returned to our hotel or *chambre d'hôtes* in the Luberon. It was our base and we were becoming increasingly aware that this was where we wanted to live, and it wasn't long before we abandoned looking anywhere else.

The trouble was that this neck of Provence was, and still is, much sought after and consequently expensive. The houses we would be shown round here within our budget, would be either in need of major renovation or in poor positions. We consoled ourselves with the fact that as it was a good catchment area for work, we were quite happy to throw ourselves into a renovation project (poor innocent fools). Having already met some like-minded people, we felt that the area suited us well but to make things more challenging, the rate of exchange had gone off its rocker. Everyone knows, give or take, that there are ten francs to the pound. There have been ever since I was a kid and the franc was devalued, and there still are as I write, but in that little pocket of time when we were getting ready to pounce on Provence, the pound sank. It practically drowned in the English Channel. Gurgling and spluttering, it went down for the third time at a commercial exchange of something like one for seven. When you are about to move a grown-up amount of currency between two countries this kind of thing knocks the stuffing out of you. It forced our house buying power down by nearly a third and spoilt the fun, but we persevered. I even started to learn a bit about the area.

The Luberon is in the province of the Vaucluse bordered by the Var to the east and the Bouches-du-Rhone to the west, and has Avignon as its capital. Pope Clement V, a Frenchman, brought the papacy to this beautiful old city in 1309. It remained there for seventy-two years, before returning to Rome. As archbishop of Bordeaux Pope Clement V had gained favour of the French king Philip IV, who engineered his election to office. He also did much to further the cultivation of grape growing. The Chateau Neuf du Pape wines still tickle the taste buds of the bacchanalian everywhere, enjoying popularity that other wines of the region can only dream about.

To the north lies the snow-capped Mont Ventoux, the highest peak between the Alps and the Pyrenees, and to the south, the drawn-out range of the Luberon hills. It was probably the Greeks who gave Provence its olives and vines, and the Romans, its architecture.

In more modern times the beauty of Provence attracted artists. Championed by Cézanne, Van Gogh, and to an extent Piccaso, it continues to play host to painters, architects, writers, directors, composers and even the odd gardener. As the coastland and the terrain directly behind became increasingly over-subscribed, the creative communities moved to the more sparse and remote villages of the Luberon. More recently the area has attracted millions of tourists and dozens of settlers from all over the world, which is a mixed blessing. They have pumped up the economy and brought the beautiful old villages back to life, but at the same time have glossed it over and unfairly given it a somewhat hackneyed reputation. It won't be long before the hard-working farmer will have been forced out, and the lands taken over by people rich enough to indulge their elegant daydreams and whims. Wine making will be an amusing tax loss, but with your own label, fruit trees will be looked after by contract gardeners and lack of profit will be of no consequence. Tractors will work the land more as a moving sentiment than as any practical ideal, whilst ungainly crops like the disingenuous carrot will be banned despite its fast return on investment. The essence of Provence will be retained untarnished but have no more reality than fantasy island.

The house we finally settled for was an old *mas* that lay in a hammock of land slung between the medieval villages of Catholic Bonnieux on one side and Protestant Lacoste on the other, slightly favouring the latter with its position. It was a tired old place that had had the top floor renovated thirty years before we saw it in a style much appreciated by the *paysanne*. It had hollow wooden doors and disproportionate fireplaces, floor tiles more suitable to a motorway public loo, and the windows, whilst matching one another, clearly held the vernacular of the building in contempt. The wallpaper, impregnated with wood chips, held deep secrets that we would only find out about when we started stripping it off. The downstairs swaggered around with earth floors, blocked up windows and stone walls that had expelled their pointing. It was dark, dank, uncompromisingly challenging and, until recently, had been the home to various animals, mostly rabbits, which are widely kept for Sunday lunch. The roof, wheezing with exhaustion, and dipping alarmingly, at least held on to its original old russet tiles, or did for the most part. There were huge tracts of space for the sky to blink at us through, and other bits were only pretending to be covered. In fact the house told boundless lies, deceived us with false promises of strength, and sniggered at us behind our back as we became ensnared by its capricious charm. We would sneak up on it from behind, hiding in the woods, and watch silently to see if the spell had worn off. We would drive past slowly and then faster to see if it still winked at us. We would sit on the terrace of the Café de France up in Lacoste, looking down on it nestling into the folds of the slope beneath, and dare it to turn against us. But always it remained there, wrapped in an indubitable air of tranquillity.

Exactly why this old ruin had caught our imagination was probably explainable for three reasons. Firstly it was within budget, or at least it was within budget to buy, but only the blessing of ignorance put it in budget to renovate. Secondly it was located close to a village which made my lady of the high heel feel reasonably in touch and secure. Thirdly it was highly visible from Lacoste and that, we figured, would give people a chance to observe how I could storm a seven acre plot, which would inundate us with masses of work, make us a fortune and let us live happily ever after. Oh and three b), the place enchanted us.

After part one of the deal was completed, we retired back to England. We had made our offer, and negotiated its acceptance. We had drawn up dates for completion, and had shaken a lot of hands. We then passed a happy few months in the bosom of Wiltshire, with a parent and step parent-in-law, awaiting the gestation period of three months to pass, before we became the proud owners. It was a hot and happy summer, but my memories are of a slightly surreal period. We had sold our house, and bought another that we couldn't get our hands on. We lived a family life but not at home, we lived intimately with others and shared a daily routine, but it was a measured existence wrapped up in the knowledge that it was temporary. Having virtually given up on work, we let the lull ennoble our spirits, and behaved for all the world like early retirees in a Poirot movie. We trundled up to London occasionally on the branch line, lunched with friends, shopped for things we thought we would never see again, and looked at left-hand-drive cars. A well-placed advert in the local paper quickly sold our current car, and before long we had bought a 60s Citroen DS complete with leather seats, multi-change CD, air conditioning and freshly painted bodywork in dark blue with a white roof. It was classically graceful to look at, beguilingly awkward to drive, and persistently expensive to maintain. It was backed up by an elderly beetle convertible in matching colours which was impossible to reverse with the roof down, because you couldn't see over it, as Nicky would explain when we occasionally found bits of Ford Transit van attached to the rear bumper.

As August bowed its head the date of departure became ever closer, we had to be in Bonnieux to sign the final papers on 16 September. The desire to get cracking was paramount. We had rehearsed the scene in our minds but when the moment came it was electric with excitement and panic, with a slightly sickening sense of no-turning-back. The two cars were laden down with things to make our first few days passable. We would have none of our full-time possessions for at least three weeks, so we had packed an inflatable double bed, a microwave cooker, a sound system and of course 'Bobble' our dog. She is a black Labrador, given to Nicky by the Chef. We had decided that Nicky would drive the beetle in convoy, with me and the mutt in the Citroen. We said our tearful goodbyes to the family as if we had landed a contract to pioneer double-glazing on Jupiter. Being one for a smartish getaway, leaving out lingering farewells, I was half way down the drive before I looked round to see mother and daughter blubbing for Britain. Len the gardener wept softly into Bobble's ear, and Toby, the twelve-year-old half brother was warning the cars to watch out for trouble. Which they didn't. We had hardly travelled for more than half an hour before the Citroen threw a shoe. The front nearside tyre punctured and we were laid up on the hard shoulder with a frisson of tension building up like a geyser. Citroens have strange suspension. When you turn the engine off, the whole machine unashamedly relaxes onto its haunches. It quite literally sinks to its axles and goes to sleep.

The following half hour was taken up with me unloading the

washing machine, three-piece bedroom suite, double-door fridge and a pack of dogs, digging around for some tools and a magic jack, discovering the manual was in French, and practising a little Tai-Chi to keep calm. Even without professional help I managed to change the wheel, which astonished me. It was not done, I am certain, in quite the way that the head designers of 60s Citroens had in mind, but it was achieved none the less and a little under an hour behind schedule, we were on our way to Dover once more. The convoy settled down to a steady gallop and an air of composed expectation resurfaced. Three quarters of an hour before our checking in time at the docks the Citroen blew another tyre. This was a bad omen surely. A bad idea to be going to live in the South of France. Somebody up there was trying to tell us something. This time there was no point in unloading the deep freeze, grand piano and horses, because I wasn't going to find anything useful in there to put on the wheel.

The frisson of tension matured into ripe hysteria. As I sank my teeth into the quirky steering wheel I caught sight of the lady with the convertible looking as if she had just had a face lift she was so fraught. There was a desperate lack of humour in evidence and it was with a heavy demeanour that I kicked myself out of the car and headed off up the hard shoulder in search of an emergency telephone. It was only five years ago but mobile telephones hadn't yet started growing out of everybody's ears. An hour and a half later Bobble and I were sitting in a breakdown truck heading up the motorway in the wrong direction, with the beetle driver following. We arrived at a back street garage in the middle of somewhere, and after waiting for an enthusiast to have his tyres changed, balanced and buffed up on his Mondeo Evo VI, we had no choice but to buy two new tyres. The first puncture was not mendable, and due to our car being prehistoric, the garage did not stock the exact size that our wheels needed. The helpful young delinquent took it on as a personal quest to try and find the right tyres within a thousand miles of his own domain. As the minutes dragged by and our stomach muscles became as tight as fully loaded cross bows, and after our blood corpuscles had finally turned white, he conceded that if we wanted to get anywhere that day we had better take the smaller size. We had to sign a piece of paper indemnifying him from incompetent service and pay in cash. Needless to say, our garagist was also foxed by the Citroen's suspension. But there must have been something in the way that Nicky hissed at him. Something in her poise that made him realise that even if he had to lift the car with one hand, and change the wheels with the other, he had better sort it out in the next thirty seconds. Faultily shod and gravely frayed, we took off for the Dover ferry delivering a threat to the big man in the sky that if he so much as thought of another little puncture joke, we would convert to Buddhism before he could say Sunday. We checked in without incident and having parked on the loading apron. We slipped Bobble the sleeping pill the vet had given us to soothe her nerves, and make her sleep on the boat.

'Give it to her about thirty minutes before you leave,' he had advised. An hour later we were all boarded up, the car neatly sandwiched between an inexpensive van and a flashy little coupé. Bobble was sitting up fizzing with attentiveness and vigilantly watching everything that was going on. Clearly eager for a dustbin or two to ransack, a sandwich to borrow or a quick race round the block, she wriggled with impatience. With apologies for deserting her, and a certain mendacity, we left her to sprint round the inside of the car and went up to the appropriate deck. After about forty minutes I crept down and peeked from behind the van to see if she was now anaesthetised. Behind the steering wheel, two razor-sharp eyes stared out from between a pair of erect twitching ears, as she tried to puzzle out why the car was obviously moving but wasn't, if you see what she meant. She was neither insensate nor in the least fazed by the rumbling boat.

As the journey drew to a close we made our way back to the car deck as ordered, and found Bobble reading some road maps and calculating how long it would take us to find the car-train.

There was no way that we were going to drive our historical motors, our bits of automotive wonderment, all the way down through France. It had already knocked ten years off my life getting from Marlborough to Dover, and I wasn't about to introduce myself to a triple bypass just for the pleasure of acquainting myself with the autoroutes and péages. After a few scenes like out-takes from a Jacques Tati movie wherein we drove round in circles, passed the same warehouses six times and went up several one-way streets, instead of down, we arrived at the car-train departure spot. Due to our shilly-shallying on the UK motorway, we had missed our connection. Not to worry, there was plenty of room on the next train for both passengers needing sleepers, and cars needing trailers. And yes that was correct, it did leave in approximately two and a half hours, and with luck the café might open for business if they thought it worth it. We sat down on the car park floor and pulled on a carefree attitude and let it all flow over us. There was nothing to do but unwind. After an hour or so I took Bobble for a walk down a siding, was shouted at for trespassing, passed the unopened café, peered in through the windows of a few cars, and returned to base.

After an interminable interlude, a loud speaker announced the departure of our train. It was getting on towards eight o'clock and we thought a bunk might be quite welcome. We gathered up our bags and belongings, bent over to put the lead on Bobble's collar only to see that she was lying flat on the ground with her legs splayed out like an abandoned cuddly toy. The drug had finally kicked in. Her chin was glued to the tarmac and her eyes seven-eighths closed. There was just the faintest hint of a lugubrious awareness, but basically the lights were out. I staggered off towards the train, carrying, dragging and stumbling over the luggage. There were no trolleys of course, and a few paces behind, Nicky carried, dragged and stumbled along with an elongated labrador that cared little whether she was in England, France or Ethiopia.

The moon was showing off that night as we trundled down through France. It tossed brilliant shards of silver light deep into our compartment and in the flickering midnight shadows, we picnicked on soft bread, local cheeses, pickles and fresh fruit, encouraged by a bottle of vin de pays. With the clattery rhythm of the carriage wheels our stressed-out souls were soon soothed, and it wasn't long before weary eyelids crashed shut and we joined Bobble in the land of sleep.

The next morning an amiable conductor came by and announced that we would be arriving in Avignon in half an hour. He passed us a tray with a plastic cup of instant coffee, and a biscuit he must have thought wanted to escape; it was tied up in a cellophane bag that needed surgical equipment to release it. Lamentably gone are the days of a delicious pot of fresh hot steaming black coffee running in cahoots with newly baked croissants and confiture. We downloaded ourselves, our cars and our dog into a wet Provençal morning, and drove briskly to the little hotel where we were going to stay. We had a few days' run-up to the final signing, and had booked ourselves into a small *chambre d'hôtes* close to our new acquisition. Run by the wife of an architect who would be retiring from his Paris practice within a few years, the second string to their income proved friendly and efficient. The Architect's Wife, an elegant Englishwoman, had lived for many years in Paris but was now happy to hang her hat up in the Luberon and work hard to make their venture work. The house was beautifully converted, as you might expect from a professional as experienced as Mr Architect, comfortable and completely convenient. Later that day the rain clouds shrank back and gave way to a warm and sunny sky. Floating in the swimming pool we blinked in disbelief at the surrounding countryside. It looked, through the lightly steaming water of the pool, as engaging as any photograph we'd seen, mauves and silver greys of the background hills mixed with the biscuit-coloured grasses of the plain already tinted by the earliest autumn tinges. The leaves of the cherry trees had a smudge of buttery yellow about them. The lavender, still damp, was soft green drying to a whitish silver, the vines heavy with fruit glowed as if they had been polished, and the storm had left the earth scented of freshly ground walnuts. We were looking now through the eyes of people who lived here and not at a photograph of memories. We needed pinching. Just up the road a wicked old wreck awaited us. We were ready to attack.

After the final signing was completed, we retired, as is the custom, to drink pastis with the vendor. Everybody was on fine form, relieved and grateful that all the t's had been crossed and the i's dotted, and that we could all get on with the next stage. Actually the vendors had already moved themselves into a small, single-storey house that had recently been built on the slopes of Bonnieux. It sparkled like a jewel, was equipped with all manner of mod cons that they certainly would not have had before, and I remember thinking, how much more simple it would all be if we could have been content with something similar. Momentarily I envied their together little house.

We left the *notaire*, the vendors and the agent getting deeper into the charms of pastis, and returned to our old farmhouse. At last we had the keys and it was with a touch of trepidation that we opened the shutters on the front door and eased ourselves in. It had been left spotlessly clean and even free of the smell of lingering garlic. We opened all the windows wide, and dumped our bags in the room we intended to sleep in. Following instructions, we turned on the electricity and water. There was no need for heating yet, besides which we didn't have any, other than one huge fireplace in the sitting room. The next few hours were taken up with eating and drinking at the old stone table underneath the almond tree, and taking stock. We took photographs and blew up an inflatable double mattress, which I was heroically near to completing, albeit painfully slowly, gasping and wheezing like a patient from a Smoker's Anonymous rebellion camp, when up walked Nicky dangling a foot pump.

There were no props beyond what we had squeezed into two cars, which included some basic cooking and bathing equipment. We inherited an old Formica-topped table and matching chairs. We arranged them as carefully as if old Louis XVI himself had given them to us, and went for a walk around the estate. Seven acres! It seemed like ten times that. We picked some sun-warmed tomatoes and artichokes from the *potager*, apples and blackberries from the *verger*, and a bunch of grapes from the *vignoble*, and sat down on the terrace to eat, dreaming of, amongst other things, the furniture van. It would be at least ten days before it arrived and the interim period promised to be challenging.

Our first night was always going to be strange. But as some friends of the family who kept a smart little house in one of the local villages had invited us to a rather grand dinner, it promised to be even stranger. They knew we had just landed and through waves of sympathy and understanding, insisted we join their party that night. Trying to dress so that we didn't look like something out of *The Good Life* was tricky. Trying to find their house was tricky, and keeping to the right hand side of the road whilst fighting about directions, was tricky. But all of that paled beside the harsh and cruel warnings of a German woman who, exhaustively, and continually, told me I would never find work down here. That was much trickier. She said that it was dangerous to think, at my age, I could rip myself out of my native land, and simply pick up tools and get on with it in the South of France. I can't believe that I was flashing like a beacon of self-confidence, and prompted this attack, or that I was fizzing with complacency, or being arrogant about my abilities. Quite the opposite. Having given up my practice in the UK and moved to a whole new dimension, I was much more of a 'riddled with insecurity and praying to whoever might listen' type of person, absolutely hoping for the best, but at the same time certainly not wanting to seem unconvincing. I have worked in many parts of the world and know the basic ropes, I'm aware of new rules and regulations that different countries throw up, and that learning curves can be arduous, but that night as we drove home I was much flattened by this woman's pedantic preaching.

'You'll prove her wrong,' yawned Nicky.

'I sure hope so,' I replied, and turned over heavily, my full weight coming down abruptly on our temporary mattress and pumping all the air across onto her side. She shot upwards and practically hit the ceiling.

A few days later we made contact with another architect friend. He had been living and practising down here for about five years, and he helped us sort out the planning permission for the alterations and renovations we had in mind. We had bought a survey of the house, plus a ground plan that had been commissioned by a previously interested party. It had proved to be a useful document to have during the summer months leading up to our arrival, giving us the opportunity of trying out all sorts of ideas, different arrangements and possibilities. By the time we were talking to Andrew Architect, we had a very clear idea of what was wanted and some basic plans and elevations had been drawn up. Andrew took the information, enhanced it, filled in the forms and sent it up to the Mayor's office. It was stamped, endless copies made, forms filled in, numbers issued and signed for by all parties. Before it could be sent to the big office in the big town so that the big person could make the big decision, we had to meet the regional architect to discuss everything in detail. A date was set and, wonder of wonders, there he was waiting. We took along our Andrew so that the French architect-speak was clear and fully comprehended by all. Sitting in that smokey little office surrounded by brown filing cabinets, reams of paper, and the chatter of old-fashioned typewriters, I looked at the fading aerial photographs, and charts of what you could shoot and when, pinned to the wall. I listened to the background noise of an endless discussion on the minutiae of the *fabrique* of our conversion. I hoped very much that the French high command didn't have any mandates as complicated, and daft, up their sleeves to deal with when it came to making a garden.

They did.

Whilst waiting for the permit of construction to materialise, which we had been told would take about three months, we had turned our heads to the garden. One morning, Nicky was poking around with a torch in one of the downstairs 'caves' which we referred to as the cattery, because that was where our semi-wild little kittens liked to hide and sleep. It was a room with no windows, slightly crumbly bare stone walls, an earth floor and no door. There was, however, a rather fine old stone arch leading into it, and it was this that was being investigated. As the torchlight beamed its way round the perimeter of the room, on the far wall she noticed the outline of a blocked-in window.

From the outside it was impossible to see any such thing. Soil had been piled right up against the house to the first floor nearly all along the south side, goodness knows how many decades before. This was an exciting discovery because when we had been busy

planning and designing back in England, we had assumed that these black holes would only be usable as storage, or utility, using borrowed light. Suddenly we could imagine ballrooms and banqueting-halls, temperature controlled environments for ageing wines and Ferraris. Adjustments were made to our planning applications, new drawings completed in double-quick time, and a few pertinent questions asked just to make sure there was nothing silly in the rule book about excavating soil away from the side of an old *mas*.

The *Mairie* assured us there were no problems with making a garden, chortling quietly, they evidently thought it quaint that we should even ask. Our builder introduced us to a young digger wizard who could drive his tractor like ringing a bell. He was an intelligent and diligent kid who would quickly see off any opposition should he ever enter a digger competition. Over the years I've worked with dozens of these guys and none came anywhere near Patrick's ability and agility. Further, he can work a theodolite, that rather complicated tool used by surveyors to gauge levels, he knows how to grade banks, put in irrigation ditches, alter manhole covers, and delegate when necessary. Compared to some of the ex-convicts and sweaty alcoholics that turn up in depleted JCB's to push a garden around, this boy lives in a league of his own.

Because our house is situated on a slope anyway, any extra levels had to be carefully worked out. It would need form and balance to avoid looking heavy. The new banks would have to be pushed far enough back from the house to let in light and give space for terraces, not be too steep but still be split up gently so as not to ape a cliff face. It was a big job and not without its trepidations. Patrick gave us two quotes, one for straight-forward excavation, and another, altogether more alarming, price to cover the eventuality of finding a rock bed. This involved blasting with explosives and huge heavy-weight tractor-driven hammer drills. We were not confident that the poor old house could stand the excitement, and thought it would probably fall down. Anyway it was decided that I would get on with the drawings, and if we did find massive rock, we would try and make a feature of the blessed thing. There was a small room down at one end of the house that I had procured for my office. I managed to squeeze in two drawing boards, a filing cabinet and computer. There was hardly room to move but it anchored me a bit, and until I had work, I might as well get on and practice with my own back yard.

One morning in late October Nicky came back from a walk with another dog besides our own. He had picked her up about a kilometre away. She says that one moment she and Bobble were just trotting along on their own, and the next, from nowhere this chap had fallen in like an illusionist trick. He was slim with a mongrel's pedigree. He had a splash of wire-haired collie mixed with a slender slice of labrador, eyes that were a little too close together like Bjorn Borg's, a heart the size of a giant valentine card, and a very bushy tail which he wagged a great deal, and *voila*! He accepted an invitation to join us for lunch, was well mannered enough to hang back until Bobble had sat down, then with minimal intrusion seated himself underneath the table. He had no tabs on his collar and no markings in his ear so we temporarily christened him Maurice. We talked about what we were going to do with him and although he was a fellow of considerable charm, we did not really want another dog at this time. We decided not to worry too much and just wait and see if he moved on.   Later that afternoon Nicky was outside trying to dig out some particularly aggressive weeds that spread like butch vines across the big bank, when Maurice went up and offered to help. He grabbed the tendrils of the vine between his teeth, and with front paws pushing into the ground, and some jerky movements with his back, did his best to help her yank them from the undergrowth. Pulling with all his might he habitually reversed straight in to Nicky's face, he would look round, grin apologetically, reposition himself, and try again. The useful axe had to be abandoned for fear of chopping off his little feet. He especially liked to sit down as near to Nicky as possible, preferably on her hands, all the time wagging away and gazing up into her eyes dreamily, certain that he had met his dream human. When I went to see how it was all going, he bounded over to greet me like a long-lost friend, smiling a great big silly smile, he darted around my legs in a figure of eight. Cleverly, he never forgot to flatter Bobble from time to time, and deeply endeared himself to us.

Where had he come from? Whose was he? Suddenly, having obviously decided he had done his best to help, he trotted off. That's that I thought. Later, Jacquie Neighbour turned up and we were discussing log chopping or something, when out of the woods bounded Maurice. His tail wagging over time, he rushed across the lavender field and presented us with, oh Lord, a freshly caught and throttled chicken. He was as proud as punch with his prey, evidence of a successful hunt and ran round with great glee, his front legs like a trotting horse. He dropped it at our feet, pushed it forward with one of his paws, and was, without doubt giving it to us as a token of his appreciation of our hospitality.

'Mon Dieu!' shrieked Jacquie. 'C'est mon poulet!' and proceeded to lurch into a hopeless chase. Hopeless because Jacquie couldn't catch a cold let alone a fit, youthful, street-wise mongrel. Maurice dashed about out of reach, occasionally circling back and sitting on my feet. He would look up at me beseechingly: 'Get rid of him,' he whispered, out of the corner of his muzzle.

'Naughty dog, you mustn't kill chickens and things,' I said feebly. But his English wasn't that hot, and, seeing Jacquie making a last desperate flying tackle in his direction he made off. He paused at the top of the bank, looked back at the mayhem, and wisely trotted out of view. Later it began to rain. It chucked down as if God had just discovered the trick. The evening drew in, dark, windy and wet wet wet. I was in the kitchen and noticed that Billy, one of the kittens, sitting on the window ledge, looked as spooked as if she had just seen a dog. She had. I peered outside, and the wind nearly removed my ears, the light flickered and the trees were bent double. There, about fifty meters away, lurking in the shadows of the house lights... Maurice! Soaked, bedraggled and apparently half his normal size. His bushy tail now so wet he could only just move it enough to back up a contrite little grin. He waited.

'Oh Maurice, you old mongrel,' I called. 'You had better come in.'

So, as Nicky prepared a prodigal-son size helping of doggy food, I dried and rubbed him down with an old towel. He gobbled the grub gratefully, slurped some water and, as if he were at home, stretched out in front of the fire contentedly. Leaving space for her highness, naturally. He spent an impeccably well-behaved night in the spare basket, didn't whine, didn't pee or anything, and was at the bedroom door at seven thirty along with Bobble, wagging furiously, waiting for breakfast and a cuddle. I, meanwhile had tossed and turned all night worrying about what to do with him, where his owners where, and how much they might be fretting. I needn't have bothered. Later that morning, to extremely mixed feelings, he left. With a jaunty toss of the head and a wink, he was gone. It had been a fair exchange and maybe one day he'll use this inn again. Strangely it took me some time to get over Maurice. I thought about him a lot and without wanting to sound too fey, I felt as if there had been more to him than just, stray dog. It was as if he was powered by some existentialist spirit. The night that he stayed with us was the night that Theo was conceived, and oddly the only time that Maurice came back, it was for an hour or so on the day that the doctor confirmed the pregnancy. Let me tell you what happened when a brace of golden eagles landed on the lawn ...

On a freezing March morning an army of digger tractors with varying sized buckets, heavy lorries, dumper trucks and low loaders assembled outside. They parked roughly level with the windows of what we referred to as the sitting room. The exhaust from the chugging diesels spiralled up against the frosty morning sunshine, and an atmosphere of major manoeuvres hung in the cold air. I dodged around dipping under the huge swinging arms, making sure that the stakes that had been banged into the ground to guide the drivers were still in position The noise was formidable but results were immediate. When you have equipment like this on site things happen quickly. You have to stay on your toes to make sure everything is going to plan. Drop off for a moment and some irrevocable mistakes can occur. Service pipes; electrical cables, mains water and drains, all lurk under ground and even with common sense prevailing, they are easily pulled out.

Around the middle of the afternoon, on the second day, we were in the kitchen when we heard a terrible scream. Rushing to the window to see what had happened, we were horrified to discover that the caterpillar tractor with the biggest scoop had managed to capsize into the hole he had just dug. This huge ungainly piece of machinery lay on its side at the bottom of the pit like an undignified dinosaur, its long hydraulic neck desperately seeking purchase. The scream had come from the unfortunate operator as he was tossed out of his cab. The God of Earth Work drivers was looking after his own that day, and one badly shaken jockey clambered up and out of the abyss to be bunged some brandy and banter. Everybody was rattled by the incident and deeply thankful that no emergency calls had had to be made.

That evening after everyone had gone home and as dusk was slipping its way in, I walked slowly round the site. It was a bizarre experience. There was a roaring silence. The endless revving and roaring of the day's activities still echoed in the ether. The land looked as if it had been abused. It was coarse in its outline, and raw from its attackers, and there lying in a pitiful heap, was one of the abandoned perpetrators. It took a big bag of confidence, bolstered by imagination, to see our way through this one.

In the end we dug out about a thousand tonnes of spoil, around a hundred lorry loads. It had to be put somewhere. In the landscaping parlance we talk of 'cut and fill'. That is to say, having dug a big hole, you try to find something that you can fill in, or up. You try to be creative with a lot of old dirt that would cost a small fortune to have taken away. It wasn't all beautiful rich, loamy earth, indeed ninety per cent of it was sub sub-soil and as much use for growing things in as a stagnant pond. But it could be used for forming banks and barriers. In the plans it was designated to be used as an embankment, giving the house a bit more privacy from anyone using the minor road that goes past the end of our driveway. Patrick skilfully shaped and shoved, compacted and covered with top soil, until we had a magnificent new base on which we would sow prairie grass and put in hedging plants to compound our new-found seclusion.

Despite the rude and unrefined presentation, we were really pleased with the whole operation. We now had a proper two-storey house, a big ground floor terrace, and some shapely young banks to work with. Jacquie, our neighbour, dropped by a couple of days later and we coerced him into clinking glasses of pastis, which is probably about as difficult as persuading the Pope to take communion, to celebrate the extra dimension the house and garden had gained. He was just a wrinkle bit reserved in his appreciation, and whilst agreeing that everything was certainly better, and that it was well executed, he didn't come out with the fully blown song and dance routine we thought he might. Well, maybe he was a bit staggered by what had happened to a house he had known since childhood. Perhaps a little perplexed that we thought such an exercise was necessary. Dropping the subject we moved back indoors and let the bottle loose. We talked of this and this and that and that. Suddenly he said that the Mayor didn't like it. His weathered face was deeply furrowed as he continued:

'I think you are going to have to go and talk to the Mayor about this new bank you've made.'

'Why?'

'Well,' he said slowly and not looking very convincing, 'there's been a lot of complaints in the village about what you're doing.'

'What, complaints about making a *garden*?'

Jacquie looked awkward. He was, he told us, good friends with the Mayor and assured *us* that he had assured *him* that we were not up to anything subversive. We tried to prise more out of our man in the middle, but it was unsatisfactory. The next day Nicky went up to the *mairie*, imagining that this whole episode would be over quickly once she had explained that her husband was a professional garden designer, and knew what he was doing (most of time). That we were, after all, only removing soil from the house that someone, at some stage, had put there in the first place, and that it would all be lovely and green in no time. She realised that a bigger task was on our hands when she was told by the Mayor's assistant, that the village was up in arms. Not so much about us taking the damned earth away from the house, but that we had chosen to make such large banks. That we were impairing the view the village enjoyed of the Luberon, and further, that one of our neighbours had added fuel to the fire, by reporting that we were blockading ourselves in against attack, and that we were paranoid and obsessed with privacy. That night we sat at the kitchen table with our heads in our hands, gazing into our glasses of local wine we buy in five litre jugs at the local co-operative *vinicole*. This is where the wine-growing farmers take their trailer loads of grapes to be pooled into the vats that make the local *vin de pays*. It's nothing to send post cards about, and it probably doesn't like to travel, but at a few francs a litre, not many would complain. It was hard to comprehend that a bit of inoffensive landscaping had brought the parochial *paysans* down our necks with such force. To say that we were blocking the view of the Luberon was such enormous nonsense, we would have laughed if we hadn't been crying. The village is about fifty metres above us, and the Luberon valley fifty metres below, so their argument was founded on aggression rather than logic.

We went into battle again a few days later, after the Mayor rang to say that he was coming down to talk to us. A likeable, moustachioed little fellow, with a portly figure, wearing glasses, he warned us to expect him directly. He also has quite a reputation as an electrical talent, having gained regard for his engineering wizardry during the war. It was tiring and disconcerting trying to wrestle with his expansive reasoning, he had an ability to talk very quickly without drawing breath. Soon we concluded that we would, as he suggested, have a meeting with the expert from the regional offices of the 'Parc Naturel Régional du Luberon' in whose jurisdiction we were located.

There was a smattering of thin white cloud screening the early morning spring sun, as we waited for 'The Expert' to come. New fresh grass pushed its way up through the bric-a-brac of last year's dead weeds, and above, the small buds of the white oak and hornbeam prepared to slip into their unblemished coats of verdant green, ready for the upcoming summer season. We were anxious to get this meeting over with. Hopefully, it would clear the air and we could finish off the work we had started. It was hard to think that all this fuss was more than just a tempest in a tea cup, but clearly we had to play the game. Just after nine a small convoy turned up, escorted by the Mayor in his little red Peugeot. He was followed by Sweep, the village guardian, in one of those ubiquitous small white vans that seem to come free with national-insurance contributions. It is Sweep who diligently keeps the cemetery and ditches free of debris, puts up the necklaces of colourful lights for all the festival do's, and generally maintains the village in a correct and proper fashion. We are also inclined to think that he probably monitors the behaviour of incoming foreigners who may be getting out of their prams, and in true Big Brother style reports back to 'The Office'. That is, people like us, who might want to make a garden, with an area that is not completely open for microscopic scrutiny, by all and sundry. After him, scurrying along in a mini jeep, came the French architect with a youth who I thought might be his son, but no sign of 'The Expert'.

Bobble rushed up to the procession roaring like a hound with rabies, then quickly turned into a one-dog welcoming party, greeting them all like long lost pals, as she does with most strangers. I re-introduced Nicky and myself with considered restraint. The Mayor lurched off into full flight, his swivelling head and gesticulating arms demonstrating his point of view like a great orator in the chamber, inexorably pulling his audience to his mandate. We all listened respectfully, shuffling the gravel under our feet, and in my case, letting my mind wander off down the lanes of listlessness. Finally, after a monotonous rally of inconsequential blather, he proceeded to introduce the earring-wearing, gum-chewing acned adolescent as 'The Expert'.

'Monsieur, bonjour,' I said shaking his hand genially and giving him a full frontal shot of me smiling ingratiatingly. But inside I was boggled that someone of his tender age should be put forward to give opinions, and make judgements, about matters of what does, and does not, go on in The Luberon National Park. With the best will in the world, it was stretching the credibility factor to suggest that he could have enough experience to offer intelligent conceptions. I have nothing against earrings in men's ears, I used to have one myself when I was in my early twenties. I would tell people that my lobe had been pierced on a drunken night spent with gypsies in Greece. They heated the needle up over a campfire you see, dipped it into the rough brandy I was drinking, and with a cork in position behind my ear, had driven it through the floppy disc with the force of a stake being lunged into a vampire's heart. Or was it actually in the ear-piercing cubicle of the fake jewellery department in Selfridges on a wet Monday morning? I can't quite remember. I have nothing against chewing gum either. I am generally pretty sympathetic about the growing pains of acne, but the combination of these things so skilfully collected and arranged in front of us, and about to pass judgement on my garden design capabilities, started to cook up the oil. This boy, looking bleakly at his trainers, hands in nappies, filled a window of silence by announcing that we would, indeed, have to remove the bank. There was a unanimous nodding of heads, shrugging of shoulders and pouting of lips. The jury had called guilty and the sentence had been passed. I expect they gave the kid half a litre of petrol for his *mobilette*, guaranteed a pass on his first traffic offence and told him to go back to the crèche.

We did pretty much what we were told, and lowered the banks in places, and improvised in others. Nicky was feeling really ropey in her first months of pregnancy. She didn't want to eat buddleia sandwiches with horseradish or anything, she just didn't want to eat at all, and was sick if I even opened the kitchen door. So we let the dust settle, sowed the grass seed and waited for the scars to heal over and the baby to progress peacefully.

CHAPTER THREE

Gloves in a Cold Climate

As February cantered towards March, strangely hot days arrived that belied the time of year. Inquisitive little shoots of iberis and alyssum appeared, and whilst not really ready to perform properly for another month or so, they seemed quite happy to be seduced by the temperate breath of the day, completely forgetting how cold the nights could be. The small yellow stars of the winter jasmine were already fading out, and the daffodils and narcissus were loosening up in the wings. The primroses looked prim and the *Viburnum tinus* was about to explode with a showy bunch of white flowers. The philadelphus was not going to flower yet a while, but the camellias liked to tease with their big voluptuous buds, and then, just as they were about to come, they went instead, their ripe unfolding blooms bitten off by the lingering frosts.

Faxes and e-mails from New York suggested a meeting in Ménerbes next week, just to have an update of where everything was at. The answer, as far as the garden is concerned, was nowhere very much. The poor darling sat neglected, still trying its best to hibernate under its skimpy covering. The tree people had still not turned up to prune the fruit trees, fell the dead cherry, or shape the quince. When Eric, the eldest son of a continuing line of arboriculturists, gave his estimate, he shrugged off the work as run-of-the-mill stuff. That was, until I showed him the fig tree that had sown itself into the old wall overhanging the valley, at the bottom of the garden. It was fairly obvious that he didn't look forward to abseiling over the edge, a chain saw dangling from one hand, the other mapping crosses on his chest to the Virgin Mary. His price, and reluctance to turn up, reflected his excitement. It was no surprise, and I fully expected to have to hustle on this one.

The meeting was held but it didn't really run to much. Mr La Bour had yet to apply his talents to the swimming pool, and he was dragging his heels in the house. Richard was relaxed about the progress, or lack of it. He runs a sizeable design and building business in New York and knows how things unfold. He also knows, having had a house in Provence for fourteen years or so, how they unfold down here. Slower than they do in Manhattan. We adjourned until next month and the next visit.

Meanwhile the forlorn garden was to be left to its own devices. No doubt it would start to look better soon, because of all the natural greenery that would jump in, weeds mostly, but still welcome after such a big strip. Slowly it would put on the very same coat that we did our best to remove last autumn.

Where does a flower end and a weed begin? Certainly some weeds are rude and coarse, and knowing that, they appear all the more determined to put down roots that defy belief. One aggressive variety, that ironically has very pretty mauve flowers that last all summer, will, if left to mature, sink an anchor 80 centimetres long. When you pull that out in one piece, you have the same sense of achievement as peeling an apple without breaking the skin. But there are others that should be welcomed into a garden. Just because they are invasive, there is no need to write them off. Convolvulus is a case in point. On one side of the family you have it invading and twisting the night away, whilst its cousins have been tamed to behave with decorum. *Ipomea* or morning glory? Imagine if that was left to it own devices, and if it came back perennially. Whilst others that have settled comfortably into the catalogues turn out to conduct themselves badly. *Gaura*, for example. That lovely long-lasting delicate pale-pink flower that fills out and grows to a metre tall. Dig it out to move it, or reduce it, and back it comes the following season, fighting its corner. Artemisia self-sows abundantly, bulbs naturalise, and grass creeps. The cross-over line is pretty thin sometimes.

La Chasse, the hunting season, would be over soon. It is not so much the fact that it's the mating or nesting season coming up, that persuades the Frenchman to hang up his machine guns, or put the twin-barrelled revolvers back into their holsters. It's more the fact that they have shot everything. There is nothing left. 'If it flies it dies' is the adopted motto, and it rings from November through to March. When the season opens, quite suddenly all the local farmers and countryside workers take on a whole new bearing. Off go the worn-out jeans and torn jackets, and on come the slick army fatigues. New haircuts, snazzy squeaky boots and an upright posture complete the icon, as they fall in for a paramilitary onslaught on the local fauna. There's something of the 'put a man in a uniform and he'll become a dictator' syndrome going on here. Take the dog or children for a walk if you dare. A carefree ramble through the countryside can turn into an ominous and downright dangerous escapade. You're walking along happy as Olivier, when suddenly out of the creases of the hedgerow crawls a demonic-looking soldier, with a heavy-duty firearm. He'll either be pointing the thing at you, louchely, or holding it by its stock, cocked, as it rests precariously over his shoulder. His gait is confident and assured and he knows that happiness is a warm gun. Whilst it's a sobering experience to go eyeball to eyeball with this untrained mercenary, it's arguably better than running the risk of being shot at because he hadn't seen you properly, thinking you might be something to roast on toast.

I was once told that it's really best to stay indoors during this madness. But if you do go out, keep shouting out loud, so that they can hear you, but I'm not sure that's absolutely sound advice. If they can hear you, they can get you. Paranoid? No, totally noid. Every year at least a dozen people bite the dust because of 'accidents' during *La Chasse*. Remember, this a country that will drop a murder charge against you if the chap whose head you have just removed, turns out to be your wife's piano tuner. Anything to do with 'G' strings, 'G' spots, and middle 'C's is fine with the *Regie*. This oddity is augmented by the fact that the hunter has the right to roam free over anybody's land, and will blast the dying night lights out of everything from an adder to an owl. A friend thought it might deter the infantryman if he put up one of those witty little signs that you can buy in the big supermarkets that says : *'Chasse Interdit'*. Hunting forbidden. It hangs on the shelf next to those other irresistible little plaques that demand you disobey them. 'Private' and 'No Entry'. His wife was worried that a frustrated psycho might evacuate the life from one of her cats. Easier to bag than a thrush. He dutifully nailed up a couple of signs in strategic spots, and whilst not totally confident that it would persuade the rapacious cowboy to back off, he was none-the-less, a little fazed to find that the very next day they had been peppered with shot. They had clearly provided good target practice, and the grouping was high score.

One animal that seems to survive the carnage relatively unscathed is the wild boar. From the reported sightings, their numbers are on the increase. I saw a family cross the road up in the hills the other day. They jogged out of the undergrowth, trotted over the tarmac without looking sideways, and disappeared into the woods. Mr was probably about a metre high at his shoulders, brown with grey coarse hairy hide, his wife much the same but predictably smaller, whilst the three boarlets were as cute as pie in their stripy baby clothes. It was as well for all of us that the car wasn't going very fast. It was interesting to see them out for a walk like that, as there is something disquieting about spotting evidence of their existence, or hearing stories of their aggressive behaviour, without actually having a clear image to fit the facts. The first indication I had of their presence, was when I went to talk to a new client up in the *garrigue* behind Bonnieux.

I was having a quick shoofty around, before the owner came out of the house, when I discovered this long, gently slopping bank that looked as if it had been attacked by a rogue digger tractor. It was ploughed up like the operator had found a secret, extra-destructive burrowing device, and had yet to gain control of it. Great troughs and ditches, cavities and chasms gaped from the injured terrain. Massive rocks had been spewed around the place and the roots of the struggling almond trees had been torn and grubbed out. When it was explained that it was the work of a group of wild boars nesting down for the night, I changed my mind about having one as a pet. I saw the signs again in much more salubrious surroundings. There is a hotel not far from here that wallows in bourgeoisie bliss. A large old *mas* that was converted by some doubtful character, who allegedly met his maker when he was shot down at Marseille airport. It was taken over by some representatives of the affluent French middle class, and turned into a chic and dapper place to lay your head. The dining room is full of stiff, over-dressed, middle-sized people sitting at stiff, over-dressed, middle-sized tables but the food is good and the service impeccable. Once, while waiting our friend, an actor who divides his time between Hollywood and Provence, and his family to arrive for lunch (it *is* good for kids), I took Theo for a look around the garden. The pool nestles between rows of perfectly clipped lavender and rosemary, interspersed by olives and oaks, overlooking the Luberon. It is the very model of a picture of Provence. The nurtured lawn swoops up towards the house, bordered by well-heeled shrubs and trees. However, in places it had been badly bullied by boars. Craters and fissures cracked open the grass, spilling the debris onto the weed-free paths. A neighbour tells me that once he heard a scuffling noise outside his house in the middle of the night. Whatever it was, was not at all discreet, and seemingly had no worries about being heard. He ran down the stairs and was just about to open the door, when he realised that he had nothing on. Not wanting to surprise anybody too much with his nakedness, he shot back up stairs, rummaged through the designer kit, slipped into something not too formal, yet teasingly fashionable, and in no time was back at the door into the garden. He checked his gate and moved forward with caution. Bravely shining his torch, he advanced down the lawn. A grunt several octaves lower than a baritone with bronchitis could manage, came from the velvet darkness. Then a few more grunts at varying distances were added. Eugene suddenly wondered why on earth he had come out into the garden at all, and what on earth had made him think he was big and brave enough to deal with burglars or boars. The torch picked up the outline of something moving very fast indeed. It was his own shadow, belting back up the garden as quickly as he could muster.

Hunters are now cross-breeding the *sanglier* with the domestic pig, and calling it a *cochonglier*. Why? Well they are easier to shoot, and not so likely to sink their tusks into your bum, that's why.

An altogether more gentle pursuit is the hunt for the truffle. The truffle is a subterranean fungus, which lives in symbiosis with certain trees, mostly evergreen and white oaks, but also the hazel, beech and chestnut. It is born by spores, and is a dark brown swelling found about twenty five to thirty centimetres below the surface of the ground. The French truffle production, mostly in the south, has shrunk considerably during the last century, due in part to the diminishing forests and the use of pesticides, and probably in part to the rubbing off of land that would have supported these extraordinary victuals. Around the beginning of the twentieth century, records show that something in excess of one and a half thousand tons of the mouldy old fungus were harvested annually in Perigord alone. But by the start of this century numbers had withered to a measly couple of hundred tons in the whole of France. People have been trying to breed the truffle for years, but it is elusive, and doesn't seem to produce the quantity and quality a connoisseur would embrace. A bit like salmon farming, a good fish certainly, but not quite the aristocrat we know and love from the great rivers of Scotland. There is a firm control over the production of young trees sold in pots, or root balls, that have been dusted with the spores of the magical *Tuber mecanosporum*. They can only be grown under licence, are monitored by a government authority and are all given an individual number.

Truffle is an acquired taste and after five or six seasons of eating it in various guises, I am now quite a convert. It's like the product of an illicit love affair between a hardened old mushroom and an uptight Jerusalem artichoke, conducted in a dank and dangerous compost heap. The passion and commotion the thing can cause is a little baffling to the uninitiated. It is inordinately un-prepossessing to look at, has a strong, lusty smell of degenerated earth, and goes off within a few days, unless jarred up and kept in the fridge, whereupon it will cause havoc unless hermetically sealed, flavouring all and sundry for weeks to come. Apparently the Egyptians ate truffles dipped in goose fat, whilst the ancient Greeks and Romans swore by their aphrodisiacal qualities. Well they would. They were so buzzed out on their orgies; gulping down industrial quantities of wine; they probably found Homer horny, what with all that hexameter verse. One can just imagine old Claudius coming to terms with the more subtle results of eating a finely prepared truffle. Lightly seasoned with salt and pepper, cooked in a covered black cocotte, and left to dance in the boiling liquid for twenty-five minutes with twenty or so lardons. Like Tritons playing around a black Amphitrite, which give substance to the cooking juices. Actually, however much I have eaten, it hasn't made me feel any more tender and loving than I would after eating some horse droppings.

One evening we were having supper with some friends. We were eating scrambled eggs cooked in olive oil, with some scrapings of the old kernel tucked in, when a man said to the middle-aged lady sitting on my right, how much more attractive she became after drinking a few glasses of wine. I don't think this had much to do with the food as such. More likely it was how much more attractive she became after *he* had drunk a few glasses of wine. But who knows, something might have tickled his truffle. It is not entirely surprising therefore that in the Middle Ages they were looked upon as a manifestation of the devil, but they bounced back into the charts, like all good old Rock and Rollers, during the Renaissance. They have been going in and out of style ever since, like Tom Jones.

There are many people who say that pigs are the best animals to employ if you want to find truffles. Trouble is they have to be muzzled, otherwise the old porker tends to gobble them down before the poor *paysan* can get his hands on them. Actually pigs are rarely used in preference to dogs. They are awkward beasts to move around, have no understanding of retrieving in the labrador sense, squeal and shout, get grumpy and unhelpful, and need to snooze regularly. Whereas a dog will go about the discovery with the enthusiasm of a rookie customs officer sniffing out crack at a provincial airport. Tail wagging in circles, propelling her towards the veiled trume, her unmitigated loyalty will keep her at it until dusk if necessary. When the wee treasure has been found, it is important to carefully replace the clods of earth so that no other traces remain. The other truffles must be left to mature and, equally important, the curiosity of poachers must not be aroused.

I asked my friend Monsieur Marcheur, a Provençal, if he would take me for a walk in the local truffle woods. Having managed a degree from Sydney University, he spent forty-odd years working in the East before gratefully retiring back here in the Luberon. He loves his countryside and knows it well. I knew he would be informed on the foibles of finding, the quirks of cooking and the possibilities of poaching, truffles. So, providing I kept my mouth shut, my eyes open and my mind liberal, he agreed to take me.

'Shall I bring Bobble? I asked, secretly hoping she might turn out to be a truffle finding champ, raising her game to one of hushed admiration amongst the locals. We could use a little extra credibility. Mr Marcheur looked at me in the way a seasoned rodeo rider might look at a first-time bronco boy, but said kindly, 'We are not asking to draw attention to ourselves.'

We parked the car in the driveway of a mutual friend who we knew to be abroad, locked the doors and shuffled away from the vehicle. Just two guys taking a lazy, aimless amble, but I felt like a smuggler walking over the borders between unfriendly frontiers. In his hand he held a long whip of a stick which he flicked from time to time with a practised wrist. As we walked along he explained

Marché aux Truffes. Carpentras

many of the secrets and lore of this strange practice. Truffle cultivation is speculative and limited. They are neither sown nor planted. They spring up spontaneously, when the fungal spores, or mycelia, encounter the rootlets of a sympathetic tree. They form a mycorrhiza, which takes its nutrients from the tree; the truffle itself is the fruiting body of the fungus and does not appear to be connected by any filaments to the mycorrhiza. Allegedly there are over sixty varieties of truffle of which more than half are found in Europe. But the best, the ones held in the highest regard come from Périgord, Vaucluse, Lot and Gard. This is the black/dark brown, white-veined variety we have around here.

Inevitably, in the truffle world there are truffle snobs, just like in the wine world. The connoisseur will tell you that a good black truffle must be well rounded and in one piece, is not really ripe until after Christmas, and will have peaked by the first week of March. They are eaten raw or cooked, shaved, sliced, or cut into strips, diced or shredded. They garnish risotto, scrambled eggs, meat and chicken. They are folded into sauces and slipped into salads.

The first time I saw a whole one, I thought it was what we used to call a 'temple ball.' That strong, black hashish from India that had been rolled and rolled round the palms of some stoned dealer, and then sent over to England via Russia, to space everybody out so the Communists could take over. Carpentras Truffle Market, the second biggest in France, the other being Richerenches, is held on a Friday morning. From my point of view this is fortuitous because it coincides with the flower market, also only held on Fridays, albeit at a different corner of the town. Having heard about the *Marche aux Truffes* on countless occasions, I thought it time to go and see what it was all about. Laziness had slipped in on this account, because our neighbours had always generously supplied us with more than we could hope to cook. I set off early, one cold mid-February morning. As I drove along the narrow lanes that cut through the vineyards, the dark trunks of the robust old vines stood out against the silvery ground, and a breath of frozen air moved slowly over the fields like a retreating coven of ghosts. I arrived at about seven thirty, and already the town was behaving as if it were mid afternoon. With the car deposited, I moved through the throngs of traders, busy setting up their stalls for the regular Friday morning market. Rows of giant umbrellas spread themselves across the town's small streets and out onto the carparks. Nestling underneath, a magnificent assortment of edibles, wearables, collectibles and forgettables arranged themselves invitingly. Deep benches of olives mixed with anchovies, red and green peppers, garlic and local herbs, vied for attention against a variety of sausages of varying sizes and backgrounds. Cheeses galore and hearty salads, meats, fishes and fruit, home-made confitures and pickles, wines, apple and pear juices and freshly baked pies, tarts and cakes, all winked, as I passed down the lines of stalls. China plates with sussy designs, dog leads, bowls and toys, DIY tools and picnic tables, even Soleiado fabrics, still going strong after all these years, beckoned from stands and tables. You could, surely, be forgiven for thinking that the world might have Soleiadoed out by now, but still the demand continues it seems. Straw baskets, hats and shoes, hand-painted plates and cups, plus a plethora of thrilling little oddities, things that prove completely useless, come at you like escapees from a free insert magazine in the Sunday papers. Finally, rack upon rack of cheap, practical clothing in sizes for all comers complete the happy emporium. Not being absolutely certain of where to find the truffle dealers I asked a taxi driver, who kindly, and without impatience, explained that I was virtually standing in it. Must be small I thought, turning round. There, about ten metres away I could see a large huddle of people gathered in a circle, all bent over and looking at something with great concentration. Maybe it's an enormous truffle, or a big bag of them, I wondered to myself. A truffle sect about to make a sacrifice?

I moved over towards the small crowd. Not wanting to be too pushy or intrusive, I edged in as discreetly as I could, and being tall I was able to look over the heads of some of the audience. To my surprise and amazement, standing proud in the middle of this group was a giant Harley Davidson. Glittering chrome, black tasselled leather and a cowpuncher's engine drew gasps of appreciation and awe. Local tractor drivers, garage mechanics and *mobilette* riders came together as one, all harbouring their Kerouac fantasies of wild parties, girls, drink and drugs, mixed intoxicatingly with the fear of uncertainty and loneliness, fused by bop. Monsieur Moriarty was not thinking truffle, so I moved my search on a little further. Round the corner I came to the Café Universal. Outside, just beyond the awning were a row of collapsible trestle tables, stretching about fifteen metres along the pavement. On top, sitting proudly in an assortment of plastic dishes, ranging from Tupperware, decommissioned ice-cream tubs, and recycled fast food foil packs, were a collection of muddy little truffles.

Their colours and sizes varied from the grand black to a slightly sorry brown; from near perfect squash balls to gnarled rabbit droppings. Prices were scrawled on torn-off pieces of cardboard stating anything from 1000 francs a kilo, to a wrenching 2000 if you were silly enough to pay it. The people selling these offerings looked a bit like buskers outside a cinema queue, and kept eyeing each other warily. I moved down the line trying to look like an old hand, picking one up here and squeezing it, smelling another one there, asking the price and feigning shock and horror, probably fooling no one except myself. Then I noticed, tucked under the awning, a quadrangle of narrow tables forming a kind of worktop, accessible by a small gap at one end. Curiously there was nobody standing very close to the tables, although the crowd seemed to be waiting patiently for something to happen. They were clearly not there just to buy from the tinker sellers at their plastic-topped counters.

At nine-o'clock sharp, a shrill whistle broke through the air, dominating all noise and pulling us to attention. There was much shoving and shuffling, and a platoon of professional truffle growers swifly moved onto the outside of the trestle tables. Each was clutching their sacks, baskets and pillow cases bulging with protruding promise. They peeled or folded back their portfolios, and guardedly displayed their wares. Nobody was going to show too much too soon. A full house was going to be kept well up the sleeve and a straight flush would only revealed at the climax of pricing. A more divergent and unlikely group of characters (*les caveurs*) you would be hard pressed to find. Some, rather grand looking, displayed an air of confidence, whilst others seemed more clandestine and veiled. Old boys with deep, smile-lined faces, watched with seasoned patience, whilst a supporting back row of luckless legionnaires, looking like furtive wrecks whose only bonanza happens once a year, tried to hustle in on the proceedings. Down one end, a small group of farmers had gathered. Similar to a bunch of hopeful bidders in a saleroom, they readied themselves to catch the auctioneer's eye with blood-shot winks, cap tipping and nose tapping. Additional players looked like good, honest, well-rounded chaps who were thoroughly enjoying their slender months of trade. A few ladies handled their big round truffles with a beguiling expertise, and a small selection of opportunists, evidently quite new to the game – probably only been in it for four or five hundred years – completed the cast.

Next, another crew arrived making their way into the interior of the square, the inner sanctum. These are the brokers and dealers. They are genial, well-versed in the game, and are the ones who set the price. Usually, in markets it is the seller who dictates what their product will cost, but here it's the other way round. After much dipping into sacks, squeezing, fondling and occasionally sniffing and fiddling, like a vet with a million-pound stallion, the broker will scribble something down on a piece of paper. It is presumably a price, only marginally less than the stud fee of a champion, and pass it back to the trader. There is something quite masonic about the ritual. Impossible to crack into from the outside, but fun to speculate on nevertheless. After everybody had either felt or been felt, the judges huddled in a circle in the middle, apparently doing little more than nodding, twitching or oscillating a hand. They break like an American football team after an on-pitch strategy conference, and without further ado the price of truffle is set. Today it was 600 francs a kilo. By the time it reaches the smart restaurants of Paris, London and Milan it will have climbed up to 3,500 francs a kilo. That probably equates to about £40 added to your bill for a measly scraping over your risotto in a minimalist, famous chef, famous reviewer, eatery in Notting Hill.

Mr Marcheur and I were musing over these fungus facts when he quite suddenly stopped. With his whip he began brushing the surface of the ground, swatting without malice at a reddish brown insect. This, he explained, was the mouche fly and it lays its eggs on a truffle spot. Marcheur, an elegant man in his late sixties, is not prone to behaving in an undignified manner. Not for him the noisy snuffling swine, or the over-excitable dog, but instead the far more refined swish of a crop that disturbs the fly from its rooty procreation pad. Sometimes on the ground you find a lightly defined circle of about a meter or so across. It is invisible to the newcomer, but the practised eye will spot the thinned out thyme and the sprouting shoots of the Orpin elegans. It might be up to thirty metres from the nearest tree, but will be a favoured spot for the fly.

'If one was looking,' he continued, 'one might drop on to one knee a bit, let the small trowel slip down from the inside of your sleeve a bit, then having extracted the jewel from the jaws of the jungle, seamlessly stand up and move off a bit, covering your tracks without too much ceremony.' The smile in his kindly eyes and the tiny break on his lips told me that he knew what he was talking about, a bit.

When we had been house hunting, and had looked at about two dozen houses, none of which fitted the bill, and were beginning to despair of ever finding something suitable, we were advised by an acquaintance to get in touch with an American lady, Madame Darke. She, we were assured, knew as much about the local property market as anybody, and more than most. Having been married all her life from a very young age to a mélange of men that included three psychiatrists, a policeman and a professor, she was now on her own. In need of money she had applied her formidable brain to the game of house trading. Joining a local firm of *immobiliers*, she had quickly risen to the top of the pile through hard work, no-nonsense dealings and an ability to put the right house to the right person, particularly at the top end of the market.

Although not fooling her about our position on the ladder of wealth, we arranged to meet her one May morning outside the local *vinicole*. She had organised three houses for us to look at, one nearby and two a bit further away. Uncharacteristically, Nicky was suffering hangover syndrome. Bruised from the Ventoux rouge of the night before, and deprived of much sleep, she was not set up properly for a day of travelling around in a hot car looking at properties. Especially properties that turned out to be too far away, too close, too expensive, too cheap, too much work, too isolated, too crowded and too too. So after an exhausting morning she and I took our estate agent out to lunch. A little correctional fluid eased the situation a bit, and we agreed to look at one more house locally and then call it a day. It turned out to be somewhere we had seen before, had liked, but figured that to get it up to scratch, in a style we would want, was beyond the shrinking pound in our pocket. We said our goodbyes, and left to go poolside, feeling flat that even the queen bee hadn't managed to produce an answer.

We didn't meet Madame Darke again until quite some time after we had moved down here. We went round to have supper with The Decorator. In her eighties, she has had such a successful career as an interior decorator that she was gonged with an MBE a few years ago, for services to an industry that doesn't feature very often in the honours list. Understandably perhaps, under a Labour administration, but even the Tories seemed reluctant to award any recognition to the decorating game. It is even worse with the gardening profession. I don't, off hand, know of any one who has been knighted or lorded for being a good gardener. And I don't know why not. Many gardeners bring a great deal of pleasure to thousands of people, inspiring and calming them, entertaining and enthralling them, amusing and educating them. Perhaps it's because, generally, they don't earn enough money to be able to slip a few turkey necks into the party's election campaign coffers.

Anyway, Madame Darke was at dinner and I found myself sitting next to her, and by the end of the evening she had a new admirer. Before long, we were good chums, and when Theo was born she agreed to become his somewhat grown-up godmother, albeit in a secular sense. The godmother has also been enormously supportive and helpful by putting me up for work projects, and introducing us to a variety of people. She suffers no fools, is quite frightening and her acerbic tongue can win her enemies. I once told her that some people found her a bit, er, intimidating. 'Good,' she hissed from behind her dark glasses. Better to keep her as an adviser and not an adversary.

When I got back to the office after the truffle-hunting expedition there was a message from Madame Darke saying that I should meet her for lunch. She had a new client near St Rémy who has just completed the purchase on a wreck of an old house, and was looking for someone to help sort out the fifteen or so hectares that go with it.

St Rémy is a pretty market town at the feet of Les Alpilles. As a base camp goes, it is an expensive little diamond, which is kept shiny by habitation taxes paid by some of Provence's leading jewellery wearers. The town centre is organised into a circulating one-way system, and in summer you are required to sit patiently on the periphery, waiting for a break in the moving chassis of executive comfort so that you can ease your motor car into the procession.

Like New York, there is nowhere to park of course, so when a little something in a bijou shop catches your attention, you simply stop the car in its tracks, and abandon it. You sail into the boutique whose doors are already helpfully open, ready to embrace and encourage your retail therapy. Most things are deliciously overpriced, exquisitely inessential, and often outrageously unoriginal. Quite why this immodest hamlet should still find English Victoriana, for example, such a thrill is baffling. But the distressed candlestick holders with their witty candle shades might be a must, as are the strings of little paper boxes filled with fairy lights, that you can't get your hand into to change the bulb, but look divine dribbled over a mirror or lying along a mantelpiece.

It was Friday, and being a lapsed Presbyterian in a Catholic country, I arranged to meet the Godmother in the café in Lumiére, famous for its *aioli* lunch. *Aioli* is a local word derived from *ail* (garlic) and *huile* (oil). It is a sauce that is served with a dish of boiled salt cod and shellfish, boiled potatoes, boiled carrots and leeks. A few artichokes are tossed in for good measure and the whole thing served lukewarm. If you don't think it sounds very tempting, try eating it. It requires a bit more training than truffle consuming and the garlic sauce has enough power and potency to remove the cap off a carthorse at two hundred metres.

A couple of months ago, another of our neighbours came wobbling down to see us on a bicycle. Had something stirred in his conscience about getting fitter? Saving the planet from diesel fumes? Or was he just enjoying the gentle pace of an old-fashioned velocipede? No. He had lost his driving licence for two months after a particularly liquid *aioli* lunch.

Lumière is a small village about five minutes from Lacoste. The drive over the hill is always a big pleasure. The countryside was looking mesmerisingly beautiful, and I dawdled along at a pensioner's pace. Everything seemed dusted by a pink powder puff of blossom as the cherry trees erupted into flower, and underneath, a blue and yellow carpet of muscari, dandelions and wild narcissus stood out against the bright green, calling for attention. That morning I had taken one of the cars to Bonnieux for a service and had seen a photographer, out early, taking a close-up shot of an icy stalactite dripping from the blossom-covered branch of an apricot tree. Because February had been so hot, some people had turned on their automatic irrigation systems a drop too soon. The photographer had caught the frozen spray-water hanging from the bough. The rising sun shone through the thawing icicle with the pretty pale pink blossom just on the turn, ensuring that he had caught a moment unlikely to be repeated again that year.

The café in Lumière is exactly correct. It has a droopy awning shading a few metal tables and chairs outside on the pavement. Inside it has a bar and *tabac* up at one end, where the bar evidently requires holding up by anybody who's passing, preferably using one hand only. The other must be free to grip the glass of pastis, smoke the Gauloise, gesticulate meaningfully, and shake the hand of all comers. The mini tumblers of water and wee cups of black coffee are snappily drunk to fill in time, whilst glasses are refuelled.

We sat down at one of the tables covered in a plastic imitation of gingham, and shared with a young mum and her four-year-old son. He was a cheerful chap and really quite adept at flicking slices of baguette across the room and onto the football table. The girl had just bought the French equivalent of the *National Enquirer* from the magazine stand, and was contentedly oblivious to the shouts of 'off side' and 'foul' being hurled back across the room at her froglet.

The Godmother and I exchanged gossip, scandal and the state of our soles. We smiled weakly at an unknown diner, smiled winningly at someone we knew, and exchanged ruderies with the waiter. By the time the bucket of garlic sauce, propped up by a small fish arrived I was well briefed on the wreck of St Rémy. It seems that the owner, a professor of research from the Royal College of Whatsit in London, had bought this enormous piece of dilapidation. She commissioned a French architect to do the restoration, and had believed that he would bring somebody of some repute in to do the garden. His wife. The couple seemed to be hard to get hold of and somewhat diffident. The Prof. had had enough of waiting for the garden-designer wife to deign to show an interest and wanted to get on with things. She was involved with the architect to the point that she has commissioned him to start drawing, but with the wife, no such stricture or professional agreement was in place. She had asked the Godmother to recommend an alternative. As I was up to date with my protection payments, and had rendered my respects to Pushkin, her Persian kitten, my name was put forward.

'She is o-kay, a bit demanding, but attractive,' the Godmother had said in a slightly detached way. 'She will probably ring in the next few days. Check it out.'

Our conversation continued, oscillating between committing suicide, the worry one has about not dying soon enough and the joys of life. One more carafe of rouge, a slice of pudding, and we were out of there.

After I had left London, I missed my badly behaved Friday lunch-time friends. Impressively practised in the art of having a little something to eat with their drink, their conversation would always be erudite and humorous, convivial and wrecking. Now with the Godmother, things were very nearly back in place.

The Professor did ring, and I did go and meet her. The mistral was blowing up a rumpus that morning and the small figures of the Prof and her French-speaking assistant, had to lean heavily into the wind to avoid being swept away. In the disused old barn, attached to one end of the house, I showed her my recent portfolio, blinded her with my client list, and assured her of my full attention, once commissioned. I liked her; she was forthright and completely unpretentious. Sure, you usually want the job, but you also want to feel in tune with your employer. For all the interviewing the client is doing, the designer is interviewing as well. By the time I got home I had a fax from her in which she stated that she felt comfortable working with me, and would let me know how things progressed. Meanwhile, could I let her have an estimate of how much it would cost to make her garden.

'Don't bore me with details, just a bottom line. And soon.'

The property has about fifteen hectares, which is about 38 acres. To just flick your fingers and come up with a budget figure, without any thought to its design, its rationale, or its intrinsic structure, is not easy. You can give a basic unit cost, a development price per square metre, and multiply it by the area, and shock the hair off the back of everybody's necks, but really things need to be thought through quite carefully before committing anything to paper.

Besides, she wanted a lake, irrigated parkland, swimming pool and boule court, re-routed driveways and an inner courtyard. Don't forget two dozen mature olive trees, and a line of cypresses for the new drive. Oh, and a fence round the whole thing so the cats don't get out.

To start the ball rolling for the Professor, I arranged to meet a contractor on site to discuss some preliminary lines of action. There had been talk of putting the outer fields down to wheat, but when the Prof. discovered that it would leave a large part of her estate looking bare and uncared for during much of the year, she had changed her mind. Fruit and vine had also been considered, but getting contract farmers to look after your produce is a difficult and frustrating game. There isn't much profit in fruit, so there is a habit of doing as little maintenance as possible and just enough to produce the harvest. Without the pride of ownership the land and trees then tend to be neglected until the following year. So that idea was dropped as well. The solution seemed to be to sow prairie-grass seed, and perhaps cut it two or three times a year giving the hay to any horse owners who might want it. Trouble was, without irrigation the grass would never get established, and the field would soon turn back to weeds. It would cost an arm and a couple of legs to irrigate the whole place with an automatic system, like you might find on a golf course. However, we were lucky because we had the canal des Alpilles. This is a series of ditches and small canals, through which the rainwater off the mountains finds a course. It is controlled by gates and weirs, and is a blessing to the area. But to make it effective and 'flow' over the fields, the land needs to be graded to allow the water to run. It looked like this might well be our route. It would involve scraping off the topsoil, setting new descending levels, then putting the soil back in place again.

We looked at the old conifers that had been planted some time ago, to act as wind breaks. They marched across the fields in straight lines and were some thirty feet tall. Many of them were giving up the unequal struggle with the *mistral*, and falling over. What had happened was that the farmer who had planted the trees, understandably, set up a drip watering system to encourage their growth. This it did with spectacular success, and the trees grew quickly. But there is a down side to this watering business, in that if you leave the irrigation in place after the roots have established themselves, they become lazy. The tap root, that's the main anchor, does not bother to burrow deep down into the ground looking for water, because it knows it will be getting it for free. Therefore the root system remains very shallow, and as the height of the tree increases, it becomes top heavy, and with no proper mooring below, will topple over in a strong wind. It was a bit depressing looking at the remaining upright trees knowing that, very soon, they too would measure their length.

We talked lake for a while, but decided that until we knew exactly where it was to be located, we would give a budget price for a thousand square metres and leave it at that. Boule courts, swimming pools, driveways and mature trees could be added to the initial working costing based on experience. When, and if, the commission came through, we would get a proper plan sorted out and figures would be tightened up, or down, depending...

March was coming to a close, and the land needed rain. The soft blue flowers of the periwinkle coiled themselves round the pale yellow daffodils, threatening to choke the living daylights out of them. The fruit-tree blossoms faded and the next generation of leaves announced their arrival. *Teucrium fruticans*, applied at our home as a hedging plant, rather misguidedly, started to flower with its little spots of blue against grey green foliage. I say misguidedly, because having seen it used to good effect, mostly as a shrub, we thought that it could be the fellow for our maze. I checked it out with nurseries, and they assured me it was not too fragile, and given a good clipping from time to time, would grow vigorously. The maze manifested itself partly because we had a field near the house we were not too sure what to do with, and partly because, since childhood, I have been fascinated by both mazes and labyrinths. I have passed happy hours designing killer patterns, complicated enough to worry the amazing mazer, Mr Fisher. I have studied books on this historical, political, religious and intellectual folly. I have even, for example, watched *The Shining* several times just to enjoy the scenes of Nicholson going tonto in between the walls of hedge. The clever ones – mazes which are laid out flat – can only be regarded in the way you might a game of chess; they certainly tease and amuse, but lack the twist of commitment that their three-dimensional cousins demand. People take their maze-making very seriously. Mazists should marry crossword composers.

Anyway, I started to map out a design for a simple labyrinth that would fit into the confines of this little field. I had in mind something that would amuse Theo, without disconcerting him. I wanted the hedges to be his height as he grew up, so that when he was three, four and five, he would hardly be able to see over them. Drawing the design is a doddle compared to marking it out. I had elected to work on a grid rather than a circle, and the whole process nearly drove me to another drink. One particularly demanding day, I threw down my marking-out tools, rushed in to the house, and opened the telephone book, hoping to find the number for Mazes Anonymous. Actually, the French call them *labyrinthes*, and there was no listing.

When we arrived all the fields around the house were laid to vine. They started about five yards from the house, and wrapped themselves around the property in a continuous line. Our first September, we were encompassed by tons of grapes. As they came on line, we couldn't think what to do with them all. The previous owner shied away from having a helping, the neighbours passed, and we hadn't made any friends that we thought might be interested. So we regretfully had to let them rot in situ. We picked a few to squeeze, but they were not table grapes, and had tough skins. We couldn't harvest them all ourselves, and didn't have any rights to take them to the local *vinicole*. It wasn't the most pressing problem we had, but it concerned us none the less. Just after Christmas, an Englishmen, and a friend of a friend's friend dropped in to say hello on behalf of the mutual buddy. He had been in the South of France wine buying for a chain of restaurants, and the Luberon was included in his itinerary. He told us that the French government was trying to encourage farmers down here to stop growing vine. They wanted the quantity to go down and the quality to go up. To this end they were offering compensation to the growers to give up their quotas. 'You'll probably get about 40,000 francs for this lot if you dig them out,' he told us. 'That could help you pay for a few trees and shrubs'. This sounded sensible and worth looking into, which we did the next week.

I need hardly tell you that the old lad we had bought the house from, had, of course, sold the quota as soon as he knew we were about to buy his house. He hadn't mentioned it, and it was only when he came round to tell us that a tractor would be arriving the next day to rip the old vines out, that the matter was ever discussed. You can't get your cheque from the regime until a man from the ministry has come to the property and seen for himself that the old vines are out of the ground, and past being replanted.

After this little operation had been accomplished, we were left with a small mountain of gnarled and twisted old roots. They were quite sculptural in their way, and when wet, looked very dark, almost black. Piled on top of each other, their wriggly trunks and stems made an interesting form. For the next few days Nicky planned ways of using them, of displaying them in a funky kind of ground-cover pattern, of maybe painting some of them, and those that were not included in the 'installation' could be

stock-piled and used for fire wood. We were wrong on all counts, again. A lorry turned up a few days later and removed the whole lot. Another deal had been struck behind our backs, this time for firewood, and that was that. Nearly. I did manage to persuade the tractor driver who was ripping them out to leave forty or so plants for us to have in a decorative capacity. I marked out a circle about twenty meters in diameter bang in the middle of the field, so clearly that a pack of sky-divers could have landed in it with their eyes closed, and yet the Don of Diggers left me with an off-set square.

I made plans to plant a lavender 'river' that would run down the banks and terminate when it arrived at the vines.

The general awakening continued apace, and the days were throwing off their winter bearing and although there were still a few frosts, they were getting lighter. Our two ducks had survived the sub-zero shock of winter, and were beginning to look at each other with a new-found affection.

Oh, oh.

CHAPTER FOUR

Be Prepared

The early-morning Easter light, clean and clear as a polished sapphire, back-lit a ribbon of mist hovering over the Luberon plain. The almonds had burst into blossom and the cherries were hard on their tails. The roses were just coming out of bud, whilst the dying spidery flowers of the witch hazel took a final bow.

Finally confirmation had come through from The Owners. All the drawings had been approved, changes accepted, budgets set and outline plant plans agreed. I was keen to clear the studio, let the drawing board relax and the colouring crayons cool down. It was almost time to get practical. But first contractors needed to be notified in writing, drawings sent out and schedules made. For my own part I needed to start sourcing the plants we required, a laborious job, as not everything was to come from the same place. We would be ordering some of the mature stock from Italy, smaller herbaceous plants from the Ardèche, and aromatiques from the west of France. Later I would be buzzing around the markets looking for all sorts of this and that, all of it at a good trade price. Plant ordering is complicated by the fact that, outside of the main giant trade suppliers, the smaller growers have hardly got their heads around writing a letter, so are foxed by fax and failing @ e-mailing.

First things first; the owners wanted another set off drawings, so we dug out the originals and hoofed it into town. If you want A4 or A3 it's a doddle, most *papeteries*, photographic shops even supermarkets will accommodate you. But if the plan has to be drawn on A1 because of scale, you're kippered. It becomes necessary to find one of the elusive *reprographie* outlets and they are about as scarce as a truffle in August.

An architect had told me of Monsieur Dyeline more than four years ago. He was the most surly un-user friendly operative I had ever had the misfortune to meet. He scowled at me when I entered his shop as if I was something off the streets and was about to trash his machines whilst daring to interrupt his slothlike progress making blueprints. His work required him to bend over most of the day, so he had an old man's stoop with the attitude of leaking acid. There were two possibilities, and I'd tried them both: one — ingratiate yourself, flatter him, thank him profusely, apologise for your existence, give him sweeties and allow him weeks to do the prints for which you will tip him extravagantly, or two — overlord him with swanky confidence, treat him as an imbecile, snap at his heels and demand instant fulfilment, and for good measure tear up a sheet or two just to show him who's boss. Neither works of course and you end up diluted, compromised and meek, all for the cause of your client's well being.

Cavaillion is an attractive market town with some snazzy shops, my dentist and a huge crane that has been building a building that we are not quite sure what kind of a building it will be. But it gives lots of pleasure to my little boy and me to watch. Just round the corner is a toyshop that keeps me happy for hours and him for slightly less when it is his mother's turn to have her fillings seen to. It is also on the banks of the Durance, our biggest and proudest local river. Any big river lends excitement and commerce to its community, but the Durance scores further. It is one of the sources for the great and wonderful Canal de Provence. Started in the fifties as an irrigation system to help farmers, it has, over the years, spread its network to cover an enormous area of Provence. In our region alone, the Vaucluse, it stretches from Saint-Pierre in the east over to Robion in the west, from Saint-Saturnin in the north down to La Loubière in the south, enabling some 15,000 hectares to be irrigated under pressure. It has not only allowed farmers to flourish but has also granted gardens to a community that hitherto had not entertained such frivolity.

It is fair to say that the true Provençal probably still thinks that the likes of me are bonkers. Anybody trying to make a garden in a climate that enervates you with temperatures up to the 40s in the height of summer and lowers to a terrible minus 12-14 in the depths of winter, must be of questionable sanity. However, there is a word in the French language for us professional gardeners, or garden designers and that is *paysagiste*. So working on the principle that if you're tagged with a title it must be acceptable and even possible, I am deeply grateful to the assistance that we can usually draw from the Canal de Provence.

And how we need it... What else can you wash, drink, swim in, keep fish and ducks happy in, make plants grow, grass green, use decoratively, enjoy the sound of, light spectacularly and keep your car clean with? To make a garden down here you need it badly, and if you can't get it, think desert. As it happens we can't get the Canal to our house, or garden. The nearest point, the nearest tap as it were, is three hundred meters away. By the time we had dug trenches, laid pipes, changed the aperture of the hose, added pressurisers and pumps to get it up the hill, bribed local farmers to let us cross under their land, it all added up to a 'not worth it boyo'. As you would expect, town water is prohibitively expensive, so we called in a diviner.

Monsieur Sourcier arrived one sunny morning (we have a fair deal on sunshine, average 320 days per year, and anybody that feels like committing suicide usually does it on one of the remaining 45 days) ready to check things out. A small, ragged old boy with damaged teeth and an accent so buried in local twang that any conversation would be forever denied to an outsider, not helped of course by the escaping consonants through his missing tusks. When I had asked the German friend who had introduced us to Mr Sourcier how the divining was done – was it with hazel, or a metal rod – he replied,

'No, he doz it wis his ballz.'

Understandably Nicky was more than a little curious to see what wizardry he hid behind his flies. But of course she didn't want to put him off his stroke by asking too many questions.

'Best leave him to it,' she said, peeking out from behind a curtain.

The truth was soon revealed. Monsieur Sourcier walked determinedly across the fields with a fine crystal ball hanging from a thin strand of silk. As and when it spun in a circle he would mark the spot. The faster and wider the spin, the deeper and fuller the well. *Voilà!* Suddenly we had three source points, two basins and a well, supplying adequate water for our inflated concept of a rural provençal garden.

'Oh your making an *English* garden,' some local wittered one day.

'No, Madame, I'm just making *a* garden.'

What she meant of course was that I was being a bit flamboyant, if not brassy, in daring to work outside the familiar local palette; lavender, olives and thyme. There's nothing wrong with these chaps, quite the opposite, they are mandatory stuff, but it doesn't have to end there. Whilst it's important to work with indigenous material we shouldn't be intimidated out of experimenting sensibly with a multitude of other plants.

From 5.30 am on Friday mornings there is a large trade market held in the disused train station at Carpentras. I often troop off here, to sniff round the shrub and tree stands, the flower stalls, to check out what's available, and for how much. It's an essential experience and very often rewarding. Like most early-start markets, especially on a cold April morning, it can be difficult to find a stall-holder. You stand around wanting to buy something, hands deep in pockets wondering why he isn't there, why he doesn't want to sell anything, then it clicks. You have to go into the café to find him. Passing through the big swing doors into what must have been the old station foyer, you are engulfed in clouds of Gauloise smoke mingling with the aroma of the strongest of fresh coffee beans. The room reels with an aggregation of men of the earth, their flat caps glued to their heads, sitting and standing around laughing, chucking back glasses of red wine, lager, coffee or all three, chewing on omelette baguettes, croissants and pain au chocolat; the camaraderie reminiscent of a regiment reunion. The serving girls, looking like decommissioned floozies, are well used to the bric-a-brac of hoary horticulturists. It's an atmosphere of pure Frenchness and as an outsider I find it hugely happy making. As time goes on I find one of the real pleasures of working down here is knowing some of these people, and whilst not sharing the intricacies of their language, I do find myself jostling along with their bonhomie.

There is a temptation to start buying small plants in February, when it is often very warm, and the dealers are putting out their wares. But unless you have a greenhouse to keep things well protected at night, the frost will fatally wound the tender young things. In my innocence, I tried this once, and lost hundreds of pounds worth of stock over night. Even in April you need to be careful. *Osteospermums* delivered at the beginning of the month will be brutally murdered.

I don't have a lorry or a pick up, and the stall holders and growers rarely make deliveries, so I have had to organise my own. Enter Monsieur Camion. He is a retired farmer with a well-maintained old lorry who likes to keep a bit occupied, or at least his wife likes him to keep a bit occupied. One day I had ordered 26 three metre tall, Cyprus trees for another big garden I was making. These are tall, thin, often caricatured in Italian and Provençal illustrations, and a vital contribution to any new project. I asked Mr Camion if he could help me collect and deliver.

'Bien sûr, Monsieur Alex.'

We arranged as always to meet outside the main gates so that I could pay for his entrance. This accomplished, we then continued on to the tree-growers stand. My heart had sunk, and my mouth had whispered for a flask. A mini mountain of evergreens lay stacked one upon the other each with their wired root balls nearly a cubic meter in size. We would never get more than ten of these giants onto the lorry without serious complaints from the suspension department. We needed a lot of help to lift them, a forklift perhaps, of which there was no sign, and come to that, there was no sign of Mr Camion either. He had taken one look at the consignment and legged it…

I discovered him pretending not to be anywhere in sight. As my roll of notes became lighter in my hand and heavier in his, he adjusted from a 'no-way, mate' to a 'let's get cracking' mode. I coerced a couple of other unfortunate passers by, and after a struggle of horrendous proportions we had loaded a great deal of the consignment onto the back of the unlucky lorry. I reassured the supplier that we would be back before ten for the remainder, and Mr Camion and I set off in convoy towards the site where they were to be planted. Unloading the other end was only marginally easier, and by the end the exhausted old boy lay breathless in the back of his truck, propped up against the cab. The way his tongue seemed stuck to his lips and his eyes lolled around with a hazy lack of focus, sent me running for refreshment. Coffee lined with Cognac, a pain au chocolat and a few cigarettes later, our hero was fit enough to scamper up behind the steering wheel, hammer the accelerator, and deiseled out of there before I had a chance to say:

'Want to help me plant the blighters?'

At least he left richer than he had expected, even if he was a little closer to meeting his maker. I had hardly dared call him again, but another occasion did arise where he was just the man for the job. Although it required no great effort this time, just the space of his lorry, he said he couldn't remember who I was, and added that he thought it extremely unlikely that he ever would.

During that late spring and early summer I ambled off to market most Friday mornings. The route takes you through some beautiful countryside, and you are virtually alone on the roads. The sun usually keeps its appointment with Provence, and it is a quiet, reflective journey. The daily stresses of running a business, keeping everything in place, maintaining a balanced and soulful outlook can be a dastardly task. But working with plants, be it selecting and buying them, or arranging and planting them, brings a joy to the spirit that reminds me why I'm a gardener, professional or otherwise.

The market is convivial, tempting, and quite often full of the unexpected.

I had bought a couple of hundred 'aromatiques' from a supplier late last autumn, and although he ran a big business he insisted I pay cash.

'I can only do that if my client pays cash,' I said. 'Anyway, I need the VAT invoice,' I went on.

'Cash,' he said.

Frederique is a big man. He isn't that tall, but his gut is slung round his middle like a sack full of oats, and if I am feeling a bit porky, in need of weight attention, I just think of Fred, and I feel fine. His arms are muscular and his neck, if he had one, would be at least a size thirty. His face looks belligerent when he smiles, nefarious when he doesn't. This man is not so much a scrum half, as half a scrum.

'Cash,' I agreed.

Well, I don't quite know how it happened, but happen it did. I overlooked paying him the full amount. I must have given him some with order, some when I had the plants delivered, and forgotten the balance. Silly move. I was standing with another gardener, Joel, at the bar in the café, when I was aware of a rhinoceros standing next to me, scratching its hoof on the floor and about to charge.

'Frédérique!' I cried. 'How nice to see you again, do you know Joel?'

He shook his head without looking at my friend.

'You owe me four thousand francs,' he said.

'Four thousand francs!' I exclaimed. 'Whatever for?'

From his back pocket he produced documentation, proof and pudding all in one.

'Sugar,' I thought to myself.

I quickly assured him that I would bring the booty to market the following week. I didn't have it on me, or would he prefer a cheque, settle it now, have it all over with, kind of thing?

'Cash.'

I apologised. 'Sort it out next Friday.'

'Friday. Cash.' His vocabulary was menacingly short. He was probably minimising the possibility of misunderstanding, but the way his scalp moved back and forth, he could have been putting it up in neon. As he departed, he gave me the sort of look favoured by the prohibition racketeers. It wasn't what one could call attractive, and yet it made you feel deeply grateful that you were able to continue in business for at least another week.

The following Friday I found Frédérique talking to another man outside his lorry. He didn't stop the discussion with his colleague, he didn't look at me, but his stumpy set of fingers attached to a leathery, cupped hand beckoned me in with an impatient wave. I bunged him the pay-off, and melted back into the fray.

Being some kind of glutton for punishment, I went to his nursery a few weeks later to get some more *anis, basil, corriander, origon and marjoram*.

'You owe me a thousand francs,' he said.

' Très droll, Frédérique,' I managed.

'Cash.'

'Excuse me, but I paid you on the 17th in the market.'

'I wasn't in the market on the 17th.'

'Listen you fuck,' I said. (Quietly, in English.) 'You were talking to another man, I came up to you and ...' (Out loud, in French.) 'Thousand francs. Cash.'

Now, because he hadn't signed any bit of paper, because I hadn't a clue who he was talking to at the time, and because I was trapped in his office, which is balanced above the potting machines some forty feet below, I said, 'Fine.' I didn't understand his game, but I'd play it this time, but we don't get fooled again.

I have found somewhere else to buy my aromatiques.

Because of the pandemonium caused by irreverent lorry parking, and abandoned vans and trailers, all ignoring a limp attempt made by the market organisers to produce signs and directions, it is best to park your vehicle, and walk everywhere. Do your buying from here and there, and then go back to collect later. Trouble is, if you are not careful and well organised, you forget where you left your car, then after you've panicked but found it again, you can't find your plants. It is easy to waste half hours searching blindly for your acquisitions, find them, round them up into a safe bay, then lose your car again. There are few landscape fixtures to take your bearings from. You might note a certain lorry, its colour or graphic, then just as you are about to move towards it, you see it leaving. Take your readings from the café, turn away, and by the time you look back again, it has moved. The man that deals in axes and saws, always in the same position, decided not to come that week, or had swapped his pitch with the strange looking fellow who flogs elongated rubber funnels.

One quite lazy market morning, I had completed my purchasing, had greedily chomped my way through a lightly cooked herb omelette, folded into a freshly baked and buttered baguette and fixed with an espresso, and was ahead on time. I caught sight of the man who sold the chickens and ducks, along with some guinea fowl and a few rabbits. I wandered over to have a closer look and felt a tinge of the 'Animal Rights' campaigner well up inside me. The way the poor things were packaged, squeezed together like a bunch of rush-hour Japanese commuters. There's no doubt that the French do support a different attitude towards animals compared with us, with the possible exception of dogs. It may not be quite as harrowing as the Spanish, but they certainly didn't invent the word 'anthropomorphic'.

With a few misgivings, I bought two ducklings. I have always had a soft spot for them, and I thought, we have a fair-sized pond now, besides which, Theo might like them too. Plus of course I was liberating this lucky quartet from a dubious existence that would end, almost certainly, in the roasting tin.

'Which ones?' asked the beaky little man strutting up and down beside his truck, his head jerking back and forth. I pointed through the basket cage rather vaguely at two different colours. He stuck his hand in, wrenched the alarmed creatures out by their wings, folded them up like little parcels and unceremoniously buried them in a tiny cardboard box. He stuck the lid down with tape and stabbed the sides with a dreadful looking sheath knife, presumably to give them air, although I wouldn't have been surprised if he had given them death. I dared not look. When I got home, I opened the carton gingerly, expecting the worst, but all was well, apart from the fact that he had given me two browns.

Despite the wonders of the Canal de Provence, and our magical diviner, we knew that if our garden was to flourish, some sort of irrigation system would have to be organised. There was no point investing in a portfolio of plants only to have them behave like St Éxupery in the desert. The previous owner, Mr Vendor, had explained that using town water would be prohibitively expensive, and the very thought of the theoretical bill had made his face crunch with pain. A slow and worried-looking man at the best of times, his expression at that moment had put the fear of the devil into me. We had no idea how much 'expensive' meant as far as water was concerned, but I had strong images from those stories by Marcel Pagnol.

Knowing that Britain has had to suffer hose-pipe bans, even if it was more to do with the scandalous mismanagement by the people in charge of leaky pipes, than it was to do with the blistering, endless hot days, we were very aware that we would have to address the matter down here, head on. We rather grandly rang up the biggest, and probably most expensive, irrigation company we could find. They duly came round, looked at my plan, suggested joining up to the Canal de Provence, made up a map, and sent in a quote. The man had ignored my bleating about the cost of joining up to the canal, and the estimate they offered would have had their stock holders clapping in the aisles, like soul-soaked gospel singers at a Sunday morning session at The Miracle Church. It was more expensive than a swimming pool and so complicated I got a headache trying to understand it. This would have to go on hold for the moment, and any plants we might have would be treated to the best water the village could supply.

I was outside watering, ironically enough, when the first bill did come, something we had been looking forward to in much the same way as a tax bill. It covered six months, most of which had been winter. Nicky called out from the window:

'The water bill's come, and it's even worse than we thought.'

'How much worse?'

'It's over a thousand pounds.'

Mr Vendor was right. That was expensive. It would have been cheaper to irrigate with bottled water.

'How much over?' I asked

'Its 1220 pounds ... no, hold on a minute, I think I may have got this wrong. Yes, no, it's .. sorry, it's one 1220 *francs!*' That's about 120 pounds, and after the fright, a positive gift. We had been so geared up for a horror, that Nicky had automatically presumed the worst.

On one of Mr Vendor's many visits, he took me down to his *ex-potager* and showed me that there was a trickle of water that arrived via an old bit of guttering pipe. It kept all his vegetables irrigated and never dried up. He didn't need a lot, admittedly, but the good thing was, it was free. The old boy had had great difficulty letting go of his house, and he would continue to come round, slightly dazed by the fact that it was not only not his any more, but also that it was fast becoming unrecognisable to him. He would arrive, wobbling on an under-powered mobilette that strained with the effort of pulling an old bastardised pram that had been converted into a trailer. It provided a comfortable carriage for his garden produce, complete with a cabriolet roof and Prestige springs, but wrenched horribly on the donkey power of the bikes little engine.

Monsieur Vendor continued to tend our or 'his' garden generally, and the potager specifically, for many months after he had sold up and moved on. He seemed oblivious to the transferral of ownership and would spend happy hours down in the lower garden encouraging his courgettes. He would often come up to the kitchen after a hard afternoons toiling and hand us huge amounts of newly picked produce, all of which would be roasted, boiled or turned into thick soups.

This odd proprietorial behaviour is actually quite a common occurrence amongst the Paysan. Although they welcome the strangers who arrive, buy their ruins, and make them feel like Loto winners, they are inclined to still carry on driving over the land as if it is their given right. Pruning trees, taking fruit and seemingly denying your existence. Some do it with an irresistible charm, others with a disingenuous spirit. Vendor didn't have it in him to be anything but innocent. His mind wouldn't bother with a conundrum regarding the rights of strangers over families that had lived here for centuries. He is a simple, kind man with a generous heart, and I used to watch him looking after his patch; his mind apparently running in tandem with nature, and his wisdom of the earth, consummate.

I asked him whether this trickle of water was coming from the spot that our Sourcier had previously found. We set off through the larger of the cherry orchards and over to the furthest corner of the midfield. As we approached the wood, he pointed out a trench that was very wet and muddy. As the weather had been completely dry, it certainly suggested that water was in the vicinity. Sure enough, Mr Vendor was soon pulling back a dishevelled old bit of plastic, the remains of a fertiliser bag, that had been kept in place by a couple of rotting tree trunks, to reveal a big and presumably deep, puddle. From this watery hole about four feet square ran a piece of plastic pipe similar to the bit that nestled in amongst his vegetables.

'This is the source,' he said without any sign of emotion. I would have thought it might have brightened his rather expressionless face. But no. It was a matter of fact to him. It gave a sufficient trickle to keep his tomatoes *et al* in health, and that was really the end to it. To me of course it was like discovering oil.

Understandably, I got very excited by this well, this Hole of Hope, and immediately made plans for a digger truck to come in and make it bigger. Not just any digger, but Patrick of course. We booked him for March. We would have started it earlier, but being that he's the best driver on the planet, we had to wait for his world tour to finish. He and his JCB were probably giging around Japan, the Americas, and the African states like an international entertainer.

The day that he was due to arrive it decided to rain really hard. It almost always happens like that. You have weeks of dry weather, the ground as hard as a week old loaf of bread, then just as the digger is about to come and do its thing, down it comes. It made everything slippy, slidey, and virtually impossible to achieve the goals. So we waited a couple of days for the clouds to clear, and then set to. Nothing very grand, after all we didn't know the strength of the source. It could be fine for a dribble down to the kitchen garden, but perhaps not up to fulfilling our fantasies. Rather than making the surface area to big, we went for depth. The scoop bucketed out sludgy old soil, spent plastic containers, decommissioned metal bars, and assorted bits of rubbish reminiscent of a dump. Patrick modelled it into a passable part of the landscape, and we waited to see what would happen. It didn't take long for the hole to fill, to even start overflowing. The newly formed banks greened over quickly, and we were looking good for an irrigation solution. I spoke to Mr Gazon, a gardener who occasionally came and did a bit of work for us, and he assured me that he could install a suitable irrigation system, that wouldn't take too long to put in and wouldn't cost too much. Naturally enough he was wrong on all accounts. It cost a lot, took a couple of days over forever and didn't work properly at the end anyway.

Well, there was no end as such, just me losing my control valve and hissing enough venom for him to think it wise not to turn up again. That summer I spent six months filming with the BBC all over Britain and France. I came back for small snatches of time, but basically it was down to Nicky to keep the fledgling garden alive. This she did with undying dedication, moving hoses and sprinklers endlessly around the place, adjusting this and pampering that. The pressure from the town water only allowed for one sprinkler at a time, and it nearly drove her to her knees, but she managed. The plumber later told us that he could have easily increased the pressure, enough to run three or four sprinklers, but we hadn't thought to ask him. I promised her that next season we would have the damned thing sorted out. It came as no surprise to discover that the network of pipes, sprays, drips and sprinklers Gazon had installed demanded far more water than our little pond could provide. Three possibilities were put on the table. One, we could make the pond much bigger. Two, we could dig a well. We had after all had the diviner tell us the different spots where he thought the water was. And three, we could go back to the idea of using the Canal de Provence. That was the expensive option that we had dropped as too hot, at the very beginning. Is this all too much? You wait, we've hardly started.

Making the pond bigger was easy enough, and didn't involve bank emptying, capital outlay, so we figured we would start there. Back came Patrick astride his digger. His new digger to boot. The tall elegant cab, air-conditioned with CD player, multi-positionable seat, sun-dim windows, telephone and computerised kitchen sink, was hermetically sealed to the body. Outside, some industrial designer had cracked how to make a very basic, functional machine look quite sexy. It rode on four enormous tyres set on black wheels with extended mudguards; the rakish line to the bonnet complemented the flared-in headlights. Two chromed hinges held his off-road motor bike, and the glossy red bodywork completed the presentation. I swear Patrick was wearing Porsche sunglasses, St Laurent overalls and a Louis Vitton man-bag.

It seemed unreasonable to ask him to actually use this status symbol of his art, to get it covered in mud and stuff. So I suggested he park it somewhere conspicuous, and bring back the old yellow job. It had cracked windows, a torn seat and a squint, sign-written advert that would have broadcast his phone number, if only it hadn't been obscured by years of compressed dirt. It could chug away without concern, do the job perfectly well, and I could shout directions at him that he might hear. He didn't agree and took his engine over to the pond. He programmed 'Make Pond Bigger' into the computer, adjusted his shades and slid up the CD volume. It was Schubert's *La Truite* and it swam incongruously out across the orchard.

A couple of days later we had a small lake of sorts. A muddy, mad and dangerous-looking corner of terrain it was too. The surrounding ground appeared bruised and beaten up, but at least we now had a big bag of water and the area would soon heal over.

After a miserable week, we realised that our problems were not yet resolved. The natural source kept on flowing as it always had, but now the catchment area was so much bigger, it was taking forever to fill up. This meant that if we put the irrigation pumps on for the required amount of time, fourteen channels running between ten and twenty minutes each, we drank the poor pond drier than one of the Queen Mother's aperitifs.

We now had to consider option two. To dig another well, and pump the water from that into the pond. Then pump the irrigation.

We found Mr Digadeepi, a weathered old boy with black teeth and an unfaithful waistline, to help us. He arrived with a convoy of enormous great drill bits mounted on specially converted tractors, a compressor lorry, and various support vehicles. His crew were dressed in the kind of protective clothing that suggested they anticipated finding some sort of chemically dangerous mineral.

I had asked the Mayor's office if I needed permission to dig this well, this hole. Best to keep in after the earlier 'dispute', I thought, just in case.

'Yes,' said the lady running the office.

'No,' said the Mayor.

So it was on.

'The first seventy metres we go down, are free,' Digadeepi had told me when we met. 'If we don't find water, no charge. Then if you want to go on after that, then it's whatever it is a metre.' He then scribbled something horribly expensive down on a scrap of paper, and waited for my acceptance with a big grin. He knew he had me.

As the diviner had estimated about a hundred and twenty meters, I could see we were in for a fair old clobbering. Whatever way you looked at it, it sounded like a very deep hole. It was a nerve-wrecking business.

A client who lives high up in the hills near a mountain village called Caseneuve, had sunk a drill four hundred meters down and found nothing wetter than the driver's armpits. They were left with a mound of unrecognisable material that was useless, heavy and awkward to dispose of, an equally heavy and awkward bill, and capped off with a sense of failure. Who wants to punt forty thousand francs on a fifty-to-one outsider? Gardeners, that's who.

Provence continued showing off its weird sense of humour. When drilling began, so did the rain. It bucketed down whilst the rig started its speculative flight down towards the centre of the earth. It took a long time, and the small side bets running on whether we would find water before the seventy meters were shaping up nicely. The odds were long, but a flutter was irresistible, besides it helped pass the time. The time dragged on interminably as the machine had extension after extension added to its probing arm. It was a like waiting to hear if you had passed an exam or been accepted for a job. Monsieur Digadeepi was fast asleep in the wicker armchair I had given him. He had looked so uncomfortable leaning against the plum tree, watching his workers with heavy eyelids, nodding off, falling over, and struggling to his feet time and time again. When I had offered him the chair, and an umbrella, he had taken them both with immense gratitude.

As the drilling spun on, it seemed we would never get to water, and the tediousness of the afternoon dug in. The droning of the machine, the constant drizzle and the lack of result settled over our head and shoulders like a damp mist. This was boring, I yawned. Cups of coffee were drunk without much expression and even Bobble gave up and went indoors. Theo had long lost interest and had gone to look for Mum so he could shoot some rubber arrows at her.

Without warning, and quite suddenly there was a whole lot of activity. People rushed hither and thither, engines stopped, drills and bits were lifted, silence fell, and Digadeepi scrambled out of his chair,

'Success?' I half yelped. 'You found something? A puddle? A drip maybe?'

'No, no,' he said with an experienced sympathy. 'But we have reached seventy metres.'

'Good, good,' I said, slightly confused as to why I should feel such a sense of achievement. 'That's at least something.'

'Do you want to continue?' The French speaking Italian asked me.

'Of course!'

I was like a drunken gambler now. At about three bottles of whisky a meter, I felt dizzily good for at least another fifty meters. 'Let's go to work boys!' I exclaimed, with that tingling feeling that creeps up your spine when you start to move towards the outside of the envelope.

'Spin the ball.'

It had stopped raining by now, and the sandy-coloured sludge exacerbated by the day's downfall splattered itself everywhere. Streams of profitless mud oozed across the ground like a scene from *Giant* crossed with a science fiction B movie. We all settled down for part two. As the time toiled passed, and the day began to close down, the incessant grinding started to frazzle the nerves, and dull the sense of humour. Finally, after some 110 metres, Digadeepi called it a day. The machinery was turned off, the overalls removed, and the crew retired for the night. It was hard to think of much to be bright about over supper, and the dreams that night were infested with endless tunnels full of desiccated powder.

The next morning was bright and sunny, and the heroes from 'Sludge' were back on the set with the sparrows. There was a sense of urgency now, and the drilling seemed to move faster. Digadeepi rejected his chair and took up position at the masthead. The chugging turned into something more like a whine and a prevailing sense of moving into outer space took over. We were into the last few metres before more decisions had to be made. More chips bought and thrown on odds or evens. Then suddenly the whine changed to a whistle, the drill speed increased, and up the neck of the bit rushed a new-born flow of water. It announced itself into the world with a long striding arrogance, confident in the knowledge that it would be welcomed with open arms, raincoats and umbrellas. It whizzed everywhere like a full hose with no handler. Smiles broke out, hands were shaken, a bottle produced, and weak jokes about striking oil were told.

With the hole dug, and water availing itself at something around a thousand litres or a cubic metre, an hour, we now needed a pump. The plan was to push the water from the well along an underground pipe across the edge of the orchard and over to the newly enlarged pond. Then, as that filled up, we would put it into the grand irrigation system, via another pump, and the whole garden, like us, could give a sigh of relief, and live happily ever after.

A thousand litres an hour sounded like plenty, but to have made Digadeepi really do the rain dance, he would have liked to see three times that much, although he had always said we would be 800–1000 litre people. He was also a trifle worried by the sand content. He had a single bushy eyebrow that stretched itself across his swarthy old face. He shot it up at one end, looked at us directly, and did his best to assure us, if not himself, that it would probably wash itself out after a few days. Aching for the damned thing to work, I readily agreed.

When he had given us the quote for digging the well, he had brought a chap along with him who ran a business supplying and installing special submersible pumps etc. Equipment that would control the flow of water, and direct it over to the pond. They too had given us a price that would put hairs on an onion, but because he was recommended, because we were in a hurry, and because he had lied so convincingly about how quickly he could start, I had accepted his offer.

The little toe rag didn't show up on the date he had given. He had demanded a 50% deposit, which was OK with me, I sometimes do the same thing but I told him that I would give it to him when he turned up for work. His disagreeable secretary, who I later discovered to be his sister, told me that he wouldn't come to our house until he had received the cheque, banked it and seen it cleared. Still, I thought, he's probably been burnt some time in the past, and is playing very safe. One does. So a cheque of impressive dimensions was dispatched.

I heard nothing for a few days, so rang them, again, to be reassured of their starting-date.

'Next Monday,' I was told. 'Nine o'clock.'

Remember, the weather was now getting much warmer and the plants gearing up for maximum thrust. They needed fertilisers and gently dug over soil for aeration. They needed pruning and staking, with lots of love and encouragement, but above all this, they needed water. The mixture of sun and northerly winds would soon be drying out the soil quickly, so I was not in a patient mood. Monday came and went. Tuesday morning. Again no show, no sign, no call. I began to think the worst. I drove into Apt, and the went to the bank.

George's basin

'I want to stop a cheque,' I said to the lady at the desk.

'It's been lost?' she asked.

'No, I don't want to do business with someone. I've given …' I went on and explained the situation as tightly and quickly as I could.

'You can only stop a cheque if it's been lost,' she said.

'Okay, its been lost,' I agreed.

Two weeks, and three hours later than agreed, they turned up, and I gave them their cheque. The engineer couldn't have engineered himself out of a hollow tube and his mate had cut one of our mains water supply pipe within half an hour of arrival, cleverly flooding the terrace. Later he continued to entertain, by revealing that he had in fact buried another pipe just under the surface of the ground, when we all knew perfectly well that it had to be at least fifty centimetres down. The whole show skidded along over the next few days in fits and starts, until the mechanic was seen sitting on a wall, his head between hands in deep despair. He couldn't get the programmer to work, and was getting a bit more tetchy than suited a man of his alleged abilities. The assistant, kept speaking to me in a dreadful broken French, very slowly, backed up by gaga arm movements. This was his way of telling me the latest news. Keeping me up at the cutting edge of their progress. His fat round face, smashed by an imbecilic grin of condescending patience, came ever closer to having a high pressure water hose inserted into its unattractive centre piece.

The sand never did clear satisfactorily, and the flow of water remained indeterminable. It had been a tiring and costly experience that left us feeling heavily downhearted and despondent. After all this effort, all this slog, still no proper irrigation system. There was only one option left now, and that was to reconsider the Canal de Provence route. The one that made a Bentley look a bargain. And even if we did decide to spend the family fortune on this formidable folly, it was on the cards that they, the people who made the system work, would not be able to connect us because of the technical difficulties.

Out of the blue came a fourth option.

Neighbours and brothers Georges and Joel dropped by one morning having heard about our debacle, and with their usual calm, quiet manner, simply offered us some of their water. They told of their own source, unknown to us, that runs down the ridge of their land, that was plentiful and had never dried up, had never even slowed down in the height of the hottest summer. They said they probably had a better supply than the village. It flowed through a number of reservoirs, could be directed into various basins, and if we wanted to set up the pipes and pumps, they would be very happy to let us tap into it. So with that short, uncomplicated little meeting, our watering problems were resolved.

That night we went out to dinner and relaxed. There is a very good little restaurant in Bonnieux called Le Fournil, and it lies deep in our affection as it was practically the first place we ate at when we arrived down here. That night Nicky had sea bass with fennel and I hit on a herb risotto first, then dived into a *Gigot Farci*, leg of lamb stuffed with mushrooms, bacon, chopped parsley and fresh chervil, a bit of thyme, a pinch of nutmeg and some garlic. And a healthy helping of sliced roast potatoes. The lovely big claret glasses were filled with an ageing St-Julien.

We continue to be deeply grateful to Georges and Joel for their kindness. It is just a pity we didn't have the conversation a few months earlier.

The Owners of the patient, tangled garden in Menerbes were coming over in the first week of May to see the next stage – the detailed plant plans.

These plans always take ages because every time I think of a plant; be it a tree, shrub or flower, my mind drifts off to where I might have seen it used previously or incorporated into a scheme. One thing about gardening is that you go on and on learning. I suppose you do with everything, but there is such a big game being played out there in garden land, that you just know you will never get it all on file in your mind. It becomes blurred as to what is original and what might have been thought up by yourself. What, or who, might have influenced your thinking. Like most things, whatever you come up with it has probably been tried before, but the thrill is to endeavour not to be like most things before.

Originality! What a rush on the wild side. To be completely non-derivative and still get work. Ah, these are the precious stones of talent. Walking round grand gardens I always make notes of things that impress. It stands me in good stead. This might be plant association, that is to say, plants that are dynamic together, bringing out the best in each other, or it may be the clever use of texture, shape or scale. Sometimes people plant so inventively it puts you in mind of a talented painter, wealthy with experience. It is very warming to the spirit to discover someone out there who can work in such harmony with nature. Working without aggression or pretension, turning in a little number that lies deep in the art of gardening. It makes me feel inspired for about thirty seconds, before it turns into a gladiatorial envy. So with this mixture of spiritual enlightenment on one shoulder, and a wickedly sharpened pencil on the other, I get on with it. Trouble is that I have grown up within my gardening career certainly loving plants, but also seeing them as only one side of the gardening coin. It has always been equally interesting to look into the hard landscape as much as the soft. The way plants are presented, whether it is stiff and formal, or loose and free, depends on where and what they are growing from. The art of gardening entails the ability to understand composition, colour and time. Composition is the basis of all satisfactory viewing. It matters little what the subject is, or how well it's made. It might be a dirty 12"in knife plunged into the heart of an inflatable love doll, or a comfortable and secure little cottage garden. Both will shoot their image towards the bulls-eye if they have an equivalence that is readable. It matters not one iota if one is collected by Saatchi and the other by the militant wing of the WI. It comes to the born artist as a free gift, whilst others struggle to take it on board.

With a garden, the successful construction is made from a balance between bricks and mortar on one side, and the life force on the other. The inanimate object finding its divine counterpart. The walls, steps, paths and terraces making up the 'hard', with lawns, trees shrubs etc., contributing to the 'soft'. Both are vital components, each showing the other off, and giving to the whole a sense of completion. Get the layout right with the solid bits, and your picture has a starter for ten, before the soil has a single inhabitant.

Nicole de Vesian, a much celebrated local gardener, who died recently after an active eighty-five years, left behind a wonderful simple garden on the village slopes of Bonnieux. Looking down the valley it had, and still does, a remarkable textured background of pine trees growing on the hills. She picked up on the natural contours and shapes and reflected them in the clipping of her essentially evergreen shrubs; rosemary, box, yew, lavender, *Viburnum*, *Ligustrum* and santolina. Everything was allowed to grow into each other, constantly being checked and snipped tightly. So much so that many of the shrubs had started to take on a bonsai characteristic, with miniature leaves growing out of thick trunks. Having spent much of her life as a stylist and designer for Hermes in Paris, she brought a unique non-gardener sense of artistry to her back yard. Always sitting in amongst the planting would be a bit of stone. It might be a Doric crown from some ecclesiastical salvage, or a broken font; it could be simply a piece of local river stone, but the juxtaposition of hard and soft breathed extra life into the vignette. She wasn't a great one for colour. She always claimed that her garden was best in winter, and although colour might be the most profound and exciting exaggeration of black and white imaginable, she preferred to keep it at bay.

Time also comes into the garden equation because trees, shrubs and plants need continuance to come to fruition. They have limited lives, grow at different rates, come out and go in, dance with the seasons, and expand according to the way they are treated. Trees are planted to be enjoyed by a generation not even born, whilst some flowers are so fleeting that they have gone in a blink. Working out the equation to keep a balance that will last for more than a season, whilst remembering to allow space for their development, harmony for their shape and colour, and time for their maturity is a juggler's act.

As The Owners' garden has much the same view as the de Vesian garden, albeit from a different angle, the idea was to keep the stronger colours and shapes close to the house, and gently let the planting become more muted and simple as it floated out to the yonder. High on the 'want' list were roses. The few existing ones dotted around the entrance level, were old and tired. They had been neglected for a long time, and had the dark brown spots of the elderly. We pruned them back last autumn and they were still stoically trying to keep up appearances. They would be included on the plan, or at least the one's that didn't need to be moved, but contingencies for replacements would be made. One of them is 'Ena Harkness', that exquisite, soft-claret-coloured favourite. Many gardeners here think that red is out of place in Provence. The dazzling, sharp, clear-blue light lies uncomfortably with the hot-tempered, argumentative redhead. They feel it is intrusive, and misdirected. I agree that this is true up to a point, but I have had a deep affection for the rich and voluptuous red rose ever since I was told the story about how they all evolved from a single white flower.

Once upon a time, Dawn Frost had not only been the first white rose in the whole world, but it had also been the only rose that flowered in winter, and it was forbidden to pick it. Generations of gardeners had tended to its every need, but had never tried to reap it. People would come from miles around just to look at its loveliness, and if they were really clever, they would come at dawn, and watch as the rising winter sun flickered across the almost translucent petals covered in sparkling frost. The purity of this rose cast peace and tranquillity into the souls of all who saw it. Then one terrible day when the gardeners and children were either asleep or at market, there arrived in their midst a wandering poet. He stopped when he saw the rose, and, bewitched by its beauty, he thought of his loved one, and how much she would adore this brilliant creation. He pulled from his pocket an old, rusty knife and hacked at the plant with a determined struggle. The rose fought bravely to stand its ground, but as the cruel blade slashed and sawed at the heavenly shrub, it felt itself weakening, and with a desperate reluctance, yielded to the superior strength of the misguided collector. The poet tugged and pulled, and finally the mutilated flower came free, but not before it had buried a thorn deep into the hand of this romantic fool, who, sensing that he had done something wrong, ran off with his prize before anyone could see him.

As he passed mile after tiring mile, the day darkened and it began to rain hard. The small wound in his hand became aggravated, and began dripping slow drops of blood over the poor dying white rose, which he grasped onto tightly. As the hours advanced, he became weaker and weaker, wetter and wetter and sadder and sadder, and he could feel his life ebbing away. Soon he stumbled and fell heavily onto the damp grass verge at the side of the road, and lost consciousness. His hand let go of the blood-soaked rose, and it lay there, limp and dull, amongst the wet meadow plants. But as life faded out of the troubadour, so did it flow back into the rose. Soon small roots had formed and the rose began to grow. It grew tall and strong with many stems, but this time the flowers were a deep luxuriant red, the colour of burgundy, and soft as velvet, with a sweet and mellow scent. It continued to flourish on this patch of ground for many years, ennobled by the compost made of the bard.

One day a beautiful maiden was galloping past on a chestnut stallion, and out of the corner of her dark, mysterious eyes she noticed the enchanting rose. She pulled up her steed and dismounted. She walked slowly over to the plant, lifted the flower with her dainty hand and gently inhaled the delicate fragrance. She kissed it sensitively, and after a long, lingering look, during which she felt an accountable stab of sorrow, she withdrew. As she moved back from this most handsome of blooms, she noticed to her absolute horror that the plant had started to wilt. She looked on hopelessly as it continued to shrivel and finally disappear, leaving nothing behind but two perfect white rose petals, fluttering on the ground like the wings of a butterfly.

The Owners have an old ruin on the edge of their first level terrace. The building, about the size of a small stable, is a rickety structure with no roof and trembling walls. Inside a fig grows out of the damp pointing of the wall. On its north side, a buddleia performs the same trick, and between them they show how tough and undemanding some plants can be and it again raises the point about what is a weed and what isn't.

The plan is to turn this quaint little room into an 'auvent' or summer room, to use against the *Mistral* when that wicked wind is behaving like a bored teenager. The centre of this terrace will be paved, with borders surrounding it. Because the level drops down beneath, we can incorporate plants that will hang over the edge of the walls adding interest and softening the stonework. It is a shame that most climbers like to remain just that, climbers. They tend not to take too kindly to being turned into trailers. Many will carry on as ground cover: the honeysuckles, the clematis family, and *Rhynocospermum jasminoides* with its glossy evergreen leaves for example, but suggest that they might like to tumble and fall, and they reject the idea as out of hand. Rosemary, is penned in. *Rosmarinus lavandulaceus escens* with its dark-blue, spreading flowers that last from February to the end of April. It will also grow over the edge a bit and its thick green leaves with a silvery underside will give an all year performance. Parked next door is an evergreen, *Cotoneaster, dammeri radicans* ('Eicholz') a low-growing (40cms) vigorous spreader that mixes well with its cousin, *Cotoneaster x lacteus* whose long, arching limbs will be allowed to droop over the edge. The foliage turns to carmine in the autumn and the height will be controlled, but it will lend a bit of enclosure to this first level.

Next come a pair of box balls, *Buxus sempervirens*, at about 60–70cms in diameter with *Teucrium fruticans* again, in-between. These too will have been bought as ball shapes. They clip easily and don't cost much, which is as well, because they have a mean little habit of dying back if the frost gets too hard. The roots will survive, but the top growth is quite likely to need cutting off. However, their grey-green leaves and small blue flower in March and April make them good companions. Further down the line come the first of several little *Pittosporum tobira nana's* ('Nanum'). Like their big brothers, these shiny, dark-leafed evergreens are immensely useful border fillers. Their own white flowers in April/May are a trifle insignificant, but they make a good backdrop for greys and silvers.

They are also planted here as standards, just to lift the eye up occasionally.

Froth is needed next, so in goes some catmint, *Nepeta* ('Six Hills Giant'), which will show plenty of free form, counter-acting against all the balls. Clipped back hard after flowering, it will come back with a vengeance later in the summer. Add a little purple with *Berberis thunbergii*, and then between the various greens, in goes a little *Senecio cineraria* (once known as *Cineraria maritima*). The jagged, silver edges of this perennial bounce contentedly off the mixture of darker colours. We will probably remove the acid yellow flowers before they come out, as they are not needed here. On the edge, between the shrubby plants and stone, we have some silver ground cover: with *Tanacetum densum*, its tightly knit leaves only attaining a few centimetrers in height, mixed with *Arteimisia caucasica* (syn. *A. lanata*), whose performance is nearly the same. Joining them come *Convolvulus sabatius* (syn. *C. mauritanica*) with its low, spreading habit and jolly blue flowers that seem to go on forever, and behind, their second cousin once removed, *Convolvulus cneorum*, showing off with its very pretty silver grey foliage and white flowers. This one will grow to 50 or 60 cms and is always welcome. These guys have a strange bent for packing up and leaving without saying goodbye or thank you. Pulling them out of the ground often reveals very shallow roots that have clearly decided not to try. Disappointing but worth persevering with.

Two *Taxus bacatta baccata* balls at 40–50cms in diameter are dropped in for good measure and grown with a little more purple *Berberis thunbergii* x ('Atropurpurea Nana') around their edges. Against the house wall we are going for pale pink climbing roses and

Wisteria sinensis ('Alba'), whose long white panicles showed up well in contrast to the slightly terra-cotta tint of the stone. A few gaps are left for annuals, or plants that we have to treat as annuals, and there might be a couple of pots added later, but that basically covers this inaugural terrace. It will have some garden furniture on it, so the centre is being kept clear. Nothing particularly unusual in the planting but it is all well tried and tested.

Inside the ruin we have decided to leave the fig and buddleia for the moment. As there are no immediate plans to convert the little building, it will have to wait until stage two. It is deemed best not to do any disturbing, lest by removing them we loosen the already dodgey stone work. It is agreed however, that some kind of external pointing should be carried out to at least keep the structure standing. Normally, it would be sensible to get the work done now so that the garden doesn't get carved up by mindless brickies at a later stage. However budgets are running a bit thin, and realistically, some kind of financial punctuation needs to be introduced into the scheme. So the ruin runs on.

Next flight down, the terrace is fundamentally all swimming pool, so planting space is at a premium. One of the first considerations is to increase the privacy factor, and this is to be done with hedging rather than walls. We need something evergreen, fast growing and tough. All too easily the card turns up the ubiquitious x *Cupressocyparis leylandii*. There are people who would rather die than have a leylandii in their garden. There are development companies that have signed affidavits from their purchasing clients, swearing not to incorporate them into their planting schemes, and there are garden designers that have struck them off their horticultural registers. They have even logged into the vocabulary of non-gardenists, people who wouldn't know a *Ceanothus* from seaweed, and are generally derided by gardening snobs everywhere. Well, I think this is unfair. Used correctly in a suitable location they can be just fine. I am not suggesting that they should be the focal point of anyone's garden, or that they should be used where a decorative hedge is required. But when it comes to hiding an unwanted telegraph pole, forming thick screening or creating windbreaks without waiting for a couple of generations, this poor, much maligned conifer can hold its head up high. They are cheap, and come in sizes from a few centimetres right up to ten metres and more. They are grown in pot sizes to cover every possibility, have been grafted onto root stock that virtually eliminates disease, will survive pretty awful conditions, and make as good a place for a thrush to build its nest as anywhere. So what's the beef? Common. That's about all you can hold against them. And ignorance. In these times of equal opportunity and middle-class values, they are being discriminated against, and getting cold-shouldered undeservedly. Plant them where you want privacy, I say. Make sure they are staked and protected, then sure in the knowledge that given some water they will grow quickly, they can be topped out in no time, and the lateral branches will soon be bound together inextricably. Use them as a backdrop. Then you can get on with some creative planting in front of them.

But that's quite enough about something we are not, as it happens, going to use here. We are going to spend more money and plant *Quercus ilex*, the ever-green oak, or *chêne vert* as it's known around these parts. We talked about this versatile tree earlier on in context of the truffle, but here we are using it to add some discreet charm and privacy to the pool area. Also known as the holm oak or holly oak, it is, along with its stepbrother, the suber oak, or cork bark oak, indigenous to the Mediterranean area. The small, slightly jagged-edged leaves are mid green and numerous. The fresh, young pale green leaflets in spring make one of the sweetest sights, contrasting stunningly with the older leaves, it makes you want to be a herbivore, if you aren't already.

I was working out in Germany some years ago for someone who would have been the King of Bavaria had the Americans thought it a good idea after the war, but they didn't. I was making a garden out of a disused bear moat that surrounded the Prince's *schloss*. He organised for us, that was me and a dozen crew, to stay in a local guest house. It was grown-up grim. The provincial little hostelry hadn't heard about soothing architecture, or simple creature comforts. It was basic and exhaustingly German. The locals would come in during the evening, drink kegs of beer and play cards. They would shout and bang the table with such force that anyone of a nervous disposition would have had an on-going out-of-body experience.

One morning the Prince asked me if we were comfortable. This was an awkward question to answer, really. We were billeted in a guest house, that was true enough, but as is often the case apparently, it doubled as a butchers with its own abattoir attached. Each morning we would be woken to the blood-draining screams of pigs being dragged, kicking and yelling, to their end. Goats and sheep, not much less reluctantly, added to the mayhem. We had no alternative but to pass death row on our way to the dining room.

The smell was terrible, but the sight of the hatchet-waving, Teutonic meat dealer, splattered in the vital fluid of life, was bad enough for the carnivores amongst us, but the majority of our number were vegetarians, with a sub-division of vegans. So when the good Prince enquired after our comfort, I blithely related our predicament. Unexpectedly, he found this deeply funny. He shook on his chair, slapped his knee, and managed: 'Ze gartners are vegtarians?'

'Well, yes, most of them.'

'You mean zey spent all ze day looking after little planties, and zen at ze night time eatings, zey svallow zem?'

He was now mopping his brow and trying to regain his composure. I began to see what he was getting at. It would be understandable for a vet to be a vegetarian, but surely a gardener would be averse to munching his way through a plate of plant life? I went back to tell Nick, my head assistant, about the jolly romp I had had with his Highness, but he was busy levitating at the time so I left him to it. Our next job was in Calne, Wiltshire. The same crew came with me, and we moved seamlessly into a small hotel not far from the green. Considerably more comfortable and well appointed, but when I looked out through the window, and across the street, there bang opposite us was: The Harris Pork Pie Factory.

Around the middle of May, in Provence, a virtual non-stop frog blather starts over at the pond, at ponds everywhere actually. The green frog, or *la Grenouille de Perez* is warming up for action. Endless calls of Grabbit, Gottit, and Beddit emanate from the reedy water. Considering that this sizeable collection of jumpers and leapers seems to mate for a good three months, it is hardly surprising that their eyes are popping out of the top of their heads. In the few moments of respite from their procreational activities, the boys sit on the long leaves of the bull rushes, puff out their cheeks like over-inflated balloons, and watch the girls breast-stroke their way past. Every now and then a young male vaults off his base and lands squarely on a young female's back, practically sinking her with his zealous amour. All this watery copulation and showing off obviously got to our ducks. One afternoon when I was making sure the water flow was working, and the pond filling, I noticed that Donald was eyeing up Dippy. Some time ago, we had decided that they were both definitely drakes – they are the same size and build, have the same butch characteristics – and that the bonhomie clearly enjoyed between them was just that: in short, they were two old ducker muckers. But on this day there was a leery glint in Donny Boy's stare as he cocked his head, and winking conspiratorially at his mate. Dippy, evidently catching the vibe but not feeling quite as ducktile, eased himself off quietly to have a muddy paddle around the inner reaches of the lagoon, and keep out of harm's way. But our Don would have none of it and his libido was up and pumping, and before you could say 'Jemima's your Aunt', he took off from the bank with a poor imitation of aviation, and crash landed in a clumsy heap, mostly astride Dippy. Grabbing the hapless bird by the neck with his beak, he determined to have his depraved way right there in front of an astonished audience of frogs. They were so surprised that they didn't know whether to hurriedly put their pads over their little tadpoles eyes, or shout brave words of encouragement. The ensuing moments saw a flurry of feathers as the chaps dived up and down and round again, the poor, long-suffering Dippy doing his absolute best to quell his chum's activities. As I lay awake in bed listening to the sparring euphony of frog echoing across the water and floating out onto the still night air, I sometimes wondered if old Dippy might in fact turn out to be a girl, although I doubted it.

I had planned a lavender 'stream' to run down one side of the garden, about two metres wide. It will drop from level to level, and run against the edge of the boundary on each terrace, linking the planes. When it arrives at the bottom, it will open out into a small lavender 'pond'. The idea is to use a mixture of varieties. The backbone will be *L.avandula* x *intermedia* ('Grosso'), the basic *lavandin* with its violet flowers. *L. angustifolia* ('Edelweiss') will give highlights of white to symbolise the foam, while clumps of *L.* x *intermedia* ('Super'), which is like the 'Grosso', but blue and taller, will be perfect to plant at the base of the wall. It reaches nearly a metre in height and will grow up to meet the other on its way down. On the face of the stone parapet that retains each level in place, we have integrated some planters at about 40cms beneath each other, and when these are planted, using the pale-blue *L. angustifolia* ('Nikita'), the effect of the lavender pouring over the edge, on and down, will be continuous. The lavender 'pond' itself will be circular and might have two or three large rocks to focus on, if I can find the right stone. I have to be careful here or it could look contrived and gnomish. The point is, you can't get away from the Provence/Lavender connection. It is, to all intents and purposes, the national flower. So rather than fight it, why not use it in the garden as expected, but display it in a slightly different fashion.

On the second level, planting space is at a premium because the swimming pool commands most of the area. Naturally the screening is paramount if a sense of enclosure and security is to prevail. There are concerns about planting the hedging so close to the pool because the roots might try to be a nuisance. The power of a taproot is formidable, and will, if compelled to do so, crack its way through concrete. The problem will be discussed with Manuel when the pool specification is finalised, but basically as the roots can wander off in the opposite direction we should be all right. Other planting will have to be containerised. Near the sides we have a series of rolled metal planters. They are between 40 and 70cms high and look like the paper a bunch of flowers might be wrapped in, rolled on the angle, so that it is cone shaped with a pointed collar. Into these are planted the sensational *Ophiopogon planiscapus* ('Nigrescens'). A low and slow-growing plant with lots of small black, blade-shaped leaves, it will look very smart developing out of the top of the metal as it begins to rust. I never treat the outside with a preservative, until it has had at least a year to develop that beautiful matt, reddish-brown colour. The other planters will be cylindrical, about 50–60cms across, much the same in height, and will have rubber-tyred castors plugged into their strengthened base plate. This is a good wheeze for several reasons. It allows you to move plants back to make more space, as well as offering the opportunity to alter the composition, to change things around. It also means that plants can be pushed into and out of the sun at will. The only down side is that they will have to be watered manually, as any umbilical irrigation leads will be long, untidy, and potentially hazardous. These 'mobiles' will support mostly plants that can be treated as annuals, even if they aren't. The colour range will be kept minimal and the gardeners, to coincide with The Owners' visits, can change them when necessary. White narcissus and green flowering tulips, *Iberis sempervirens*, and its family friend *Iberis semperflorens* for a splash of white for early spring. Replaced later with trailing pale, pale pink pelargoniums, or geraniums as they keep getting called, tied in with some cream-white roses. Purple sage and *dorycnium Lotus hirsutusm* (syn. *Dorycnium hirsutum*) mixed together, elegant and understated in another pot, but taken out and transplanted when they start to get too big. *Artiemisia x ludoviciana albula* and *Rosmarinus officinalis* var. *albiflorus*, make up an interesting mix of dark green and silvery leaves, with unexpected white flowers in the third container.

The steps down to this terrace have been re-positioned, and the wall that supports them has been built to incorporate space for more plants into the side of it, along with a small, recessed cupboard for a fridge. It is, after all, quite a long way up to the kitchen.

The design approach to a small garden, divided up by lots of levels, like this one, needs to be tackled in much the same way as the interior of a yatcht. Every inch of space needs to be exploited, each nook and cranny made the most of, as space is at such a premium. On this level alone we need room for trees giving privacy, decorative plants in their planters, a flight of steps, the pool itself, and of course chairs and sun beds. The space allocated for wall climbers will have, amongst others, *Solanum jasminoides*. Although it is not very tolerant of heavy frost, its delicate and pretty little white, five-petalled flower, with a drop of pale yellow in the centre, is such a joy that it's worth having and replacing each year if need be. It grows quickly, and flowers from June to first frost. Sometimes, the top growth will get beaten up by the cold, but usually the roots will be OK and fight back to shine another day. It will be encouraged to ramble where it will, tied in from time to time, for its own protection. Underplanting the hedges on either side, a small touch of the grasses are included. The blue *Festuca x glauca* is chucked in to form some gripping wee tufts in-between *Helictotrichon sempervirens* on one side, an evergreen, or ever grey, reaching about 40cms and as tough as stale rawhide, and the wheat-coloured *Pennisetum villosum* on the other.

The final two levels are going to be left for the moment, until we see how we develop with the big, lower retaining walls, and finalise the shape and length of the steps. All this depends on the amount of work that will be needed when we start to install the swimming pool, how much strengthening will be required and what weight and pressure the pool will produce. Manuel has finalised his programme for excavation, and the preferred construction methods agreed. Colour is to be black, salvaged old stone will be used for the surrounds, and the depth will be graded from one metre shallow end to two metres deep end. Things are finally shaping up. Work has been scheduled for the second week of May, and the crew are ready. Mechanical digging equipment has been booked and all the technical stuff like pumps, filters and heaters, ordered.

Then a fax comes through from New York.

Planning permission for the pool has been turned down.

CHAPTER FIVE

Highly Sprung

I had recently been to one of the local architectural salvage yards, ostensibly to look for a some metal fencing to put round a swimming pool. I had another client with small children in St Didier, a pretty market town named after the celebrated Saint, just north of Carpentras and just outside the Luberon.

There are several of these yards in the area selling rescued grandiose pillars with intricate iron gates, enormous fluted urns, and baronial flights of stone steps, complete with fancy railings that Joan Crawford would have been happy to fall down. Generally, the reclaimed material would suit a chateau up north, rather more than a discreet Provençal farmhouse. But people with president-size pretensions evidently buy these things, because their turnover of material is impressive. However, hiding in amongst the oversized obelisks and ornate gazebos, there are often to be found lesser little stone goodies, like basins, wall fountains, windows, and paving. It seems incredible that so many houses are being pulled down or blown up to produce enough stock for these yards. They never seem to run out of the stuff, and despite there hardly being queues at the checkout desks, a healthy trade is always going on. I once started to take some photographs of a few stone seats and troughs in one such yard, to show to my client, and the owner was down my neck like a ton of terra-cotta tiles. A full-bellied fellow with long hair and biceps that must have been developed over the years pulling down Corinthian columns and Doric arches. He was coated in stone dust that puffed off his moustache in little clouds when he spoke,

'No photographies,' Samson said in his best English.

'Just a few to show my client, s'il vous plâit monsieur.'

'Ze client, she comes 'ere, monsieur.'

'She does?' I asked.

I looked round, half expecting to see Madame trooping towards us. Then realised of course that he meant she would have to come to the yard, and see for herself.

'But she's in a wheel chair, Monsieur,' I lied.

'Zen you must puss 'er, monsieur.'

'Hmm, perhaps, but excuse me, monsieur, I don't understand the problem with a little photograph, just for reference?'

'D'accord, j'explique. You 'ave my petit reference, zen you picture it to an autre person, et voilà! I mees my sales. Comprenez?'

'Er, oui Monsieur.'

Okay, he was a bit paranoid about me taking snaps of his gear then rushing around trying to find the same thing somewhere else for a few francs less. But somehow this overly suspicious behaviour didn't really suit a dealer of fine goods. It was more like a man who made fakes. Then it dawned on me; he *was* a man who made fakes. Behind the scenes, this burly entrepreneur and his team were knocking out reproduction gates and urns, fountains, tables, fireplaces, arches, etc., *ad infinitum*. A bit of diligent distressing and they were out in the yard competing with the original and genuine articles. Maybe he declared their age, maybe he didn't, but it certainly wasn't going to enter into the conversation with this Brit.

I had gone into this particular dealer because it was on my way to a client meeting, and I thought I would just pop in to see if they had some decent, authentic, old stone to use on the terraces at The Owners' garden. I had found a couple of pallets of soft beige stone, well worn and full of character and, importantly, random in their size. They seemed reasonably within budget, and there were enough of them to pave all the terraces. Often you find what you're looking for but discover there's only enough to cover a coffin. I had bunged him a 200 franc note to keep them reserved for a week. But still no photographs. Actually the best way round this petty problem was to make a few sketches, and if the client liked the idea, they could, as Sampson had suggested, come and see for themselves, keeping everyone happy.

The fact that The Owners' planning permission had been turned down had thrown a major mattock into the works. What next? Was everything to be put on hold, or should we try and work out a programme that skirted round the pool? Should the workmen and machinery be cancelled, orders put on hold and the scheduled deliveries stopped? It looked like it.

I decided to go back to the stone dealer. I told him about our problems with the construction permission, suggested he held on to the two hundred francs, and if he got an offer for the flags, he had better take it, but to let me know anyway. He was semi-civil and we left it at that.

As I found my way back along the N100, dodging and weaving the fanatics who habitually terrorise all non-French drivers with their innate skills of heart-stopping, eye-popping, death-challenging, road madness, I realised that finally I was no longer wound up by these idiots. That is, I had given up flashing my lights, shaking fists, yelling obscenities and generally passing out with honours in road rage propensity. It had become so much easier to comprehend when I realised that they all drove in exactly the same obsessed way, male and female, young and old alike. So when a Frenchman, having been sitting with his front wheels virtually in your boot, waiting to see the whites of the oncoming drivers' eyes, finally pounces out on to the other side of the road to overtake, he is undeterred by the fact that there is not enough room between you and the truck in front for him to squeeze back into. He doesn't care that the road isn't wide enough for three cars, or that the upcoming vehicle is travelling in excess of 130 kilometres an hour. He doesn't have to worry too much about the absolute carnage he is about to create for himself, you, and several dozen others, simply because he knows it won't happen. These warriors of the black top, the knights of the two-lane arena, know the rules and accommodate each other's lunacy. They swerve, brake, and drift in perfect unison, without panic or pause. Considering they are all talking on their telephones at the same time, the execution of manoeuvre is balletic and demands a sardonic respect. I now relax and let the pilots dance on.

The evening bragged an almost perfect spring dusk. The sunshine lowered itself gently down on to the hills. The long shadows had folded themselves into the creases of the mountains, and the weary, dipping sun illuminated the leaves on the trees. It made a pale and dark-green tapestry, already rich in its softening weave. The car was full of music, a cheque had gone into the bank that day and I was having what a friend once described as 'a right-on moment.' Sometimes, if I'm running late for a meeting and gripping the steering wheel too tightly, with my knuckles creasing themselves towards arthritis, if the stress of dragging schedules, and no-show workmen are taking grip of my stomach, I think about how it could have been. Fighting my way through city traffic on a wet Friday afternoon, temper frayed, only concrete to look at, and moving at an average speed of a snail on Mandrax. All those people jockeying for position, hoping to pull a couple of inches from under the glistening alloy wheels of a hundred-thousand pound mobile. The main roads of France can be pretty desperate. It's just that here, when you peel off from the thrust of the highway, you land mildly back into a tranquillity that no city can hope to give you.

I took stock of my surroundings: the plodding tractors labouring away in the fields, the wild flowers in profusion, and the early fruit forming on the trees. I noticed an elderly couple, contentedly shuffling along the roadside, hats, caps and sticks in place, unaware that they were about to be scared witless by their neighbour's son as he screamed past on his super-series Yamazuki. The air was briefly rent by the howling engine as it power shifted up into third to take the left, right, left, as flat as possible, ejaculating out of the corner, changing down and disappearing with a scorch of tormented rubber, leaving a cracked silence ringing in their heads.

And I said to Louis, 'Louis,' I said, 'What a wunnerful world.'

The rejected planning consent instigated a flock of faxes and a hundred megabytes of e-mail to whiz back and forth across the Atlantic. There was no panic, but a quiet resolve had emerged ready to fight the case. All the reasons for the rejection, the unexplained turndown, needed to be studied, and appeals considered. The Owners were organising an emergency trip.

When you live in a country as a native, you don't think twice about ringing up the local authorities and rollicking them for what you perceive to be an injustice, about writing letters of complaint, or going round to some dead office to swing a bureaucratic cat around the room. Having lengthy conversations with a lawyer or local MP is your right and taken on as a matter of course if you feel that the system is ignoring you, being unnecessarily pedantic, or misunderstanding your case. But when you live several thousand miles away, don't speak the language of the country where the hassles are happening very well, or certainly not well enough to go into battle head to head with the local planning departments, it is a huge extra burden to bear when things backfire. It is a bewildering and depressing experience. You can hire professional help, employ interpreters and dual-language advocates, and beg friends to assist, but if the one-to-one confrontation is denied, the problem is exacerbated ten fold. The Owners may be deft at handling these problems in America, old hands at the game of municipal manipulations, but here in Provence they found themselves bereft of clout.

Until they remembered The Godmother.

Madame Darke had the whole story explained to her by Ros. She listened quietly, asked a few questions, and said she would ring them back.

Two days later The Owners had their planning permission. Everything was passed and agreed, *including* the swimming pool. There were all sorts of faffy excuses from the *Mairie's* office. Shrugs about simple misunderstandings, and expressions of bewilderment at the evidence of neglected attention. However, most importantly, promises were pledged and a date offered. In other words, it was all pretty much normal.

This was good news all round, and a big burden off the everyone's minds, not least Ros and Richard's. We could start to crank up the garden wheels again, and get ready for their arrival within a couple of weeks.

I set up a preliminary meeting with Manuel, and discussed the retaining walls, steps and position of the pool. He told me that although we now had planning for the swimming pool, there was a new problem. The old ruin with the fig tree growing out of it did not belong to The Owners, it was not within their rights. This meant we could not shore it up to make it safe, but worse, the family syndicate who owned it, having sniffed on the wind an opportunity for making money, had collectively announced that they wouldn't sell the deeds to The Owners. Well, they might, but what with things being what they were, the rising market prices, the lack of properties in Ménerbes, well, they would do better to keep it, wouldn't they? I listened as Manuel expounded on the problem in a knowing way. I suspected he'd met these hiccups many times before. I was informed at the very first meeting that the ruin was not absolutely The Owners'. But they waved it aside as a minor irritation, not something to take much notice of, sure that it would, as a matter of course, become theirs in due time. Their certitude had extended into the design, and the positioning of the pool on the terrace, directly underneath, had reflected that confidence.

This meant that its position had to be reconsidered. We could either move it over to the other side of the garden, the east side, where there really wasn't enough room for it, unless we extended the terrace further out. This would require an expensive operation involving new retaining walls, steps and in-fill, that would not only diminish the lower garden, literally, but also upset the balance aesthetically. Or, we could relocate down to the bottom, the lower level, where it could certainly be accommodated without upset. But it put it a long way from the house, in terms of climbing up and down. It concerned me that the positioning of this damned swimming pool was turning out to be the main problem with this garden. Having thought we had it resolved, it was now throwing up more questions than answers, and in my experience if it was tricky at this stage, it was quite likely to continue to be an irritant for some time to come.

Back to the drawing board. I set about preparing some sketches and plans of the pool showing it in another set of locations. I found it difficult to make up my mind, partly because I needed to discuss budgets again. How much money we had in the kitty would determine how much we could re-jig the levels, and the sizes of the terraces. The house was now costing more than originally planned, something that as a garden designer you get boringly used to. Also partly because each level had its own pro's and con's. Mostly though, because I needed to have client contact to chew over the current

situation. There had been quite a lot of water under bridges since the first round of discussions, and yet very little had actually been achieved. A feeling of down-heartedness was creeping in, and it brought with it a sliver of uncertainty. A blow that could floor the game plan. It's hard sometimes to keep your finger on the pulse of a project if it lies fallow for a while, and when the beat misses, a vessel tightens somewhere inside the blood stream.

I finished some sketches with my feelings being that the middle level would be my favourite spot. I liked the idea of keeping the lower level as a sanctuary. A place in the shade. Cool, tranquil and as far away from the house as was possible.

It was time to get out of doors, to shake off the office bugs and absorb a bit of June countryside. Theo was at school in the village teaching them to speak English, and Nicky was having coffee at the Café de la Poste in Goult. She was with a girlfriend who was having difficulty understanding why her boyfriend would not propose. She had managed to get him into a jewellers in Paris, had even got a few trays of glittering prizes dazzling in front of him, but somehow she hadn't quite managed to seal the deal.

I egged Bobble out of her basket and set off. The combination of wild poppies growing in wheat fields have enthralled people for centuries, and as Bobble and I walked across the meadows it was doing it to me again. The simple, single red heads were prolific and in parts seemed to outnumber the sheaves of wheat. The sky was a deep uninterrupted indigo and a dazzling little cloud of butterflies bobbed about in front of me. Amongst the collection were two tiny fellows, one as blue as the sky, with no markings, succinctly called *Le Bleu*, the other as yellow as a buttercup, *Le Solitaire*, not to be confused with his slightly bigger, ubiquitous lemon-coloured cousin *Le Citron de Provence*. Also in the pack were a clutter of *Jasons*. Brownie-orange with a white band dotted with black buttons. Sometimes I walked through them, and at other times I just watched as they lit upon the wild ranunculus and campanulas.

A local farmer had just cut the long grass and it lay sunning itself in the field awaiting to be turned and collected. There is a deal between him and Monsieur Neighbour. He cuts and bales it in exchange for having most of it for his horses. It doesn't take long, perhaps a day to cut, and a day to turn and bale. It is one of the most evocative couple of days of the year. Mr Bailer arrives on his ancient old Ferguson tractor pulling an equally elderly device to do the mowing. The little 'Fergy' chugs up and down producing an engine note that I remember well from my childhood in Scotland. It was a Fergy that I learnt to drive on, aged eight sitting in the lap of the farm manager. When all was done, and the hay had been turned into bales by an implement that would have been pensioned off by most farmers, it was loaded slowly onto the trailer by pitchfork. Later as it tugged up the hill against the setting sun, the tractor giving its all, small puffs of exhaust bouncing out of its vertical pipe, Mr Bailer waved from behind a contented smile, and a moment of melancholy washed over me. It was one of those little scenes that I would like to have freeze-framed so I could keep it in my back pocket, only to be pulled out when feeling a bit sad. The whole procedure would happen again in late July, and I would do what I could to be there.

Bobble and I sat down in the shade for a while, to take stock and to absorb the surroundings. Unless you pay attention they can begin to slither into the taken for granted mode, and that is really daft. After a bit of one-sided doggy talk we returned to the house to get on, me with my drawings, Bobble with her sleeping.

The next morning we were out again, this time with Theo joining the ranks. The hay fields looked bare and bashful, and some of the wild flowers that grew along the edges had been destroyed. They were acquaintances that I had become used to when I walked over to the basin to change the direction of the water flow. But soon there would be replacements, new stories to be heard.

Anyway a little further back on the banks, still fighting their corner, blue, yellow and mauve meadow flowers jostled for space with the grasses and low-slung branches of the cherry and apricot trees. As we reached the reservoir, the sky was as clear as pale-blue ice, and the Mistral wind was blowing up a bit, but not too hard, just enough to sharpen the air. The climbing sun filtered through the boughs of the oaks, and the long, bending swords of the bull rushes reflected off the still, calm water. The wheat was rippling and glowing like warm biscuits, the moon hesitated in the west, before fading out completely, and the day began to deepen. Bobble lowered herself into the cool water and took off for her early morning swim and Theo managed to lift the water gate and arrange it so the water began to flow towards our pond. He had grasped the rudiments of this manoeuvre most satisfactorily.

On Friday mornings, there is a small market in the square at Bonnieux, and I often drop along to buy some fruit and veg, and also to monitor what annuals, and shrubs in flower, are on offer. There is an irresistible goodwill amongst the stand holders. They all know each other well, but further, there is a genuine welcome to all comers. Graphically it is pleasing as well, the way the stalls are set out. The rows of polystyrene heads showing off hats, next to pots of jam stacked on top of each other in neat pyramids, their tops wrapped up in an assortment of jolly, sunny fabrics. The soft-coloured blocks of soap, 'Veritable Savon de Marseille', form a strong contrast to the garishly painted clock plates that have bright yellow flower heads stuck on to act as numbers. On the vegetable stand, cases of onions, garlic, cauliflower and carrots vie for space with the feathery-edged salad leaves. The lavender and olive oils that are sold next door complement bottles of local wine, painstakingly arranged. Sausages, cheeses, lampshades and pretty painted boxes all tumble into sight at the same time. At the far end of the square, Monsieur Fleure has a small but carefully sorted selection of plants. They are all in good condition, and whilst nothing very unusual is on offer, it is a good barometer as to what is now in season. There might even be a box of big yellow courgette flowers, 10 francs for six (female), 10 francs for eight (male!). He also has fresh eggs, chickens and some vegetables. Mr Fleure is a musician, of sorts. He plays a Jew's harp with great panache, and it draws people to his stand as if he had the pied piper's siren hidden behind his van. Before leaving I pick up some olives, maybe a few *Vertes au Basilic*, and a small bag of *Sevillanes au Citron*.

One Tuesday morning in late June two things happened. First, The Owners postponed their trip. They were unable to leave NY for various reasons. Second, the tractor mower arrived. It had been on the agenda to get one for about two years. We have a lot of grass to cut. Orchards, fields that are semi rough or rough, plus the lawn areas near to the house. The first year we had elected to buy a mobile '*debroussailleuse*', that's a three-wheeled brute of a lawn mower. The back two wheels are height adjustable, chain-driven, and enormous. The front is a small golf-caddy-sized thing that changes direction at the drop of a weed. It gives the machine incredible turning versatility and guides it through strangling undergrowth with an assured ability.

Years ago, I hired something similar in England to help me on a job I was doing. It was called an Allan scythe, had the same two enormous chain-driven back wheels, but instead of a rotary arm underneath, cutting the grass, it had a giant-sized pair of hair clippers at the front, about a metre wide. On either end were two shark's teeth-type blades that stuck out like daggers. It was an antisocial monster, and in hiring it for an overgrown garden in south London, I soon discovered that I had rather embarrassingly over-equipped myself. Weighing up the cost of renting equipment against manual labour, I had got my sums right, strictly speaking, but had over-looked the fact that this vicious tool needed an advanced driver's licence in the vehicles-from-hell section. Anyway, we got it on site, having unloaded it gently, and wheeled it through the side gates. Even in its slumbering state it snarled at the occupants, and scared the fur off a couple of cats. You would have thought that Dr No had sent a directive. It was basic in its design, and although only a couple of years old, it looked pre-war, and as if it had been, as one observer wrote, invented by a committee and put together by a spare-parts department, only he was referring to a gnu.

I didn't trust any assistants to drive the Allan, thinking it best to wrestle with it myself. I poured in the petrol, pulled open the

choke, yanked at the starter cord, and with trepidation held on to the clutch. It exploded into life, firing warning shots over the bows of a hundred neighbours. Immediately it began to move off, the blades with their savage hedge-clipping action, scything their way through the undergrowth like a deranged gerbil through blotting paper. As it gathered speed and began to hurtle down the garden, I did my best to pull it up. A frantic tug brought it round a bit, but before it could be turned off, closed down or shut up, it had bitten and snacked its way along the entire length of the neighbour's newly erected overlap fence, collapsing it like a row of dominoes. Then it crashed into the house wall and, spun round like one of those toys that just keep hitting things, changing direction and carrying on. It headed for the garden shed. By now I was as out of control of myself as I was of the machine. I pulled and wrenched at cables, twisted handgrips, shook levers and fought with all my might against Allean power. One last, desperate ditch jerk, and the rogue instrument ground to a halt, buried into the garden shed door, fragments of splintered wood sticking out of its teeth, and oil dribbling from broken supply lines like a deep, sticky blood.

I try, usually fairly unsuccessfully, to keep to an annual budget for the outside activities relating to our own home. In the first few years, trees and shrubs were eating into the home economy in much the same way as I was eating into Provençal cooking. To begin with we needed to find an aggressive mower that would tackle the battlefields of weeds, brambles, creeping vines and huge tufts of neglected grasses. This butch mower we had bought achieved the goals on all fronts. Strong and happy to run for hours longer than I, or Amar, could sustain, it single-handedly pulled the rough edges of the property back into shape, at the same time dealing well enough with the emerging lawns. Problem was, I wanted to be able to sit down while all this cutting activity was taking place. So this summer the tractor finally arrived.

I had hunted around trying to find the right machine for the right price, finding that the more I learnt the less I knew. Salesmen asked obscure questions about the area of mowing I was going to tackle, the gradient of the slopes, who would be riding it, etc. Anyway I had always thought you drove tractors and rode horses. One particularly boisterous sales kid even asked me if I was after variable timing. I cuffed him round the lugs and warned him to watch his tongue. I learnt that I needed at least a sixteen-horsepower engine, a 42cm cutting width, six speeds plus reverse and a choice of at least five cutting heights. By the time I had added leather seats, power steering and four-wheel drive, I needed a steady hand to write out the cheque. The deciding factor, in the end, had been the colour. Everybody seems to have red, so that was out, yellow was far too exhibitionist, mustard and light green too conspicuous, so when I saw a dark-green machine, without much badging or boasting, the deal was concluded quickly.

It arrived early one morning just as Theo was leaving for school. He saw it being unloaded from the truck, and with his eyes gleaming he ran over to me.

'Oh thank you, Daddy, thank you, thank you.'

'Um, I er … .'

With The Owners not due for at least another couple of weeks I was able to take the given time and act on a new job enquiry. When I had last been in London some months earlier, a friend had suggested I drop by his office. He had been doing a bit of marketing work for an Irish family who had recently bought a chateau near Aix-en-Provence. They might need a bit of help with their garden, and he could give me their number, that sort of thing.

I arrived just before lunch, and as I hadn't seen the lad for a while, and knowing of his highly developed nose for a glass of something cold, dry, frisky and ready to go, I took with me a bottle of chilled middle Moselle. A Piesport, delicate and slight but not soft nor faint. It was welcomed with open lips and we settled down to the briefing. He explained that the youngish couple had moved from Ireland, down to the Var, not far from Aix, and had bought a well-known chateau that was also a substantial wine business. The operation, having once been a celebrated Provençal label, had lost its grip and had virtually sunk in a vat of mediocrity, until, in the early Nineties, David O'Irish had rescued the enterprise. David, son of the legendary Irish horse trainer, Vincent O'Irish, had, after considerable success himself within the equestrian fraternity, decided to change course. With Catherine, his bright and attractive Australian wife, their three children (at that time), dogs and nannies, he upped anchors from the Emerald Isle, and set up home at the Chateau Vignelaure. Now, after eight or so years the hard work put in by both of them have started to pay off. Trade journals, food and wine magazines and social periodicals are all beginning to take notice of the product. Reports of the recovery have spread, and once again the Vignelaure is a wine to be reckoned with.

My chum continued: 'Because of the success of the venture, and because they have already done the chateau up beautifully, they now need to turn their attention to the garden.'

I was listening, but also trying to imagine what kind of state the garden might be in.

'They are starting to encourage passing trade. You know, people dropping in for tastings, as well as the big buyers showing up, and of course there is the inevitable flow of people in the business who have to be entertained.'

My friend had been pitching to get the job of helping market the wine, and was waiting to hear the result. As things turned out, he wasn't successful on that front for reasons I never really knew. We finished the wine, and agreed that he would effect an introduction by way of a 'phone call, and I would follow that up a few days later, when I got back to Provence.

In fact by the time I arrived home, there was a message that Catherine O'Irish had already rung. So without further ado, a meeting was set up.

The drive from Lacoste over to Jouques, where the chateau is located takes a little under an hour, the slowest bit being the winding road over and down through the Luberon hills. There is no chance of overtaking, unless of course you are French, in which case there are several suitably death-defying high spots that seem to be offered up as sport for *les chauffeurs du mort*. Beyond the valley come the well-known towns and villages of the region: Lourmarin, Cadenet, then Pertuis, and Jouques. I once had time to wander around Jouques, a place basically built along either side of the main road. I had parked neatly in a parking bay, gone over to a *boulangerie*, and returned to find another car parked across my beam and I couldn't go forward, there was a wall. The driver of the blockade had done what all French drivers do. Abandoned his vehicle as close as he could to where he needed to buy something, probably a pastis. The car doors opened but there were no keys in the ignition. I hung around for a while, beginning to think of those strong adhesive labels that people in London seemed to keep in their back pockets, to paper over the windscreens of inconsiderate parkers. But here it was normal, and presumably totally understandable, forgivable and encouraged, because everybody did it. So I went for a look around the town, had a beer, and then walked along the side of the river. I watched a tough fight between a couple of geckos about 15cms long. *L'Hémidactyle verruqueux*, as it likes to be called in learned circles, is a descendant and relative of the pterodactyl. This would perhaps explain their surprising aggression. They are so much part of everyday summer activities, scuttling across terraces and up walls to get out of your way, one doesn't really imagine them being cruel warriors, fighting to the death, but there definitely wasn't room in this town for the both of them. I got back to my car to find the parking culprit easing away from his spot. I didn't even get the chance to thank him for his consideration.

As I came round the corner on the final approach to Vignelaure, wheat fields flanked the road. Huge, gentle, undulating swathes of pale golden grain moving rhythmically in the breeze. It's not until you turn off the road into the driveway and see the chateau, an elegant eighteenth century two-storey building, that any sign of vine growing becomes apparent.

I parked in the main courtyard. A huge expanse of gravel, surrounded on three sides by first the chateau itself, then by the administrative block, and finally by the loading bays that front the *caves*. The quadrangle was completed at the far end by a boundary wall with a tiled toplet. I went into the office, and while I was introducing myself to a secretary, I noticed I was being watched by a chap that who looked as if he had recently been dragged in reluctantly from the fields. After a few moments he stepped forward and with his hand shaking mine warmly, announced that he was David O'Irish. He was charming, amusing, and within minutes I felt I had a new friend (he probably does that to all the girls). He explained that Catherine was not back from wherever she'd gone, but was expected, and meanwhile he could show me round.

Vignelaure, they say, means 'the vineyard of the sacred spring', and one of those alleged facts that we should be happy to accept, after all it sets a romantic tone. The land used to belong to a local aristocrat, the Marquis de Rians. Although the area appears to have grown vines since the time of the Romans, it does not seem to have really started producing wine in earnest until the 1960s. This was when an agricultural engineer, Monsieur Georges Brunet, who had amassed a fortune in property dealing, had liked the idea of turning his hand to wine making, and bought the place. He developed the estate, planting up to 100 hectares of vine. He added a wing to the house, laid out the formal gardens, and turned the cellars under the winery into an art gallery and, by the end of the Sixties, managed to produce good wines. By 1985 Brunet's marriage was on the rocks and he was forced to sell up. An American businessman, who was very much the absentee landlord, acquired Vignelaure, but he too sold up after a few years having lost money on a business venture. It passed on to an Indian in 1990, but he didn't pay enough attention to his asset, and after a few years the place had slipped out of the frame and back on to the market again. In 1994 David and Catherine took the bottle by the cork and kicked it back on to the rack. Eight years later Vignelaure has returned to the table with a vengeance.

The first thing on the O'Irish gardening agenda was to reinstate the formal gardens. These were laid out on either side of an allée of plane trees that run from the ornate front gates, on the edge of the vineyards, up to the main terrace on the south side of the house. The rectangular beds were arranged around a raised, circular pond, with the pattern being the same on both sides. What must have once been a neat, organised and slightly prim parterre had slipped the fold and degenerated into a mere ghostly outline of its former self. Beyond, a newly planted field of olive saplings stood to attention like fresh recruits on the drill quad. The stone that delineated the plant border rectangles had crumbled in places, pushed up by the continuing expansion of the roots of the tall planes. The soil was good however, having been used over the years of downtime as a vegetable patch, and the central paths, whilst devoid of any surface, other than weedy patches, could be cajoled back into life quite easily.

Catherine arrived with a little girl on her hip, about the same age as Theo. Baby talk ensued, and I kissed her brow like an American president on walkabout (the baby's brow I mean). We continued the tour that took in the reclaimed pond, the tennis court, almond orchard, and the main courtyard where I had parked. They were very keen to smarten up this bit, but owing to large lorries needing to turn and load, we were going to have to try and be imaginative against the house walls.

A cheerful family lunch out on the terrace ensued, with me happily tasting the house rosé for the first time. Light in colour, character and price, it seemed destined to be decanting itself over to our own cellar in reasonable quantities for summer use. We talked of gardens and gardening, wines and winemaking, Australia, Scotland, Ireland and Provence. By the end of lunch we seemed to have laughed a lot and learnt a bit about each other's lives in a very short time. I left after a tour of the *caves*, promising a quote by the end of the week, and thinking that my job would be a whole lot easier if all my clients were like those two.

I had quite a lot of plants, particularly mature shrubs, on order from Italy, for various projects, and deliveries were due to start soon. Aldo, the chap in charge of foreign sales, had rung to say that he thought I should go and tag the things I needed. This is normal procedure with larger orders and it makes for an enjoyable trip, one that I have been making on and off for fifteen years. I fly to Pisa, hire a car and drive to Pistoia, about an hour down the motorway towards Florence. The whole region around Pistoia is given over to plant growing. Some of the bigger nurseries cover hundreds of acres, and export their plants all over Europe. Naturally, the climate zones dictate what can go where, but there are a tremendous amount of trees and shrubs that will survive further north.

My order is basically for big 'filler' stuff, readily available, evergreen and not too expensive. I have always worked on plant plans this way. Start with a backbone of safe, non-attention-seeking, evergreen shrubs and trees that make the garden feel as if it has immediately got some shape and presence. Then add on the more esoteric chaps later using the others as the backdrop. The harder-to-find plants are unlikely to be available in large sizes, and this can be frustrating when you seem to be planting smaller, behind taller. But as they reach towards maturity they stake their claim in the height game, coming through as the catalogue promised. Naturally people do feel a bit hard done by when, having accepted a design based on clever 'come-on' drawings and pictures, the plants arrive and all they see is an array of tearful little chaps looking up from the nursery beds like lambs newly separated from their mother.

'Is that it? I thought it might be a bit more exciting than this.'

But of course everything begins to grow, providing it is watered, and before two shakes of that little lamb's tail, you have bonded, fallen in love, nurtured the wee darlings through baby school, put them in long trousers and sent them off to pollinate. The big fillers can also give protection against cold winds and even frosts, whilst the youngsters establish themselves.

So it was off to Pistoia for the 'fillers' I went. My list included the *Prunus* brothers *P. laurocerastus* x ('Rrotundifolia') and *P. l.x* ('Caucasica'), some *Photinia fraseri* or red robin, a dozen olive *frangivento* olives, that those pretty Italian olive trees with a pyramidal habit, a herd of *Osmanthus fragrans*, some topiary bits – balls, pyramids and half standards. I would be using *Taxus* (yew) or *'if'* as it's called in France, available as balls up to about a metre in diameter. They make a great impact when set in a line or in odd numbered groupings. They also come as cones and pyramids, up to two and a half metrers tall. *Buxus* (box) all sizes. That fine *Pinus, P. mugo* var. *pumilio,* a round little conifer, slow growing and a bit unusual;, an elegant *Elaeagnus* or two. You can, if you feel inclined, get them trained as pompoms, looking suitably like a French poodle, not my bag but I thought you might like to know. A few *Fatsia Aralias* which could be found at just under two metrers. They were a trifle dull perhaps, but good solid stuff for the background, and tough as a Turk. Expensive but dynamic, the huge *Ilex aquifolium,* or common holly. It's going to come as a ball with a diameter of over a metrer and a half, terribly expensive but a gob-stopper none the less. Then from the back row of the parade ground, a platoon of privets, or ligustrums. They are popular topiary plants, can be fidgety and need a lot of clip clips, but are available as standards, half and quarter standards, balls, cones and pyramids plus an endless manner of daft creations, only tempered by the grower's imagination. I've seen rather stiff-looking deer, elephants, and giraffes, but more pleasing are the dolphins jumping through hoops and the bucking-horses. I also need an enormous pair of Florence cypress trees — those long tall Sallys that are so typical trees of Italy and the south coast of France.

I arrived at Pisa early, and a little discussion was had at the airport because they didn't seem to have heard of my car reservation. I wanted the smallest car available, with air conditioning. They have only the biggest car available. A small amount of cheerful screaming, gentle yelling, and genial fist clenching ensued. Cash was put on the table, and I left in a huff, but driving a grown-up Mercedes. I doubted it would impress the nurserymen but as I was not paying full whack, I thought I might as well go with it. It had navigational equipment, an entire mixing desk of in-car entertainment, air conditioning for thirty-two different countries, including Icelandic blizzards for homesick Eskimos, Kalahari sand storms for misplaced nomads and a seeping dampness for Scots. All these goodies plus a plethora of other completely superficial dabs of perceived luxury were on hand, or rather, on voice. All operations were, you see, activated by voice recognition, which I was a little shy of at first.

In my office, I have a 500 zigabyte G-whiz big-Mac with a zipper fly drive. It boasts an inter-your-face, ram-disked laptop dancer that gets so confused by its own personality that it tends to go down on itself, and sometimes refuses to come back again for days. But it is controlled in silence, bar the dull taps of the keyboard. So all actions and commands being carried out as a result of speaking out aloud to a machine, were a bit disturbing. I pressed the English-language button, then chose a female voice, politely introduced myself, and mentioned that if she was ready, then I was too.

She said flatly, in English with a strong German accent:

'How do you do. My name is Claudia.'

She sounded decidedly humourless and a little intimidating. She welcomed me on board, and asked me if I had understood that her software could cope with Italian spoken with an English accent?

Not wanting to sound too illiterate I managed 'Yah Dankeschun'.

She told me that if I wanted to use the CD player, address book, hands-free phone, text messaging or, she cleared her throat, organise data transfer to a hand held portable, well just to let her know. Meanwhile she would be programming the satellite-navigation system.

I affected a bold, conquering attitude, snapped out a couple of commands, and rinsed in a touch of impatience for good measure. As this lady of the limo had a brittle chafe with dominatrix overtones, I thought I had better assert myself early on. After the seat belts had offered themselves to me, and I had muttered something about my destination, we moved off silkily, and were soon on the freeway to Firenze.

You know you are nearing Pistoia because one minute you are cruising through perfectly pleasant rural Tuscanshire, and the next you seem to be hurtling surreally down the allées of an oversized garden. Giant *Magnolia grandifloras* crowd in on you, droopy *Cedrus atlantica* lean over like something from a ghost-train ride, whilst regiments of straight-backed conifers dare you not to pay attention. It doesn't really matter where you pull off the motorway, sooner or later you will find yourself parked in the lot of some grower's domain. However, today Claudia was in charge of pinpointing the spot, and she cracked her whip if I even glanced at a pretty side road, and ground her heel into my glove compartment if I missed a turning. I arrived at the offices of Senior Zanucci and Sons with highly disciplined panache.

I had written my order, faxed, emailed, and phoned it through as back up, and just wanted to tag my plants and get cracking again, because, after all, I had been to the nursery a dozen times before. But it was not possible. The chances of escaping Aldo taking you round every square inch of the zillion-acre nursery are practically zero. You are loaded into a 4 x 4, and whisked round the site at phenomenal speed, accelerated down the narrow alleys between *Enkianthus campanulatus* and the *Sequoiadendrons*, drifted past *Catalpa bignonioides* and *Acacias* and on through rows upon rows of *Pinus*, *Tthujya*, and *Cupressus*, with *Acers*, *Azaleas* and *Lagerstroemia*. He is quite likely to stamp on the brakes to within a toenail of their existence when a man on a black stallion gallops across his bows at one of the dozens of intersections that divide up the planting rows. The animal rears up and the rider, pulling off a passable imitation of sitting on a Ferrari badge, looks down his fine nose, hacks the beast in the groin with his impeccable riding boots, and catapults off towards the *Chamaerops* forest. This you will later learn was the Zanucci heir, the fifth generation, out for a little bridle practice.

A 360 degree hand-brake turn slides the all-wheel driver backwards into his parking slot at the local taverna, and before you can say Benny and the Jets, lunch is happening, whether you want it or not. Because Aldo is quite irresistible, and because you need a drink, it isn't long before you are guesting without complaint. You shouldn't, but you do, drink glasses of very chilled, crispy *vinho verde*.

We were drinking this almost water-white Portuguese wine, with its refreshing little bubbles, and slightly under-ripe style rather than anything local, because it is light and useful at lunch time. Did you know that because of land shortage in northern Portugal they grow the vines up the trees to save space? I was hungry so started with a dish of Sage Leaf Rolls, where an anchovy, having been soaked in milk for half an hour to remove the salt, is sandwiched between two big sage leaves that have been dipped in beaten egg and then sunk into hot oil. I took my hosts recommendation for '*Seppie in Zimino*', a famous Tuscan dish of squid cooked mysteriously well with spinach and beet greens, and considerably elevated when shared with a little *polenta*. An *insalata verde* comes along for the ride, just a few lettuce leaves, *radicchio* and parsley, stylishly dressed in mega virgin olive oil, vinegar and salt. It hits the spot. Does Richard Branson own virgin olive oil I wondered? Most likely.

I left the nursery late in the afternoon having tagged my trees and shrubs, tired, hot and still a trifle 'lunched'. When Claudia told me to shut the door, turn on the ignition and take off my trousers, I was ready to row. Bluntly, I was feeling a little belligerent and did not want to do anything to please her. I didn't want to discuss anything, not how the car worked, how my life worked, or what I was going to do that evening.

I exited back onto the motorway in the general direction of Lucca, and tried to guess the directions to my lodgings. I was booked into a hotel about half an hour away, somewhere I had found at the last moment, and was looking forward to landing in my room, but at the rate it was taking me to find my bearings, it would be a long haul. I heard Claudia humming quietly to herself in the background, then: 'I will find ze hotel.'

'It's OK thank you, I'll manage.'

'Why don't you do as I say and we'll get there much quicker?'

'Don't worry, its just up here and … .'

'Nien Herr Dingwall, it is not.'

I ignored her and sulkily drove on.

'You are stupid, Herr Dingwall.'

'Alright Fraulein Navigator, you show me, my head hurts.'

Immediately, up on the screen came a local map with the quickest route to Lucca highlighted. I entered the name of the hotel and, before I had put my hand back on the wheel, the directions to the door were laid out simply and efficiently, right there before my eyes.

I checked in, registered, gave credit-card details, then found out they had given me a suite. Some misunderstanding, no extra charges, and is that all the baggage I have? As I moved away from the desk I reflected on my extraordinary ability to get upgraded everywhere I went on this trip. I shrugged and decided to take it in my stride. The hotel was a cavernous old building with long, wide passageways that would suite a roller-skater. The tall ceilings and windows enclosed an air of hushed respectability, and the carpets and wall hangings quickly absorbed what background noise managed to escape. White jacketed waiters progress about as if on a moving carpet, their trays held high above their heads, packed with expensive Italian cocktails. I delivered myself up to my rather grand quarters, and finding the window doors open, I edged out onto the balcony.

The garden below had some beautiful trees. A fine pair of *Paulwownias*, a magnificent plane, some old and elegant *Cupressus sempervirens*, and throwing a little welcome shade over the shallow end of the pool was a horse chestnut that any English eighteenth century park would have been proud of. I ran a bath, which took some time as it was big enough to dip a flock of sheep in. As I waited for the trough to fill, I went for a run round the rooms. Nothing too exhausting, just a gentle jog.

Setting off from the sitting room, I swerved between turn-of-the-century commodes and writing desks with their dainty feet. I took a short sprint down the outside track past the sofa, then, braking hard, headed back towards the bedroom, where I deftly dressaged my way through a chicane of trouser presses and luggage tables. Dropping down to a saunter I approached the telephone table in low gear. I picked up the book of hotel amenities and noticed that they had a Thelasotherapy massage on offer. 'Ring reception to book' it urged, for a memorable relaxation *sessionni*.

Years ago when I had been working on a hotel garden in St Lucia they had had a Thelasotherapy massage room there as well. It was all to do with the sea, and the revitalising properties that can be extracted from the salt water and the seaweed plant. It begins with twelve minutes in the sea, the minimum amount of time for the body to absorb the natural goodies, then goes on to a massage given by an expert tuned into the finer points of this particular body care. People would come from far and wide to enjoy this treat, much in the way that years ago, they would travel to the spas. The bloke who was in charge of the project explained that, whilst they knew they could find Thalasotherapists without any problems in America, and probably Miami, only a few air miles away, they were duty bound to advertise in the local newspaper first. The government insisting, rightly so, that any jobs that might be created by snazzy new developments should be offered to the indigenous islander before anyone else.

'Yes. sah. This be de classifieds.'

'I'd like to run a small employment advertisement.'

'No problem Mister. What you want to be writin'?'

'Thelasotherapist needed for new Body Awareness Centre, apply: The General Manager, The Pittons Hotel.'

'No problem, just checkin' de spelling there man, was that two t's in Pittons?'

I called down to reception, was connected to the massage room, and an appointment was made for seven o'clock, in about half an hour. I turned off the bath, no need for that now. I watched the Italian news, had a large glass of Scotch, rang home, and didn't mention the massage just in case I explained it badly, and headed off for my appointment with the master of minerals.

As I let myself in through the blank white door with Dottori Slogato's Male Massage Room written on it, I had a breath of a thought that I might be sanctioning myself into a pit of hairy Italian gays. Nothing, I rush to add, wrong with that per se, just that I didn't want to find myself in the wrong camp. The lights were so bright I was about to bolt, but was arrested by a middle aged, moustachioed, muscle maker. He had fitness written all over his torso. He had probably achieved his doctorate in bodybuilding, even the hairs on his chest looked fit. His white T-shirt stretched menacingly across his ridiculously firm chest, and his trousers looked like they had shrunk on him whilst taking part in a Persil-sponsored weight-lifting competition.

In one hand he held a card, which I was to learn later was an insurance indemnification slip; in his other, he squeezed one of those absurd little spring gadgets that I think are meant to condense your wrist muscles. Over his arm he had draped a couple of towels, not very big ones from the look of things. He managed quite good English, introduced himself as Dottori Slogato and told me to fill in and sign the form, get undressed, and he would return after he had run my bath. He had omitted to leave one of his little towels or give me a dressing gown, so I stripped down to my underpants, and stood, unnerved, in the shining white undressing room like a pea prematurely popped from its pod. A swing door swung open and the Dottori was standing there looking at me much like I imagine workers in a mortuary view the evening's intake, or a hooker at a rather disappointing trick.

'It is not advised to wear underclothes in the meditation tank, signor,' he said matter-of-factly. He stood there watching as I tried to kick off my boxers with a hint of bravado. My 'call me big boy' laconic smile was failing on all fronts.

He led me through to a clinically clean sort of bathroom. A cruel fluorescent strip light caught hold of every blemish and hiccup a body might possess, and bounced it off the white tiled walls. The floor was covered in wooden duck-boards. Large, polished copper, water pipes travelled up out of the ground in bunches of six. They networked their way over to an enormous stainless steel tank that occupied most of the middle of the room, wrapped themselves round one end of the cistern, and with much braggadocio, aided by a fleet of magnificently polished taps, gushed hot water powerfully into the spotless container. As the room filled with steam the

Dottori applied sachet after sachet of secret potions into the stream of water. By the time he ordered me into the pool of tranquillity, I could hardly see him. I lowered myself down slowly, feeling the warmth and softness of the treated liquid absorbing my ills. I was however, sitting bolt upright thinking how the hell you could really relax in a steel tub with straight sides, when the medicine man arrived with two polystyrene cushions, one to put behind your head and back, and one for your feet. He considerately explained that as we were all different sizes, he had a substantial repertoire of cushions to meet nearly all comers. He lit a candle big enough to please the most devout Catholic, threw the switch on the strip light, piped in some soft Cesaria Evora singing Paraiso di Atlantico, ordered me, rather oddly, to forgive myself, and to float. Occasionally, I heard a whisper of sound or noticed a shadow move as the Dottori attended to the water temperature and topped up the salts. What a lovely way to drown.

Three quarters of an hour later I was lying in a dimmed room face down on a slab of white marble, the welcome coldness pressing against my marinated body. I was laxed out.

Without warning or cautioning, and quite suddenly, I felt the crack of something whipping my back. I had hardly focused through the blur of tears, when another came with six more on top of that. It seared through my being as if the devil had picked up a nasty trick that involved mean little flicks, coming from a tightly wound, wet towel. I started to yelp, and tried to lift myself up. It didn't work. I was strapped down and the pain seemed to die in my throat. I could just see the man cracking long lengths of seaweed at me, raising them up and bringing them down with awesome force across my back. Then just as suddenly, it stopped, and before I could whimper a complaint, I was being pummelled with fists up and down my back. Nothing gentle or considerate here. This was a heavyweights pre-fight physio frenzy. I was then turned over and attacked again. The side of a highly trained killer's hand sliced into my upper thighs, so close to my, by now, public parts, that I feared I might never have another crack at the mating game. On it went, pummelling inch after inch of my beaten-up old frame. God, I needed Claudia to come in and stop this onslaught, this physical abuse, and pull this mad Italian off me.

In fact this last bout of Thelaso nonsense only lasted about fifteen minutes. After I had been pulled limply from the slab, had gained control of my faculties, and slipped into a warm courtesy dressing gown, I found myself thanking the doctor and shaking his hand, in fact I bloody nearly hugged him. I must have been going through post-air crash survival syndrome, where everybody who wasn't killed or maimed beyond hope instantly bonds out of an euphoric sense of survival, having all escaped from a shared disaster. A little later, I would consider ringing my lawyer to discuss the possibilities of suing Dottori Slogato for trauma.

That night I ate *Granseola al Llimone*. *Granseola* are large, very tender spider crabs found only in Venice, and are considered by many, including me, a delicacy, and are served simply with lemon and a some leaves of lettuce. Sometimes the chef might add a few capers or fish roe, but tonight it was simple. Delicious. Having thought I would keep dinner minimal, I found myself, instead, ravenously hungry. So I trotted on and ordered *Fritto Misto alla Fiorentina*. This Florentine fry-up puts a mixture of chicken, rabbit, artichoke, and zucchini flowers on your plate. Pretty to look at and very good to munch. 'A gardener *eating* flowers,' the Bateman cartoon would have screamed, all eyes popping with social indignity. Prince Bavaria would have applauded. Cooking it in extra-virgin olive oil made it exquisitely crispy, and was it so delicious I could have done a jig around the table, had my legs been up to it. A good bottle of Chianti seemed mandatory, so I chose Toscano from the Sitwell estate at Montegufoni. It sort of fitted my Anglo Italian mood, and as I sat there in a grand dining room that oozed discretion, getting ripped, I felt sad that I was there without my other half and a quarter.

At a little after ten, I called for a stretcher and went to my room to sleep and recover.

CHAPTER SIX

Going Swimmingly

A flurry of activity at The Owners' garden awaited my return from the pastures of pastaland. Richard and Ros had decided that the pool should go on the lowest level. It meant they could instruct Manuel to start work on it immediately, and being at the bottom also meant that it didn't interfere too much with getting the house finished. If everything went to plan, they might even be swimming by the end of August. That would give them about four weeks before it got too cold to use without the heating being turned on. It was also another bet worth taking a swing on. Yes, they understood that it spoilt the shade zone and that one of the big cherries would have to come out, but 'let's just allow for replanting some big trees nearby, and get on with it.'

I was concerned that the positioning of the pool had been arrived at under pressure. Because of the continuing work on the house, it would not have been possible to start installing it that soon, if they had wanted to put it on any of the higher levels.

But at least we had action. It had felt a bit like being a fighter pilot waiting to scramble. All trained up, and prepared for action, but with nothing to throw it at. I met with the builders and agreed to mark out the exact position, clear the trees, and move any plants worth saving. Manuel told me he was going to make an exploratory dig that afternoon. He needed to know what he was digging into. Back at the office I confirmed colour and depth of the pool, shapes and types of tile, underwater lighting, and a myriad of other watery details with The Owners.

At least all the planning and discussions held earlier in the year came into good use now and things moved quickly. It was nearly the end of June and the weather was good. Mr LaBour was ready for action.

The next morning there was a site meeting to discuss, amongst other things, the exploratory dig done the day before. Manuel was concerned about the project, again. This time the worry was about the rock that had to be broken up and excavated to make the hole big enough for the pool. It was a bit crumbly, very heavily stratified and layered. He felt that perhaps, after all, it would be best to commission a specialist swimming pool firm to come and do the job, professionals in the game. Pool construction is a difficult business and Manuel's hesitation was understandable.

Within days we had had site meetings with two installation companies. Firstly, a local business whose work in the area was known. Secondly, the franchised office of a large chain that operated throughout the country. I have a reservation about franchises. They may have good back up, heaps of experienced bods you can call on to get things sorted out and under way, but if and when something goes wrong, they suddenly become impossible to deal with. You end up haggling with a head office because your local contractor has passed the buck. You argue with people you haven't met or spoken to before. You are kept waiting and you're likely to get stockpiled in the 'must do' tray, probably somewhere down in the nether regions, between the underside of the springboard, and the deep end. At least with a company from the area, you should be able to get hold of them, even if it's by the neck, and apply some kind of pressure.

Neither firm seemed too concerned about the rock, although the local chap mentioned that it seemed a bit porous, but that was a remark made more to satisfy his judgement about the ease of excavation rather than any kind of geological phenomena.

The access was a nightmare of course, especially as coming through the house and down the garden was not an option. I confirmed that the neighbours had agreed to let us move equipment in over their land, or rather, through their cherry orchard. It would mean knocking down a section of party wall, but Manuel was equipped to put that back up as soon as the hole had been dug and the larger equipment was off site. This was, of course, completely untrue; I had yet to approach the neighbour about our intentions. I hadn't met them; I didn't know their name and was not even sure they existed. But we didn't want any more delays or false starts, so I chucked this little fib into the agenda in the blind hope that I would get it sorted out before it mattered.

As we waited for the quotes to come in, I started my directive towards what I hoped would be a helpful and understanding neighbour. I asked The Owners who knew little more than I did about whom to talk to. They did know that they weren't the same people who had denied the purchase of the little ruin. Small mercies.

I asked up at the *mairie* and after explaining my intentions, they gave me a name, Monsieur Abut. But they seemed a little doubtful about his whereabouts. I checked at the Post Office, and they confirmed that Monsieur et Madame Abut did live there but didn't *live* there. They did, however, have a *boîte postale*, and if I wrote a letter it might or might not get picked up. I asked at the pharmacy near The Owner's house if they had ever seen any one going in or out of the house in question. They had and hadn't, and suggested that the house I wanted was actually at the bottom of the hill. This threw a whole blanket of bananas over the facts I had collated. Maybe they had thought I was talking about a completely different property altogether.

The next day the full frontal assault began. I wrote a letter. I made three copies, one for the PO box, another to go through the door of the house that I thought might be the house that I wanted, although I was no longer certain about the name being right. The last I left with the pharmacy as a rather desperate long-shot. I dropped in to the café and had a quick *demi pression* and asked the proprietor if he had any ideas. He thought the house was let, and that the land belonged to somebody who lived near Aix.

'A Monsieur Abut?'

Perhaps yes, and there again, perhaps no.

I had a bright idea. Conceivably, if I wandered on to the land that we wanted to use to move our equipment over, stood about looking suspicious, and drew attention to myself, someone would come forward and, if not arrest me, at least ask me who I was and what I was doing. That was, if I hadn't been shot by a mad tenant or devoured by poodles. So, that afternoon I ostentatiously climbed over the stone wall, ignoring the wide opening without a gate, some ten metres to my right. I encouraged Bobble to run around, I hovered and stretched, pulled at a few wild flowers, kicked up some dust and generally tried to look unofficial. I conspicuously marked out the route that we would need to follow, and generally hung around for something to happen. After half an hour it did. I lost Bobble. I shouted and whistled, called and hollered, but to no effect. The dog had disappeared. As I stood there bellowing for her to make a speedy reappearance, I was aware that at least the side effects of my public exhibition of one man and his disobedient mutt, might just draw enough attention to encourage someone to investigate the loony in the field with no name. On the other hand it occurred to me that anybody witnessing my performance would probably assume that a person making that kind of racket must be confident of his quarter, and doubtless owned the land he was waltzing around on. Or, there again they might have adopted the 'it's got nothing to do with me' attitude, 'the guy is obviously bonkers'.

And it was true to say that the sun was probably getting to me. My mind was wandering around in increasingly meaningless circles. Bobble wasn't appearing, and I was being bitten by things lurking in the long grass. Things like big red ants, recalcitrant bees bothered by being disturbed as they work the wild flower pollen mill, backed up by aggressive, overblown anthrax flies. This was also the perfect environment for lizard-chasing snakes, *la couleuvre aux échelons* that checks in at a healthy metre and a half long, or the even spookier, *la couleuvre de Montpelier*, an irascible chap when menaced apparently, otherwise, they say, he doesn't really present much danger to man. But that's bearing in mind that by the time he gets to about twenty years old, he weighs about three kilos and is well over two metres long. If he was out there, I was certainly not looking to spoil his afternoon. I tell you, it *is* a dangerous place this South of France.

The owner was not materialising, and I was feeling increasingly stressed. Looking round for what I thought might have been the sound of a wandering labrador, I saw a man waving at me from the roadside, up the hill a bit. I waved back. 'At last,' I said to myself and scampered with new-found energy up the slope towards my new best friend.

'Bonjour monsieur.' I felt like Scott of the Antarctic discovering a sledge full of help. My friend guessed my nationality and spoke good English. He had a relaxed smile around his eyes, and he spoke softly as he enquired:

'Do you know where the *boulangerie* is?'

'What?' I gasped, looking at him as if he were a traitor to the crown.

'The *boulangerie*? I can't find it anywhere.'

I let out a low, long sigh, felt my shoulders dip, and sank down to sit on the wall. Perhaps he might like to push a baguette up his alimentary canal? In the distance, down on the plain, shimmering in the tangible heat, a tractor was moving slowly up and down between the lines of vine, aerating the soil and dislodging the weeds.

'Oui monsieur,' I said, and explained to the tourist how he could find his bloody *boulangerie*.

I set off again, this time only looking for dog. The house, the neighbour, and the access across the field could wait. I needed to find our hound and soon. Labby's, despite, or because of, their charming and gentle disposition, are not blessed with a German

Shepherd's brainpower. Bobble, although brighter than some I've known, will follow the scent of something to eat like the Bisto Kids in the gravy advert. Nothing is ultimately more important to her than food. It doesn't really matter what, but best is something that can be both eaten or chewed, and rolled in as well. I followed down the hill, dropping sharp, shrill bursts of finger whistles onto the afternoon air. She usually comes to those, they are almost reliable, but today they seemed to be falling on oblivious ears. A little further down the slope I came across a dear little chapel that had been constructed in the early seventeenth century by grateful Ménerbians who had escaped the plague. It was very small but had a dignified proportion, tucking itself into the side of the hill with discretion and charm. I went inside and discovered a small congregational area, with stone benches running round the edges of the walls, probably enough for twenty people. Across the narrow floor, and two steps up, there stood a small, heavy stone altar with a pair of simple candlesticks. Above, a triptych of religious panels, each about one a half metres by a metre, painted on hardboard, and set off by a stout stone frame, hung peacefully under a half-domed roof.

A painter by the name of de Pojidaieff had restored these vignettes in 1955 and they were holding up well. A miniature font built into the wall was watched over by a patient spider. It was calm and cool, and also contained a labrador. Bobble had found a stray bone, and had wisely decided to pay it full attention within the shady sanctions of Notre-Dame des Graces.

After a few moments of reflection, we headed back to the car, both a little despondent. Bobble because she had left without a bone and me, because I had left without a contact.

That night I wrote to The Owners explaining the blank I was drawing, that we needed to start moving in the equipment soon, and that I had fibbed to Manuel about access in order to keep the whole project moving. In other words I went to confession. Had they got any ideas? They had after all lived, on and off, in the region a lot longer than I had.

Twenty-four hours later, incredibly, all was resolved. Ros had not only found out whom to talk to, but had actually pinned them down, had a conversation with them, *and* gained their permission. So some things can be resolved from the other side of the planet after all. What a relief. And a salutary lesson had been learnt: don't pretend to be a detective. Clearly it wasn't my bag.

I got to work on the plant plan for the surrounds to this upcoming puddle. As the topsoil was clearly shallow, it made sense to get the digger to excavate the planting areas whilst he was on the job. If you made quite big pits, about a cubic metre, you could plant quite big trees. Providing the roots were given plenty of water in the first year or two, and space to develop, by year three the tree would be strong enough to anchor itself in its own environment, and the tap root could go water divining.

I hadn't wanted to put the *piscine* 'down there' particularly, but I could understand the clients' reasoning. However, it meant that all my plant plans for a shady garden were mostly out of the frame.

Starting with Ros's decision to go with a black interior for the pool, I started to sketch up some ideas for a planting scheme that would work with that. Heavy contrasts, with whatever really dark colours I could spring in among pale and silvery foliage. Also, because we had at least managed to save two of the cherry trees, there was a certain amount of shade, and that called for amongst others, *Acanthus mollis* and some *hostas*. One of my favourites is that big glaucous-leaved variety, 'Blue Moon'. 'You saw me standing alone, without a hosta my own.' A clutch or two of *Helleborus argutifolius* with its winter-green flowers, three *Bupleurum fruticosum*, a quite tall growing shrub, up to two metres with silver green leaves and yellow flowers throughout the summer. I tend to stay clear of yellow unless it's soft as we have enough sunlight to compensate, but in a shady spot, it is useful as a highlight. The *Euphorbia* x *martinii* helps in these conditions, not drinkable but it does have a dense habit and will form itself into a ball. The leaves are mid green with purple underneath, and it is evergreen, or *persistante* as the French say.

For backdrop in the semi-shade *Rhamnus alaternus* or buckthorn, again an evergreen, with shiny leaves, the vigorous growth can be trimmed or even shaped. That favourite standby, *Pittosporum tobira*, would be drafted in to help with the screening. I can't imagine a garden where this old timer isn't used in one way or another. It can be clipped or left wild, seems to thrive by the seaside, responds well to iron pellets if it's feeling a little pale, and generally puts up with inconsistent attention. There was a bit of stone wall near to one of the cherry trees on the east side that doesn't get much sun, so I've designated some *Umbilicus rupestris* to be planted into the cracks and crevices. It is persistant, survives extreme cold and shade and still manages to put on a performance of yellowy green from April until July. I would probably use some box again down there for form, as well as some *Cistus salviifolius*, a pretty variety of this big family, that is well behaved and shows plenty of grip. Growing to about a metre high, it has soft, sage-like leaves, grey tinged with green-and-white, and flowers in mid spring to early summer. It colonises in woodlands, and battles well with the snakebites of heavy winter.

Screening was an issue again, but at least 'down there' we had more space, and were further away from any neighbours or passers by. Apart from the *Pittosporum tobira*, *Viburnum tinus* and *Ceanothus hearstorium*, we would have a Florentinian cypress or two. It's hard not be predictable with hedging and screening plants. It often looks as if everybody is calling up the same agency, but when the portfolio of plants is limited, it becomes inevitable. Add in second-division conditions and everyone will be paddling the same canoe. Out in the open, away from the soft shadows and broken light, the choice opens up. Before even thinking about what will go where, I put *Gaura lindheimeri* on the list. This delicate pale-pink perennial will flower profusely from late spring all the way through to late autumn, splashing itself around at up to a metre high, and if given half a chance spread like mad. Most welcome. Another classic is *Perovskia atriplicifolia* or Russian sage. It's what is termed a shrublet. Not quite a perennial, not quite a shrub either, kind of a thing. But an asset for sunny gardens, dry or not. The elegant pale-blue panicles tower above a feathery grey foliage, and last well into the autumn, then they should get cut back in March. *Hibiscus* is the sort of plant that, in one form or another, appears on the menu of most Mediterranean gardens, and rightly so. Playing safe I'm including two varieties in the plan: *H. moscheutos* with its big showy summer flowers, available in white, pink or red, and the classic *H. syriacus* Russian Violet, again with its big simple mauve flowers. These guys need to be cut down to size in the spring, and are tolerant of our conditions.

I soon found myself over-dressing the salad. I have a tendency to introduce far too many different types of plants and had to force myself to simplify the planting scheme, edit and compromise. There are so many good things out there that I would like to incorporate, but of course, one needs discipline and a restrained imagination.

Another aspect to making up a planting scheme is the fact that for all the pre-planning and researching that goes on, there is the added dimension of finding plants on the road. It's always worth popping into a plant centre, or *pépinière* to see what they have got on offer. You never know there might be something unexpected, something that fits the bill for some project that's under way. It has happened dozens of time. It changes the well-laid plans but adds a fresh angle.

We needed some kind of folly or focal point. I would need to go and hang round the junk sales that happen all over the Luberon during the summer, and see if I could find something suitable, preferably a bit witty and to the point. I'm happy sniffing around second-hand garden furniture dealers, making excursions to boot sales, and little *brocante* markets. Often you don't know what you want, until you see it. The other day I had been looking for some zinc basins and ended up buying a weird pair of wicker basket chairs. Each of the two arms, or sides, were large elephants, the back of the seat rose up like an imperial throne, and they were wide enough for two children to sit in comfortably. Another occasion had yielded an extraordinarily ornate birdcage modelled on a Regency manor house. Complete with detailed iron work and lead roof, it was bought, not to put birds in, but as a focal point of interest. It was too big to take into the client's house in the winter, so had to sit outside. We had a cover made to measure, using a dark green waxed fabric. It looked interesting in its own right, like a Barboured box. On another occasion I found a couple of old down-on-their-luck tractors and had them dragged them back from the scrap heap, sprayed with a clear preservative, and then put out to grass. They looked quite regal sitting out on the *manoir's* long lawn, like a pair of tramps who had come across a toff's suitcase.

We also needed to look at the small cement block shed in the garden, and convert it into a place for all the filtration equipment, etc. It would need to be softened up, to look more house-like, and made secure. But this could wait — as long as it could be locked up, the decorating could come at the end.

New electrical layouts had to be organised along with lighting and irrigation. There was plenty to do. I was just about to tape the drawing paper onto the board, when Theo said, 'Dad?'

'What?'

'I love going for walks.'

'Me too, let's go for one later.'

'But we have to take Bobble for a walk now.'

'Later, Dad's got to work now.'

What ensued was a hammy demonstration of an upset child. Hammy that is, until after blowing the notes on his tantrum trumpet hard enough, for long enough, he managed to convince himself that his world really was caving in under a shower of parental hate and exclusion, and that he might as well bawl himself to death. Of course I gave in. I picked him up and dried out his tears with warm kisses, knowing full well that he would never learn about leaving me alone to work if all I ever did was hug and cosset him every time he came in to see me. (Memo to self: 'Move office out of house before we all get divorced from each other.')

The tears had soon evaporated and, purring with victory, he carried on as if nothing had happened.

'Dad, you know somethin'? Long time ago when dinosaurs were real, they used to eat this grass.'

We had abandoned the office and were taking a walk over to the field where Georges Neighbour was growing this season's courgettes, cucumbers and aubergines, their big foliage already beginning to spread out to keep the direct sun off the backs of the newly forming vegetables. On either side of the rabbit path that had been worn down, presumably by rabbits, and certainly by single-file humans, was mare's tail, growing strongly and determinedly. By August it would have spread unchecked and become a nuisance. Theo was right about its being a dinosaur nibble; only thirty million years ago, it had grown up to about four or five metres in height.

He was obsessed by these prehistoric monsters. There were dozens of them in his room in various sizes, made from plastic, card, wood and rubber. He had books full of drawings, and videos full of cute animated dino stories. The other day he had told me that he preferred the furastic period, and that carnivorts were more fun than herbivorts 'cos, their teeth were bigger'. So when he wasn't being Theo Lightyear, he was busy being Theo Saurus.

'How do you know that?' I asked, impressed.

'Mum read me a story about it last night, in my dinosaur book, it's a French book, but she was reading it in English. I prefer English,' he added ruefully.

It is hard for him up at the local school trying to get to terms with speaking French, and I worry about him being deprived of children's conversation. Somebody said to me that at three and a half, most of the talk is based around the 'gimme' factor but I'm not so sure that is correct, having seen him holding hands with Marie, the postmistress's daughter, at the end of term singsong. Also, when Miss English Actress and her director came to lunch a few weeks ago, we noticed how animated he became with their little girl of the same age. I tend to end up hoping for the best; after all, there are other children here who speak perfect French having arrived at four, five and six knowing zilch.

'Dad?'

'What?'

'I'd love a story tonight.'

'OK, what sort of story?'

'A long one.'

'How long?'

'About eleventeen metres.'

In the trees we could hear the call of the little green tree frog, *la rainette méridionale*. He has a sort of elongated bark that you usually only hear when it's going to rain or storm, and as that afternoon moved towards evening, he was singing his head off, thrilled to be the town crier. Sometimes we would find one clinging to the shutters of the kitchen window. He is a cold little fellow in the palm of your hand when you move him out of harm's way, but quite delightful.

We met Georges and his brother, Joel, coming back from the reservoir. They pulled up in their old Peugeot pick up, a vehicle that looks as if its mind is somewhere else, and probably has been for the last twenty years. They had been installing a tank that holds liquid fertilisers. The water from the 'basin' is pumped into the cistern, mixes with the 'goodie' and then passes out into the irrigation system. This is an inventive way of giving plants two things at once. George winked and assured me his cucumbers and melons were already looking formidable. We paused a moment to watch a pair of soaring eagles. *L'aigle de Bonelli* has a wing span of nearly 80 cms, the tips of which spread out like fingers feeling the currents of rising air, and are captivating in their majesty. Correctly protected from *la chasse*, it is confronted more nowadays by the dangers of electrical power lines and pollution, despite the safeguards that are offered. More often one sees a kestrel hovering above the roadside, or a *busard des roseaux*, which we know in the UK as the marsh harrier. These powerful birds of prey are also protected from man but suffer from the use of pesticides. There is another rather strange eagley fellow, occasionally found in all parts of Provence called *le percnoptère*. He is predominately white and has a pointed yellow face and beak with a wingspan of about 60–70 cms, Sadly the creature is in decline, and therefore an increasingly rare sight.

Our nattering moved on from fruit and fertilisers to the plans for *La Maison Basse.* This is a very large property that is positioned about a couple of hundred metres below our house, a little further down towards the plain and has a wonderful easy composition. It consists of one medium-sized *mas*, adjoining a big three-storied *bastide*, enhanced by an enormous stone barn. It is all roofed with beautiful old, weathered, terracotta tiles, a bit battered in places, their rusty brown surface absorbing the afternoon sun. The buildings harmonise with one another faultlessly, and the total area of usable domestic space must be some 800–1000 square metres, *if* it was usable, which it isn't. Our conversation was about the lamentable fact that this lovely building the brothers had known all their lives, and their parents before them, had fallen into such a sad state of disrepair. Very soon it would be past the bounds of renovation. People had started to pinch bits from it. The old, worn stone steps that lead to the upper floor of the barn, on the outside had recently vanished. It had already been on the market a long time when we arrived. We had learnt more about it when we had enquired about a plot of land that butted up to our own driveway. We had thought it wise to try and buy this little field and secure ourselves against any nasty, unexpected development plans that might happen. Although any new building was highly unlikely, it was so close to our house, and virtually in the garden, and we didn't want to have to think about strangers using it in any way. The proprietor had told us that he would only sell it when he sold the *Maison Basse*. He didn't want the bother of getting involved with the lawyers over such a small parcel of land. We therefore immediately developed a keen sense of interest in who, and what, would want to take on such a big project as the dilapidated farm. He was asking a lot of francs for it, and it would need a lot more to get it up and running. Planning permission had been turned down for various commercial propositions such as a conference centre, a hotel, a small factory and even a museum. Presumably the local powers that be felt that anything too commercial would bring havoc to a pretty and tranquil little corner of the Lacoste basin.

Eventually, it was bought in 1998 by The Lacoste School of the Arts, a non-profit institution that is run in association with Bard College, of New York State, who have been directing the academic programme since 1997.

It all started nearly fifty years ago when an American painter called Bernard Pfriem from Cleveland arrived in Lacoste. He had been living in Paris, but, tired of suffering from hay fever, had decided to head south, and dry out. He stumbled upon Lacoste and immediately fell in love with it. In those days the thousand-year-old village was virtually a forgotten place, being mainly occupied by the traditional population of quarry workers. Evidence of their work can be seen in the beautifully built houses, streets, and walls.

Pfriem at first stayed in the Café de France, the village's only hotel, but soon moved when he managed to buy a house for the enviable sum of fifty dollars. Over the years he added considerably to his property portfolio, including one dwelling that he bought in exchange for an American fridge. The idea of starting an art school came to him in the mid Sixties, but sensitive to his surroundings and the possible reluctance of the villagers to be overrun by students, Pfriem broke the idea to the population of three hundred cautiously. Far from being against it, they welcomed the idea, feeling that the economic benefits that such a school might generate could only help. By 1970 he had found financial backing. It came through his job at the Sarah Lawrence College, in Bronxville NY and the school was up and running. It quickly became a success and regularly had up to fifty students enjoying not only a rigorous art school but also an idyllic refuge from the distractions of everyday life.

Maison basse.

Over the years the sponsorship has changed, and was for a time in the hands of the Cleveland Insitute of Arts, but nowadays is under the capable guidance of a board of trustees, the majority of whom are American Ladies. After more than thirty years of peaceful co-existence, Lacoste and the art school have yet to regret their decision to work together. Bernard Pfriam died in 1996 aged eighty. He would have been pleased with the acquisition of *La Maison Basse*, albeit for a few dollars more than his original little house on the hill.

Once the school has commissioned work to start on the house, things will probably never be as placid again. Besides which, I had dreamt of buying it myself and keeping a fabulous collection of vintage sports cars in a climate-controlled, sound-proofed, brilliant barn. Something that would have made the Schlumpf brothers, of Mulhouse near Basel, one-time owners of the most spectacular private collection of classic cars in Europe, bleed with envy.

I told Georges that I had heard on the bush telegraph just this day, that allegedly the planning permission had been granted. A bright and friendly man, cool in a natural and self-assured way, he pointed his finger at nothing in particular, but sort of upwards, he smiled economically and nodded his head. He had just managed to say an awful lot without speaking a word, conveying a seemingly indisputable knowledge of how things are. Georges would conduct himself correctly even if he were dropped into a G8 global conference for heads of state. In fact he and Joel spend most of their days working hard, and without complaint, in the fields. His partner, Crystal, is an American, and the daughter of a science Nobel Prize winner. She came to Lacoste more than twenty years ago to teach at the art school. Being an accomplished photographer and painter in her own right, she wanted to pass on her knowledge in a convivial atmosphere. It wasn't long before she had met Georges, and never went back.

I met her the other evening at a local exhibition, and she had had her long hair cut short. It looked very pretty and made her look much younger. Oh Lord, I thought to myself, I do hope everything is all right with Georges. I worry about drastic haircuts on women – it usually means that a relationship's over. The statement of the chopped barnet is a declaration of a new-found freedom. And if there had been a new puppy under her arm, then it would have been a certainty. Happily there were no puppies to be seen.

The quote from the local swimming pool contractor, Monsieur Noir, was accepted, and he was commissioned to do the work providing he could start quickly, and get the job completed by the end of July, one month. It's possible, but is a tall order, and will take a big effort. He has openly loaded his estimate to accommodate the longer working hours that will be necessary, and is keen to get cracking. He could do this work only because another project had fallen through, so he was hungry for income, and relieved to have something to put his men to work on.

Within no time at all there was a burst of gardening business. The boundary wall was broken down, wide enough to get a small digger in, materials started to arrive by the lorry load, and the tools by the van load: picks, axes, spades and forks, cement mixers, piles of sand, cement, and stone, all seemed to come at once. Soon men had cleared away the undergrowth, which had taken up a firm residence again, scraped off the top soil, what there was of it, and drilled into a sub layer of softish rock. Within three days the hole was big enough to recognise as a potential swimming pool. The excavated spoil was removed by little dumper trucks, waddling their way backwards and forwards up through the neighbours' orchard like ants stealing grass seed. Ants are so proficient at this particular act of garden high-jacking that sometimes when you are trying to sow a new lawn, you get to feel like you've gone out just to feed them. You then manage to get through a lot of packets of anti-ant powder in your attempt to make a lawn. You Sherlock your way along the endless lines of workers, until you come to a huge mound of seed being stockpiled, before being shifted down the ant mine. Grabbing back what is rightly yours with one hand and shaking down a dose of serious powder with the other, you remind yourself that there are more than two hundred million of these little fellows in this patch of lawn alone, and that any anti anticide comments will fall on deaf ears.

The end of June arrived, and The Owners had the basic structure of their pool in place. The unwanted rock, stone, and earth was off site, the borders dug over somewhat basically by the digger, and two of the old cherry trees had been saved. The team packed up for the last weekend of the month with a sense of achievement and an enthusiasm for action rarely seen amongst the building fraternity. A happy building site is, to an architect or designer, a huge bonus and something to be nurtured.

CHAPTER SEVEN

The Sinking Garden of Menerbylon

L ocal lore says that July is usually hotter than August in Provence, and our own experience seems to ratify this. One particular early July afternoon was excelling itself. The temperatures were nudging up into the 40s (11° Fahrenheit). The air was as close as one's own breath, and you felt as if you were being squeezed between two heavy rubber balls. A stupor started to spread itself around one's consciousness like a barbiturate. It needed a big effort to talk and heads ached. People slobbed into their pools and hung out, waiting for the sky to get on and crack, for there was certainly a storm a-brewing. The sun was smudged out by a sky with a pale grey complexion. Even the cicadas were slowing down. It was very Tennessee Williams. As the day dragged itself forward and the evening beckoned, a light breeze, just enough to make the leaves shiver, fell in from the south. The storm clouds began to gather. Huge herds of black-grey menace folded themselves into one another making a multi-dimensional backdrop. There was a suspense, a tautness, and it was like watching a party of invaders inexorably making their way towards you, knowing that very soon all hell would break lose.

Parasols were lowered, shutters shut, doors secured. Windows closed on the cars, shoes, cushions and rugs brought indoors. Soon the hills disappeared behind a rolling shroud of gloom. The thunder started quietly, far off, and was more a feel than a sound. Little splinters of lightning darted aimlessly about the sky looking for a parent to hunt with. Thoughts at this early stage were of being ready to soothe children and animals, later it would be worrying about broken power lines as the lights flickered and fluttered. All televisions, videos and computers were unplugged. The power surges of a big storm can blow these appliances out like candles on a birthday cake.

Suddenly and violently, out of the jaws of disorder, the King of Thunder took a mighty crack at the roof of our house. Although we had braced ourselves, when it finally arrived, absolutely overhead, it seemed to smash into the soul with a force that humbled our existence. The house had weathered many such attacks, but it didn't stop us, or it, feeling vulnerable.

At this stage of the play you think how clever you were to replace torch batteries, or you realise how silly you were to have forgotten them. Thor had grabbed hold of our home and tried to throttle the very spirit out of it. Not content with ringing its neck, he started to stab the sky with gigantic jagged blades of silvery beaten swords.

Millions of volts of high-tension electricity crackled above our heads. This must have been a vengeance for all those gentle sunny days. The pay-back from all those people who hope that sometimes you will stop being so bloody smug about your damned fine weather.

Then came the rain. Cataclysm had struck a deal with catastrophe. It sheeted down like a twin-jet-pumped waterfall, rivered over the roof tiles and burst through the gutters. It would have impressed the Dam Busters. Quickly, great torrents had created courses of fast-moving water that took no prisoners. Top-soil, gravel, pots and furniture became dislodged, disconnected and dispersed. One last flicker and out went the lights, off went the phone, and the umbilical chord with the outside world was cut.

As the lightning wound itself up, fizzing with fury, it dazzled the interior with ghostly reminders of how nice it would be to have things back to normal, but there was no chance of that. The battle was set to last. And last it did, for eleven hours. I had always thought that storms passed over and frightened you and left you, all within a few hours, max. Not these Mammas. They seemed to select you and, as if directed by some satanic amusement arcade pilot, fire grief at you for an interminably long time. There was no sleep. No possibility, because even if you could get drunk enough to pass out, you can't because there is a baby boy who is beginning to understand that there is something out there that Mum and Dad can't switch off, and it's scaring the nightlights out of him. Bobble lay with her paws over her ears being considerably braver than most dogs, but she too was feeling beaten up. The cats had holed up in the wine cellar and the ducks were to be seen occasionally strobing against a

backdrop of trees. They flapped their wings as if they have just got out of bed after a good evening's sleep, and talked excitedly to each other about what a night it was turning out to be.

The very first storm we had encountered like this, we had, needless to say, no idea it would persist with such confidence and authority. We were lying in bed having only been here for a few weeks. As the first rumbles of thunder broke through, we reminded ourselves of that old rule about, how you can calculate how far away the thunder is by counting the time in seconds, between the lightning and the thunder clap. If you get to twelve seconds, for example, that would tell you how many miles away it was. As the numbers grew longer, you settled in the soothing knowledge that the storm was moving off, and you'd ridden it out without much mishap. We had tried it that night. We puffed up the pillows, raised ourselves up a bit and got ready to count. Suddenly, and without a hint of its ferocity, the sky was ripped open like a savage attacking silk, and a spear, a hundred metres long, forked across the sky, puncturing the heavy atmosphere.

'One, tw ....'

An explosion of such fiendish force strangled the count in our throats, and left us breathless. We looked at each other, blinking in disbelief; could nice, cosy, little Provence really manage to show off like this?

This time we all cuddled together in one bed. Theo was squeezed between us trying to be brave but not always succeeding, and Bobble, disobeying any lessons she may have learnt, had dived under the duvet muttering something about 'sharing our basket whether we liked it or not'. As the night wore on there was a sinking realisation that no tempest of this magnitude could possibly have stitched itself onto the landscape without causing a few tears.

At dawn, the sense of release, as the sky at last started to quieten down, and the mean, forbidding clouds slunk away, seemingly satisfied with the uproar they had caused, was palatable. The air was as light and fresh as a butterfly's breath. The sun appeared coyly, a little uncertain that it still had a right of way, and, gaining in confidence, puffed out its chest and shone with a warmth that spread over the wreckage like rescue remedy.

Everywhere we looked it seemed like we had been intruded upon and abused. Great gashes of top soil had been scrubbed away, taking young shrubs and plants with it, only for them to end up pathetically wrapped round a tree, or splattered without ceremony over a bank. There was no electrical power, no phone and no hope of having it fixed for ages. The driveway had been turned into a small river, and the lower lavender field was a flattened mess. I walked round taking stock, and shivered at the thought that it was quite on the cards to have two or three more of these assaults this month alone. I began to wonder about the gardens I had been working in, what damage might have occurred, and how the embryonic garden in Ménerbes and its new pool had held up.

'Could probably swim in it,' I thought to myself dejectedly.

It would have been a good test, and I pondered about how many inches or millimetres of rain had fallen during the night. It would not be long before I found out.

Just how badly things had gone wrong came with the post. Like a walking headline, the post girl told incredible stories of destruction: fallen telegraph poles, mechanics getting bogged down and the rescue services reaching breaking point. Tales of roads being broken up, drains bursting, roof tiles falling, gutters dangling. All sorry stuff but not as bad as being scorched by laser-guided missiles in the Gulf, I thought looking for the best. Then came the big one.

'There's a garden that has crashed down the hill, in Ménerbes,' the girl reported.

'What do you mean?'

'Well, apparently there's this garden, just been built, and in the storm it seems to have broken away, and slipped right down the bank, you know how steep it is.'

This was definitely not a right-on moment. I took the letters, went inside and sat down heavily.

'God,' I thought, 'it must be *our* garden.' I felt cold and disorientated for a moment. I couldn't ring anybody, no phone, and I couldn't expect my neighbours to know any more than I did. I could however get in the car and get over there as quickly as possible. I did.

There was a strong sense of 'the morning after' as I passed up through Lacoste, and drove over the hill towards Ménerbes. The gullies were still brimming with muddy rainwater; the grass was flattened, and all the trees and shrubs were still looking bedraggled. But soon with the sun warming everything by the minute, all would be looking perkier than it had done for weeks. The trees glistened, and the road itself was unfamiliarly black. I pushed the big Peugeot, holding in third for most of the way, passing dithering tractor drivers, small vans and tourists as though they hardly existed. Maybe it isn't The Owner's garden, maybe it's somebody else's, I thought over and over again. But I also knew that if there had been another garden being built in the village, I would probably have heard about it. Even if I didn't know what or where exactly, the contractors vans, the gardening equipment' etc., would have suggested some kind of horticultural activity, and that in my usual nosy way I would have sniffed around and found out. I tried to imagine the worst, and what on earth we would do about it. I slung the car into a parking bay, and ran up to the site.

As I approached the house there were no people to be seen. I had expected a small crowd of locals, police, ambulances, helicopters, soldiers, relief workers, emergency food supply drops from an overhead Hercules, screaming sirens and panic. But not a soul in sight. I tried the front door. It was open and I went inside. No one. Spooky. I thought; it really wasn't this garden, it wasn't true, the post-girl was exaggerating, it was all a load of nonsense.

The new kitchen still smelt of fresh paint, and the newly hung curtains pulled across the open windows, were moving a little in the morning draft. Some electrical cooking equipment, still in its boxes, sat on the table. Piles of plates, just unwrapped presumably by the caretaker, stood in their stacks on one of the shelves. The kitchen door was open out on to the balcony, I moved forward with trepidation.

The sun, higher and hotter, had dispersed all hints of a breeze, and the early morning coolness had evaporated. The birds were singing up in the gutters, teaching their young how to fly.

Below, mayhem.

About three quarters of the lowest level of garden had gone AWOL. Vamoosed. Packed up its belongings, tucked the swimming pool under its arm and buggered off. It quite simply was not there. Instead a ragged edge of torn soil, turf, fragments of reinforced concrete, pipes and various bits of stone, hung insecurely on to what remained of the ledge. The knock-on effect had dislodged the retaining wall of the next level up, and cracks like oversized marble veining had appeared. The steps had dislocated themselves, and the heavy, wet soil in the borders had started to ooze out. The plants, still wet enough to hang on to life, were displaced and heading for the edge. The pool that sank a garden.

I went back into the house, went downstairs and let myself out onto the top terrace, half expecting it to give way. Who in the name of the mighty creator was going to shoulder the blame for this little escapade? I wondered. The pool makers? The planning department? The garden designer (gulp)? Perhaps the good Lord Himself. That was certainly a storm and a half last night, but it could not have been so severe that it went around dismissing swimming pools, here, there, and everywhere, could it?

When I reached the bottom the mess was overwhelming. It made me think of earthquake disasters, gas explosions, or mammoth flooding tragedies. If I could have thought of a good plot, I would have immediately lost it. 'Pull yourself together,' I muttered to myself, 'this is messy but it won't be necessary to declare a state of emergency. I am not about to find any trapped bodies or grieving parents.' Well, I hoped I wasn't. Maybe a few rodents with their noses out of joint, a couple of freaked-out frogs or an exasperated snake perhaps. But the poor old Owners were going to feel like they had been under some sort of a siege. Then I wondered if they knew. Dismissing the idea as impossible, I wondered who knew anything, and what the procedure was. Who was responsible for what? Oh dear, what a to-do.

If in doubt, go to the *mairie*.

I started the walk up to the top of the village, trying to rehearse what I was going to say, or report. I had only been to this *mairie* once before when I enquired about The Owners' neighbour. I reckoned I would have to go through the whole 'who I am' thing, then tell them that we had lost a swimming pool. Not lost it like one mislays a bunch of keys, not lost it like a relative who decided to die, but more, lost it like it has been taken away by aliens. All of this would be tough enough for me in English, but having to skittle my way down the alleys of French, added to the rising stress levels.

L'Hotel de Ville, the town hall and mayor's office, is a fine, elegant eighteenth-century building strategically located in a beautiful square at the top, west side, of Ménerbes. As soon as you go in you meet the hallway leading down to a refined stone staircase, flanked on either side by large rooms with immaculate vaulted ceilings.

'Yes,' you say to your imaginary estate agent, 'Yes! I'll take it.'

I turned into the room on my right, the reception area, and was met by two ladies whose professional friendliness came as a big encouragement. They have their jobs, and keep them, because they are that rare breed that seems unfazed by dealing with endless dumb questions from tourists, and unbounded banalities from natives alike. Their geniality with me hovered somewhere between a suspicion of madness and a gentle understanding of the foibles of foreigners. To be asked about planning applications, and obtaining firearm certificates, calming concerns about the school playground, or sorting out the minutiae that any small town generates, all that was a doddle. But to know where to direct a loony Scotsman who was going on about a garden that had slopped off in the middle of the night, in not altogether perfect French, seemed to have temporarily stumped them.

A few more shots at explaining myself and my position in this sorry affair suddenly brought a total change of atmosphere to the conversation.

'Ah oui, bien sur.'

Of course they knew about it. The *gendarmes* had been called in the middle of the night, by the residents of a small house, located at the bottom of the hill. They had narrowly escaped being flattened, Tom and Jerry style, by a demented rally of rocks, dragging an unfinished swimming pool by its neck down the side of the valley. It had surged past their bedroom window at two hundred kph, at 1am, and had missed their dwelling by three metres.

This was not just a major upset for The Owners but was also a geological phenomenon that affected the whole village, and its surrounding area.

It seems, put simply, that what had happened was: the rock having been disturbed and exposed by the drilling, and being of a porous and permeable nature, had absorbed more rainwater during the storm than it could contain. It had been bone dry for months, and when the storm flung itself at the boulders, they had absorbed the water like a dry sponge. The extra weight had caused the stone to split and divide. As it started to slip, it had gained momentum, and slithered off down the bank, taking a fair slice of the garden with it. Whilst this did not indicate that the whole of Ménerbes was about to belly up and disappear like Atlantis, it did, however, highlight the importance of respecting the foundations of the long rocky promontory that the village stretches itself out along. From here on in, the requests for planning permission for a swimming pool would need to be reflected on more closely. Considering some of the more outrageous positions of some of the more outrageous pools that have been installed in Ménerbes over the years, it is surprising that there haven't been more disasters.

There was concern about the biggest bit of rock that had slithered all the way down to the roadside, stopping just short of the road itself. It was too heavy to move with a bulldozer, let alone by hand, and to dynamite it might dangerously shake up the promontory. In the end it was gently broken up by hand drills, and left to settle into the landscape. A small monument to a big misadventure.

Once the dust had settled, as it were, the whole affair soon got put on the back burner and people carried on with their lives, with little more than an occasional reference to 'the night of the big storm'.

But for The Owners some quick decisions had to be made.

Having arrived soon after the event, and having reviewed their poor injured garden, Richard and Ros decided to instruct the builders, pool makers and gardeners to pull together, quickly and efficiently, and produce some quotes. They urged everybody to stand by for a massive clearing and cleaning-up job. They wanted the whole thing back in place before the summer vacations began, and were willing to cover the overtime if required. They would, with the help of a lawyer, file an insurance claim. They also knew that such a claim would take time to reach a conclusion let alone a settlement. There were endless strands to be examined and resolved, discussions to be had and expert opinions to be heard. If they were to await the outcome, any appeals aside, they would not have a garden, a swimming pool, or an uninterrupted view for a long, long time.

Nobody wanted to walk away from the site leaving it looking so unhappy. Besides which, I think everybody felt a bit responsible, and whilst the technicalities of insurance assured that the expenses would, to a greater or lesser degree, be covered, there was a shared feeling of wanting to put the whole thing back together without delay. And so it was, that by the end of the following week, the full crew, from all disciplines, were back on site, working like Trojans.

Everybody knew what they had to do, and it was neither necessary nor desirable for me to be hanging around the garden all the time. I was at the end of a phone if required, and would be turning up every couple of days whatever. Besides, in the first couple of weeks, the surgeons of repair would be the builders and poolers, not the gardeners. We all hoped they would keep up their enthusiasm and work the long hours they had said they would. But that didn't include working through lunchtime.

You can try persuading a Frenchman to work through his two-hour lunch break, you might suggest that he reduces the time that his lunch takes, you might even get him tentatively to agree. But when push comes to shove, it is all a waste of effort. You might as well ask the Pope to convert to Islam. Lunch is sacrosanct. It is a two-hour break from everything except food, and possibly drink. A relaxation period, more important than the end of the day, and should be respected, upheld, and endorsed by one and all.

When we were restoring our house, the builders would leave on the dot of twelve. It never ceased to amaze me that whatever they had been doing, that part of the project always seemed to fold up neatly by lunchtime. The mixed cement ran out just on time, the area to be plastered was always just completed, or the shuttering finished. With the electricians, a ceremony began at mid-day that involved a fold-away table being brought out of the van and erected, a tablecloth being shaken out and put down, and the knives, forks and spoons carefully placed. Whilst the primus stove was being pumped into life, plastic containers of innumerable goodies were opened, divided up and prepared for cooking. A small carafe of red wine was uncorked, the daily paper unfolded at the racing page, the radio tuned in. Once the bib was tucked into the shirt-front, Mr Sparks and his assistant were ready to 'grab a quick sandwich'. If they talked at all it was about computer games, about Nintendo and Play Station. A little liedown on the lawn followed afterwards. A closing of the eyes and a folding of the hands, soon put our boys back on form for a cracking good afternoon.

Knowing that this unmoveable philosophy exists, is imprinted onto the very being of a French workman, it was therefore completely ridiculous to expect the builders or swimming pool contractors to finish their work before the August break arrived. To think that they might, out of some kind of exceptional loyalty, bend the rules and forego their annual sojourn to the beaches of paradise so that the Americans could swim around in small circles, was absurd. If the idea had ever existed it evaporated quickly. It might have flickered as a sentimental and sympathetic concept for a short time, but not for long. Besides which, as the days rolled on, the tragedy of the disappearing garden became increasingly old hat.

As August approached, there were clear signs that work would soon grind to a halt. Materials were not being ordered, discussions about completion dates were being avoided, and plans for the vacation being aired ever louder. The heat was making afternoon work nearly impossible, and the tourists dawdling in the middle of the road with their cars overheating and their mouths open, slowing everybody else down, added to the general lethargy that hung in the air. By common consent work on The Owners' garden stopped at the end of the last week of July.

It had at least been a productive few weeks. The dried mud and stones had been hauled back up into position. The sides of the bank reinstated, and the retaining walls, including the bad boy at the bottom, had been restored or shored up. The chasm had been turned back into a recognisable object that you might one day swim in, and the surrounding garden area had been raked into neat piles of rubbish. It looked like a building site for certain, but at least it looked like it was resting, and not abandoned.

CHAPTER EIGHT

Time Out

T here are a lot of snails in Provence. An endless variety of these creatures manage to make a nuisance of themselves through their lack of understanding of what we do, and don't, mind them eating. Generally, they are fairly unattractive, unless of course you are another snail, primarily because of their slimy habits. Although some have interesting shells, it remains hard to imagine the moment when a Frenchman first looked at one of the wee pests and thought: 'Mmm, I bet that's damned good to eat.'

He must have had both a terrible hunger and a determined imagination to have picked it up and, teased by its cheeky little trick of curling up, cracked its shell open on a stone and gobbled it down. Maybe somebody suggested with the second one that if he chucked it into the oven and flavoured it with garlic, it would improve the taste no end. Like Elizabeth I telling Raleigh that his latest discovery, the potato, needed salt. Nowadays, after years of perfecting the culinary possibilities, these factory-farmed gastropods tend to be fattened first on a very satisfying diet of pasta and salad. Then for a week before being eaten, they are starved. This gives time for the toxins to pass out of the body, and when yellowish foam starts to form around the underside, the process is complete. They are then rinsed under cold water and placed in a baking tin. A little oil and garlic, a smidgen of salt, and perhaps some local herbs are added, then they are popped into the preheated oven, alive but depressed, to cook.

Broadly speaking the snail season runs parallel to the oyster season. The first snail snatcher was probably much encouraged by the fact that this tasty slither of slime, this hapless invertebrate, could be extricated from its shell without too much ceremony. I wonder if it was he who invented that weird set of tools that helps you disencumber the meat from its armour. Or maybe he knew a dentist who was rather adept at adapting his or her own portfolio of surgical instruments. There is no doubt that some of the French eating habits take a bit of getting used to. Frog's legs, pig's nose, horse flesh, bulls' testicles. I remember I once stopped in the Dordogne and asked a lady sitting on a three-legged stool near the roadside if she knew the way to somewhere or other, and noticed that she was wearing a goose on one of her hands. Actually she had her arm thrust down the poor bird's throat. Without hesitation, and with great politeness, she told me to 'follow the road to the next junction, take a left up to the ...' all the time pointing the way with her hand that inhabited the goose's gullet. It had the appearance of one of those rather smart three-quarter-length gloves that ladies used to wear in the Fifties, only this one had flapping wings stuck to it.

The most common snail here is *l'escargot de Pise*. These are the ones you see in their battalions manoeuvring themselves around your more delicate flowers and salad leaves. They also can't resist the moisture that either an occasional rain storm, or the daily dose of irrigation, brings. They just love it, and glide their gunge across the gravel by the dozens. Trouble is, it is normal practice at our house to put the watering system on in the evening. It might not be as good as in the dead of the night, but it allows me to keep an eye on the mechanics, and make sure that everything is working. But then, as people leave after dinner, or I take the dog out for a last walk round the cherry orchard, it becomes quite impossible to avoid walking on the little pets. The scrunching noise of squashed snails is indistinguishable from the scrunching noise of damp gravel.

From time to time they are joined by another, bigger variety. *Le Zonite d'Algérie*. This Algerian moves relatively quickly, giving a bad name to the phrase 'snail's pace', and has a huge shell painted a bit like a swirling disc, the sort which if you press the handle down on it, the disc quickly speeds up, making pretty patterns. He slugs around the garden with his house on his shoulders like the Greek God of Furniture Removal. He could be the family's Sunday roast.

But there is a much stranger snail than this, he that exists in by the millions, and is – practically as limitless as ants. No bigger than a five *centimes* piece, as white as snow and seemingly capable of absnailing down the trunks of trees, they cover fruit trees, shrubs and tall grasses, virtually to the oblivion of all else. The first time I saw them was in an fruit tree orchard. From a distance I thought they were a blossom of some kind. Getting nearer I discovered these odd little snails. None of them seemed to move, and yet if you shook, brushed or knocked them off the leaves and branches, which is not that easy as they cling on tight, by the next morning they were all back in place. They must carry out their manoeuvres at night. Like all snails they are encouraged by moisture which makes for more of them, but even without irrigation, you will still find them spreading themselves around in epidemic proportions. Why not eat these little chaps too? Like sprats with shells, delicious and crispy.

One early morning, the sun hung in the air, yawned and looked at its fingernails, disinterest harboured at the corners of his mouth. The heat had already come out of its corner fighting, and the temperatures were high in the nineties and climbing. I sat on the terrace eating breakfast. Nothing too much; a handful of warm figs from the tree, fresh *fougasse* with bacon, some abandoned corn flakes, a glass of newly made peach juice and a pot of some infusion or other, the source of which was unclear but definitely included lime. I was waiting for the post to arrive and was expecting some shopping that I had done on the internet, including a book on local gardens. It was, rather feebly, the first web purchase attempted, and I was keen to see if it worked. I had received an e-mail a couple of evenings earlier wherein somebody from cyberspace had confirmed my order and informed me that my book would be delivered with the post, in two days' time. A chummy sort of note it was, calling me by my first name, and practically asking how my sex life was going.

My stepfather-in-law is a man of impeccable manners. The sort of chap who raises his cap to a lady, and would never consider calling anybody by their first name unless invited to do so. He came into the kitchen one evening whilst we were staying with him, ashen. A hard-working barrister, having just arrived home after a long, strenuous day in the Royal Courts of Justice, he had answered the telephone on his way through, to hear some salesman from a local ice-cream company saying 'Evening Pat, it's Bob from Melt-Down Limited, Ice creams for all the fam...'

The guy with the freezing cold call hadn't stood a chance of finishing. But, in cyberspace everybody has ice cream and can be called anything.com. And if you have a name like mine, you get used to giving your first name, even abbreviated if necessary. It makes things easier, especially for a local Frenchman.

My book was indeed in the post delivery, and as I proudly looked through the glossy pages of horticultural prowess, Nicky passed by, looked over my shoulder and announced that 'they have that book on sale in the *tabac*, in the village – reduced.'

'Maybe, but mine is in English,' I said weaekly, trying to cap the conversation.

'Theirs is too, that's why it's reduced.'

In amongst the letters, bills and junk mail, was an invitation to attend the end of term exhibition at the Lacoste School of the Arts, or American Art School as I tend to call it. The Sculptor and the Poetess were helping organise it and hoped we would go. They had taken up a second session of lecturing at the school, and as an end- of-term wheeze had asked all the students to fill in a single page of A4 with drawings, photographs, words, or anything else they felt inclined to contribute. It was bound together between two sheets of clear plastic, and handed out with the invitation. You either found the contents encouraging, or they made you gasp with despair.

This couple, recently returned from a posting in Beirut, also have a little boy called Alex who, at four and a bit, is just a few months older than Theo. When the two kids met, Alex naturally enough felt inclined to take Theo hostage until he had relinquished all his toys and emptied his piggy bank. The strategy employed and the force of its execution left Theo blinking in disbelief. He hadn't met anything like it, and immediately began to think of this mini-mercenary as the most magnificent model to base his attitudes on. The Poetess explained that the school playgrounds in war torn-Beirut are full of children tainted by violence. Fed anti-Western propaganda, malevolence ran through their blood. There was no polite waiting for a chance to use the swing; if you wanted it you went up to the swaying kid and dragged or pushed him off, insulted him, and if you were strong enough, smacked him one just for the hell of it. I said it sounded just like a regular Chelsea kindergarten to me.

That afternoon we dutifully walked up to the village to start our work as art critics. The main part of the exhibition was housed in a fine old building on two floors, and benefited from a large terrace that looked out over the plain. It is a big, impressive view across the Luberon valley, dropping away from Lacoste on the west, and rising again to meet Bonnieux, on the eastern flank. The detail of the landscape below is clear, and gives the students a strong sense of their Provençal surroundings. As they look down, they can see our house, which tucks itself into the foreground of this composition, forming an intrinsic part of the vista. Being that this was the end of July, the emerging lavender 'river' that winds it way down our banks made a striking blue ribbon, standing out against the pale greens and buffs of the drying terrain. Unsurprisingly, it wasn't long before we came upon a painting of this scene. Not an easy panorama to achieve, the depth of field being considerable; however, Yoko, a Japanese girl studying art in New York, and over here for the summer course, had pulled it off with aplomb. As she didn't seem to be around, I asked the Sculptor to ask her if she would like to sell it. I have always reckoned that we'll probably end up with dozens of pictures of the local landscape that include our house, sold to us by impoverished artists, reminiscent of a Stella Artois beer advertisement, and this looked like being our first. The next morning the Sculptor rang to say that Yoko would pass by that afternoon.

She duly arrived, elegantly dressed in a long, black loose-fitting dress and carrying a large hold-all. We sat at the table in semi silence whilst I waited for her to produce the great work. She smiled and said nothing. Eventually I asked if we could see it. I had called Nicky.

'I not have plicture,' she said with a big smile that split her face up into a charming parody of Mad's Alfred E. Neuman.

'Oh,' I said. 'I thought you were bringing it for us to look at and maybe buy.'

'Oh no, plicture not for sale,' she countered. 'But I make you a copy if you like.'

'What do you mean? You'll paint another picture exactly the same?' I asked a bit confused. Was she into faking her own paintings, or was she just doing limited runs?

'S'cluse me, I don't understand,' she said.

'Well, you just mentioned you could make a copy.'

'Searlox,' she said, looking at me now as if I were mad. 'I make searlox photocopy if you want.'

As the picture was certainly bigger than A3 I began to imagine I would be getting several slices of A4 through the post, with cleverly written instructions in Japanese on how to origami them together.

'Oh no, thank you, that is not what I had in mind.'

Trying to move the meeting along, I suggested that perhaps we could pass the school studio and she could show it to Nicky anyway, and ...

'It's out in the sun drying, I am taking it to Potland, Olegon tomorrow.'

'Fine Yoko,' I said, 'thank you for dropping by to see us, and I hope you have a dry painting to take home.'

She began to gather herself up, and as she did so she said:

'It's a velly beautiful garden, can I take a photograph of you both?'

Neither of us much like having our photograph taken, although I have never understood why Nicky who is so lovely to look at, and photogenic, should object. But we declined, again smiling and virtually bowing now, with our hands pressed firmly together.

'O-Kay,' she said cheerily. 'Good-bye.' And set off. Twenty metres down the path she stopped, turned round and said, 'How much you play for my plicture?'

'I didn't think it was for sale.'

'Maybe next year I slell it to you.'

'Well then, let's open negotiations with a bid for fifty thousand dollars,' I offered, looking at her, I hoped, enigmatically.

She started back towards us, her mouth falling ever closer to her knees.

'Leally?'

'No, Yoko, not really.'

During the high summer months all the local villages have their fetes. Each is allocated a week on the calendar, which ensures no one clashes. Their success varies somewhat from place to place, and Lacoste, although a small commune compared to some, manages to pack a fair punch. Exhibitions and visiting entertainers, children's play-groups, boule championships, and an assortment of stalls set themselves up. Sometimes local dramatic groups and classical musicians will add themselves to the event list. The week's activities culminate with the village ball. A rather grand stage is erected in the little square outside the post office. It stands proudly on its scaffolding legs, topped by a skimpy corrugated tin roof. A sound system is installed and strings of festive lights slung across the square from pillar to post. There are usually several acts on the bill, and by listening to them tuning and warming up during the afternoon, you can decide for yourself which might be worth listening to later on. Their musical notes drift lazily across the afternoon air, and down into the valley. Quite often, out of control, they tumble out of the sky and crash heavily onto the fields below.

In amongst the horns, clarinets and electric organs I deciphered an accordion. Being Scottish, I have a deep and immovable love for both bagpipes and the accordion. A committed pacifist by heart, I would happily drop tools and march through an early morning mist and on into war, if I was led by the regimental pipe band of the Black Watch. And as kilted adolescents, we all reeled to the mesmerising playing of Jimmy Shand, as he pushed and pulled his accordion, strapped tightly to his chest, to the limit. People stripped not only the willow, but also the polish off the floors as they whirled one another round in fanciful formations. I only need to hear a squeak out either of these two magnificent instruments and I'm anybody's. Add a Les Paul and I may never leave.

At about ten thirty on the night of the ball, I went up to the village to listen to the first set by Sammi Quaverre. He had been irresistibly billed as the European Champion Accordionist and had received rave reviews from wherever he had appeared. He was, at least amongst accordion aficionados, king of the squeeze box. Theo was asleep, and Nicky thought it best to let me go on my own. She wasn't convinced that Sammi was her man, and didn't want to wake the sleeping beauty. I had imagined that such a major artist would pull huge crowds from miles around, bringing locals and tourists alike. There would probably be stalls selling his CDs, merchandising memorabilia, T-shirts, mugs with pictures of the great man tattooed onto the side, that kind of thing. I fretted about where to park, perhaps best to leave the car at home and walk up to the village. I hoped there wouldn't be too strong a police evidence. A little crowd control is one thing, but when the *Gendarmerie* are let loose on a crowd of over-excited accordion fans, it can get ugly.

Anyway losing the car wasn't a problem. In fact, I could have driven up to the stage and parked right there in front of the maestro. I could have had the air-conditioning blowing comfortingly, the sun-roof open and watched him from the repose of the front seat. I looked around at the scattering of village people, there must have been ten of them. On stage, a large lady was belting out something I figured had its roots in a folk song, but had been sauced up with a bluesy overtone. Her voice was strong, and made the microphone a shade jumpy. She shimmied and shook, and whilst her over-made-up face was a little scary, she had a very successful bosom. As the number finished she bowed and thanked her audience, and started to introduce her friend, her inspiration and her husband: *'Mesdames, messieurs, je vous presente: "Sammi 'main lente' Quaverre"!'*

The couple of people playing at the mobile roulette wheel gave a whoop of joy, but more for their winning number than for Sammi. A small group of elderly fellows, whilst not actually stopping their conversation, did at least glance over to the stage where a rotund little man with greasy black hair stood centre stage. He was practically obscured by his enormous, flashy, pearl-coloured accordion. Without wasting a moment he burst into a virtuoso rendition of 'Under the Bridges of Paris'. The short stubby fingers on his left hand danced frantically over the sea of little black bass buttons, giving ecstatic encouragement to his other hand that seemed to have a life of its own. It flew up and down the keyboard in a blur of digits, no sooner having given life to one chord, then on it soared in search of other hidden crotchets and hard-to-find sharps and flats. The fingers intermingled with one another at such speed the eye could pick out no distinct shape. This improvised homage to the great composer of the

French classic was fussy, and bubbling over with unnecessary twiddly bits, but it was undeniably the stuff of champions. I looked around again, and there wasn't a wet eye in the house.

I left after half an hour and happily more people were arriving. By midnight it would be in full swing, and nobody within five kilometres had a chance of being asleep.

The project for the Professor over at St Rémy had moved forward over the last few weeks. Despite a few stumbles in the early stages due to misunderstandings between architect and client, his drawings were accepted and the project was underway. It had not been possible for me to really commence with any plans for the garden until we knew what the budget was going to be. And that could not be decided until the estimates for the house work had been received and debated over. Apart from a meeting with a local farmer to persuade him to cut down the fields of weeds, and a natter with my contractor about tree removal, protection of the existing plants growing against the house from insensitive builders, and one or two other small matters, little had been done. But now everything had been given a green light and I knew how much I had to play with, I started to plan.

The Prof. had set a date for mid-August to come down, see some drawings, look at some big trees — olives, plane's and fruit trees were first — and to look around for old garden furniture. She wanted me to set up a meeting between myself and the architect before she arrived, and for us to establish and stabilise our various disciplines. She warned me that he could be difficult to deal with, had a high regard for his own talent, and would probably be dictatorial about the garden. Monsieur Dictatorial, who enjoys a solid local reputation, sounded a bit daunting, but over the years I have dealt with dozens of architects, some of whom have been completely out of their prams, others who have been a pleasure to work with, and an exercise in coalition. All I needed really was to be left alone to do my bit, and to have an ally I could call on if needed. I arrived on site to find a workforce underway re roofing the old ruin, and several clusters of hard-hatted people all looking at drawings. Nobody took any notice of me as I wandered around trying to suss which one was The Man. I approached a young chap who, having established my identity, directed me to a cigar-smoking, gently spreading chap of medium height and longish hair. His father.

We spoke in French and English and whilst we didn't dwell on unnecessary niceties, we made contact and gave faces to names. He gave me a set of plans of the house, and I offered to send him copies of my own drawings. He declined this, announcing that he wanted nothing to do with the garden, and if I showed him drawings, it would only make him want to give opinions and ideas, which might not be a good thing. He mentioned that I should be aware of certain difficulties regarding the installation of a lake, and advised me to consult with the local authorities. They needed to be reassured about depths, surface areas, amount of water being used, etc. This I took as normal, but thanked him for his advice. I left feeling that we had cleared the first hurdle, and that I too had better resist giving any ideas about the house. The only area I could see where the borders of the professions might blur, would be with things like the position of the swimming pool, the courtyard walls and the types of gates to be used. But we could face all this when the project had advanced down the road a piece.

I arrived back at the house and found Nicky and Theo both worried by a larger than usual scorpion in the kitchen. It had apparently been in there all morning, mostly quite still, but every now and then performing sprightly dashes across the wall and floor.

'Dadahh!' welcomed Theo, running and giving me a huge hug. 'I don't love korpions,' he said, his voice dropping to a whisper, and his eyes turning to look at the dark menace lurking beside a hanging sieve. After five years we had become accustomed to *le Scorpion noir*. He is a frequent visitor to the interiors of houses and makes a heavy tribute to the reputation of scorpions. Seldom more than four centimetres at most, he will do everything he can to get out of your way. Only if cornered and frightened out of his shiny black skin, and forced through a desperate last ditch attempt at survival, will he sting, and it will be no worse than a wasp bite. I have yet to meet anyone who has knowingly been bitten by this little fellow. At first, through an ignorant fear, we used to adopt the attitude that the only good scorpion was a dead scorpion, and stamped on them at sight. Now we have a more lenient disposition towards them. This usually entails my sneaking up on one, quickly covering it with a drying-up cloth, or towel, bundling it up and then, hopefully, with said *Euscorpius flavicaudis* safely tucked into the folds of the fabric, transporting it out into the garden, and dismissing it with a quick flick. It has an altogether much more unpleasant cousin: *le Scorpion languedocien*, which is green, twice the size and skulks under dry stone. If he stings you, within a few hours it will be extremely painful and you should hop it to the hospital. Happily, he is rarely seen.

It was the month of holidays. Everybody else was at it so we decided to do it as well. I mentioned to a chum that we were going to do this and he said 'but you *are* on holiday'. That's the trouble if you live somewhere that people visit for a vacation, they don't think that you need to go anywhere else.

We wanted some seaside activity; some sand castling and swimming in the surf. We didn't care if the whole of France and his wife were doing the same thing, we just wanted out for a week. We booked into a smart hotel on Porquerrolles, one of a group of a small islands some twenty minutes by boat off the French coast, opposite Hyeres, a coastal town roughly half way between Marseilles and Cannes. No cars are allowed on the island so you unload your luggage, wife and child at the quayside on the mainland, then lose the car in a security-controlled car park. The ferry was mostly made up of tourists taking a day trip, and plenty of them there were too. After docking, we phoned the hotel and they sent down their driver in an old lorry, probably a decommissioned army truck repainted a jolly red, to pick us up. We rattled out of the port and down the narrow streets of the only town. Apart from a handful of indigenous service vehicles, it was swarming with people of all ages on bicycles. Kids and dogs ran free without worry, the cafes overflowed onto the streets, and the little square was bustling with stalls.

The lorry trundled out of the village, turned down a side street and set off for the headland. After fifteen minutes we arrived at Le Langoustier Hotel a fine building that sat proudly on its location looking out to sea. We waited on the terrace with its small white tables covered in pretty blue fabrics, whilst our quarters were readied. The purple bougainvillea grew over the pale red walls, and the strong smell of pine from the surrounding woods assembled an immediate calm.

I had taken a two-bedroom suite. Wised up to the horrors that a room with one double and an auxiliary child bed can bring, I had dug deeper into the pocket to ensure that we all got a bit of sleep. I had learnt from previous hotel escapades that Theo is usually out of his complimentary camp bed and thrashing around in ours, by midnight. After an hour or so of sustained body blows, and trying to nap with one of his feet in my mouth, I had generally conceded that it was probably better to leave him and his mother sleeping, albeit turbulantly, whilst I crept off to doze on his mini mattress. I had been a bit mollified when told by a friend how he had actually ended up sleeping in a cot when his baby daughter had refused to settle. Installed into our two big rooms, we threw open the windows and started to go out onto the balcony that looked down to the sea. We were immediately buffeted back inside by a violent wind that had blown up. We had felt it gathering as we came over on the boat, but now it had whistled up the troops and was getting down to business. By the time we arrived at the restaurant for lunch, they had zipped the whole thing up like a cellophane bag. All those pretty Italianate parasols had been folded, cushions whipped indoors, and the staff were beginning to look like officials at a life-boat conference. Then came the rain, not a storm that would blow over, so much as a good hard-working, thick drizzle. It was only a few moments before the floor of the improvised tent was awash and the food arrived wet.

The next day the rain had stopped but of course the Mistral always blows for increments of three. The sky will be a brilliant, clear pale Van Gogh blue, but it will blow and blow for three, six or nine days. The forecast was for nine. We spent the next few days doing the best we could with bikes, walks, eating and drinking.

The television card in our room advertised a children's channel, but it didn't actually work. They probably thought they could fib about this because everybody would be out on the beach, swimming or sailing around. The children would return and go straight to bed exhausted, and wouldn't even turn the box on. We had bullied the mini-bar into submission by lunch-time, and had taken hot baths and showers enough to keep you clean until All Saints.

We had come to play in the sea, but the beaches were closed, and were going to stay closed. We battled on bravely for four days and then quit. We might as well go home and sit in the sun.

Quite often at this time of year tourists wander down the little lane and then into our drive to take photographs of Lacoste. I have tried telling them that it is *privé*, but they seem to take no notice, sometimes even continuing further into our garden as if I didn't exist. Bobble bounces up to them barking, then quickly falls in behind them, tail wagging, hoping that perhaps the strangers might have a little yum yum in their back pockets. I had noticed in my travels around the area that very often you see a pair of stone piers about 50cms square by two metres high, erected on either side of a track that clearly indicated that it was the beginning of somebody's property. They were not attached to anything, no wall on either side, and could easily be walked round, but they formed a strong psychological barrier. It struck me as a profound and simple piece of engineering that I would adopt.

I did a quick drawing and went up to the *mairie* to see if I needed permission. Of course I did. I had been careful not to suggest any of those flashy resurrected chateau pillars we talked about earlier, just some simple stone jobs built from the materials of the region. But a committee had to consider all the implications, so I filled in the 632 forms, provided character references, thought about setting up a trust for the mayor's own benevolent fund, and swore undying allegiance to the coalition government. Weeks later and after meetings with the regional architect, my daring proposal was granted planning permission. Granted, providing I had five metres in between each pillar. I thought that was a little excessive but didn't give it any more thought.

When Thomas, or Tom-ah, our baby-sitter's husband to be, and *maçon*, arrived to build the things, he pointed something out. If we made them five metres apart, one of the structures would have to be either in mid space, due to the bank sloping down on one side of the drive, or, half across the orchard on the other side. The gravel road that we had, which had been there since roads like this were invented, was only three metres wide, if that. It had accommodated cars, vans, tractors and lorries over the years, and had been passed by the emergency services as acceptable. We had an intelligent conversation about the way forward, and decided that at a push we could stretch it out to nearly four metres. It looked a bit odd, but with some diligent hedge planting, it would be alright.

As Tom-ah was putting the finishing touches to the second pillar, a messenger from the mayor's office arrived and told us to take them down. They had not been built at five metres apart and should therefore be disassembled without delay. We patiently explained that, unfortunately due to the slope of the land, and the change of levels therein, it was not actually physically possible to make them five metres apart. Smile, smile. I was thinking how on earth do they know they aren't five metres apart? They must have been down here in the dead of the night with their torches and luminous measuring tapes, little weasels. Work stopped, Tom-ah went home, and I rang Sasha the baby-sitting fiancée and explained why her man was back early. They were about to go and live and work in England, and this job was to have been a useful little earner before leaving.

The next day the mayor himself appeared. A master of diplomacy, a giant amongst gesticulating public speakers, he explained that rules were rules. He reminded me that I had agreed to the dimensions when requesting permission, and although he could see it was impossible to adhere to the missive, five metres it had to be. I asked his advice. Would he favour the mid-air arrangement, or did he think an amusing little folly in the middle of the orchard would be better? If I had been Mr Actor I would probably have reminded him at this moment that the school had a nice new roof, and that the pianos seemed to be holding up well. But I wasn't, and my only contribution to the commune recently had been to offer to help with some plans for the renovation of the school-yard. As that scorching bit of generosity seemed to have fallen on deaf ears, I was not in much of a bargaining position. An absurd compromise was reached. I would move one of the pillars back 30cms. This involved knocking it down, digging a recess into the bank, cleaning off the cement from the stones, and rebuilding. It was now a full throbbing three and three quarter metres, but no worry, face had been saved, and besides Thom-ah got a bit more out of it than expected.

There are dozens of good photographs to be taken of Provence. The landscape is nearly always spectacular, the architecture, in its unpretentious farm-house fashion, is sort of loveable, the singular old villages dyed in angry history, are camera ready, and the big views that stretch between the mountain ranges, all make up a fine, albeit slightly oversubscribed, portfolio. But the big boy, the one that gets the shutters clicking more than all the others put together is: 'Lavender Time'.

Kicking in around the second week of July, depending on the amount of rain we haven't had, and running throughout the month, it brings a stunning overlay of colour to thousands of hectares. It fills in huge fields with vibrant mauves, blues, and purples, as it drifts endlessly over the contours of the land in a surf of gently waving brilliance. Because it is happiest growing on the higher ground, as high as 1100 metres, it often gains massive panoramic vistas as a backdrop. During the peak period, wise tourists find an old oak tree on the edge of a lavender field to have their picnics under. Some fresh bread and cheese, a little sun-warmed fruit picked that morning and a cold bottle of local white wine. Stir in the calm and warmth of a long summer day, mingle it with the scent and view, and I'd say that they would be pretty close to having a 'right-on moment', probably chased by an effortless snooze.

Often in the lavender fields you will find little windowless stone huts, or '*borries*' as they are called. These strange small buildings, with their dry stone walls and roofs usually sit isolated, amongst the furrows of the headily fragrant flowers. They were used chiefly as shelters for shepherds and their flocks, who would come to feed in them in bad weather. The shepherds used the '*borries*' as fodder deposits or tool sheds, and sometimes for rearing silkworms or for wine vats. They have been part of the Provençal landscape for many hundreds of years, dating back to the time of the Ligurians. The fact that they were still used and occupied up until the beginning of the last century makes them all the more intriguing.

By the end of June, the long bracts of lavender flowers that have been steadily growing since early spring begin to gain a hue of mauve. The intensity builds up to its full-blown glory by mid July, then, as smoothly as it arrived, it starts to recede, fading out leaving a brown and straggly shadow. Most farmers like to have picked and delivered the flowers to the distillery by the 15 August. It is a process that has been going on since the sixteenth century, and the alleged virtues of the flowers and oils produced are so diverse, they practically defy belief. We all know that a few drops of oil in the bath will soothe and relax a tired body, aiding bruises and swellings. You probably know that a little oil rubbed into the skin will heal insect bites, small wounds and burns, but it also can boast of being beneficial in much more grown- up games than this. It has been used as treatment for brain disease, epilepsy and hysteria, the recommended dose being 10–12 drops in an appropriate liquid, probably not whisky. Or, four to five drops taken on an empty stomach, in a spoonful of wine, can clear away migraine and fortify the stomach. They, who know these things, have even suggested that if you mix it with St-John's-wort-oil, it makes an excellent liniment against rheumatism, palsy and convulsive movements. If you have a sore throat and don't much like the idea of lavender tea, try some lavender honey. Some French teachers still recommend dabbing a lavender-oil moistened swab behind the ears of children to help them avoid catching head lice, and much the same applies to domestic animals. A quick dab around their necks will discourage fleas.

My elderly aunt swears she sleeps better since she started using the perfume-burner I gave her, and this gadget, like dozens of other side-products, helps make the versatile lavender business a success. The local growers have not been slow to capitalise on this and most markets and tourist shops will sell the essential oil, toilet water, shower gel, pure vegetable soap, body lotion, cushions, pillows, and dried bouquets. As if this were not enough, you can add books galore, postcards, deft little landscape prints, drying-up clothes, and, oh, it goes on and on.

But much more than this, is the fact that lavender is an attractive green-grey-leafed plant that contributes to the garden all year round. It is easily clipped into a comfortable cushion shape, needs little attention and will give its all for a good seven or eight years, and sometimes a lot longer.

When we decided to plant our lavender 'river', which is nearly two hundred metres long by a couple of metres wide, we needed to find a commercial grower who could offer us a keen price on the four thousand little plants we needed. We were directed to a local cultivator.

Being the direct descendant of a farmer who had started developing this crop a few hundred years ago, Vandula was well versed with the intricacies of lavender growing. A tall, strong young guy with a huge moustache, he lived on a rambling farmstead with houses dotted all over the place, presumably occupied by various members of his family. When we first turned up, a gang of disparate dogs, hens and labourers, none of whom took much notice beyond a cursory glance, met us in the yard. I asked an old boy where we could find Vandula and he pointed his head in the general direction of one of the houses. He had a poor deportment from years of lavandering and his highly scented cap seemed to have become part of his body. It was well worn, perfectly moulded to his head and was probably seldom, if ever, removed. Certainly not for baths, going to bed or the odd moment of gallantry.

I called out from the vicinity of the house, bon jour-ing and 'ello-ing to no avail. I tried the downstairs door, which was locked, climbed up a wooden staircase on the outside of the building, tried another door and called again. A man appeared looking bedraggled and harassed. In one hand he had a baby girl, in the other a feeding bottle. The little person was crying, and Vandula, I supposed it was him, looked as if he was about to do the same. I introduced myself, explained what I wanted and why and asked if he could help. He was a bit reluctant at first, and seemed wearied at being disturbed. And why not, who wants to do business in the middle of the afternoon? Who wants to have their crumbling quality time terminated by a client wanting to spend lots of money? After he caught sight of Nicky who was noticeably pregnant by then, his manner eased and he became all cups of coffee and do-sit-downish. Under Vandula's instructions we lurched and bumped our way down through the lavender fields in the old Citroen, its suspension raised to its highest setting, until we reached an enormous cold storage barn. The aircraft-hangar-type doors were slid open and inside, as cool as a February morning, were stacked hundreds of rolls of bare root lavender plants.

He advised us to take two or three rolls at a time, because if we couldn't plant mechanically, it would be a slow process and they might dry out. He showed us how to prune the roots and how deep to put the little plants in the ground. By now he had warmed to these two mad foreigners. It was certainly the first time he had come across anybody loopy enough to want to plant four thousand of these things by hand, and so close you would have difficulty weeding and cutting, let alone in a meandering line two metres wide, on a slope. We loaded up the boot of the old car with optimistic bravado, and left Vandula scratching his head as we set off to start planting.

I had a young lad helping me, Steady Eddy, who needed a bit of holiday work. We cleared, dug over and planted the whole thing in about two weeks. It was a slow, and at times demoralising venture. A brain-numbing, back-breaking and finger-hurting

Borie en Lavande

business. But he did a sterling job, and if I thought he was faltering, I promised him that a class of pretty sixth formers wearing short skirts would be coming to help once he passed the three thousand mark. We battled through, and the sense of achievement was manifold. The 'river' started at the top of the highest bank, zigzagged its way down the slope, flowed on through the quince orchard, and finally arrived at the 'wine lake'. That's what I pretentiously called our remaining forty vines. I had been certain that if we were going to use lavender in the garden then it had to be applied in a slightly different style.

Now after four summers or so the lavender has grown up and it is effective and colourful. Owing to the soil varying in consistency over the route, it flowers stronger in some places than it does in others, which increases the effect. I wish I had added white lavender to give highlights;, it would have been quite subtle and easy to do, but it was missed, so there we are. The whole thing is maintenance heavy and only has a life span of seven or eight years and I doubt I'll have the energy or inclination to do it again, but meanwhile it is most welcome.

Most new or renovated gardens in Provence usually include lavender, of course, but the other must-have is an olive tree.

Olives are the wise men of the garden. Heaped in legend and folklore, they found their way to Europe from the island of Crete more that two and a half thousand years ago. The Bible makes over 140 references to the tree. The ancient Greeks, Jews and Egyptians used olive oil in lamps to read their best-selling parchments, to anoint their kings and religious leaders, to cure a host of ailments, and to rub down their athletes.

I had instructions to find some big boys for the Professor. When I had taken her to look at a few that were nearly a hundred years old, she had wanted them. As you could buy a perfectly respectable new car for the same price as some of the trees, the numbers were restricted. We settled on two of the really old ones, as near as you could make it to a pair, and a clutch of younger, less expensive youths, a mere forty to fifty year olds. Olivier, the entrepreneur, had been on holiday at the time so I returned to sort out the order with him a week or two later. We set off in a jeep and drove around his fields looking at hundreds of olive trees of all shapes and sizes, types and origins. I learned more about pruning and shaping them, watering and feeding them, lifting and moving them in an hour than I would have supposed possible.

I learnt that if you accidentally put oil in the fridge, you can let it breathe in a warm environment and you will be able to use it again. I also learnt that the majority of the aces, the really old, beautifully gnarled, double-stemmed trees had already been sold. After I had thrown a bit of a tantrum, beaten the dashboard and yelled abuse, Olivier assured me he would find another 'pair' that he felt sure our client would approve of. He also showed me some wonderful old plane trees that weighed around thirty-five tonnes, as well as six-metre cypress trees, huge evergreen oaks, and some prettily shaped parasol pines. You could spend a lottery of money in there, and more if you wanted them guaranteed. As the clients' agent I certainly didn't want these mega-buck stars keeling over in the first few weeks after planting. The nursery or grower will usually offer some kind of security on this front providing they: a) transport them to the site, and b) plant them themselves. They, of course, make another killing on this little sideline, but if any retribution is going to raise its force, it's better to have the buck passed to the supplier, rather than be sitting on my desk like a dead donkey stuffed with lemons on a wet night.

As we continued to drive round, I was beginning to get olived out. The dear things were blurring into one another and I was becoming increasingly blind to their different characters. I began to wonder aloud how much olive oil could be made from this lot. Picking up the baton and running with it Olivier became more animated by the minute.

'It takes about six to seven kilos to produce one litre,' he told me. 'We produced about three thousand litres a year.'

I looked at him with a new respect.

I noticed that the new TGV train line that will soon be running from Lyon down to Nice appeared to be slicing right through young Olivier's land.

'Did they pay you compensation?' I asked rather naively.

He looked at me with a smile that tied smugness and perception inexorably together.

'Ah oui ... beaucoup.'

I thought this might be good moment to bring up the subject of professional discount, or trade prices. If I was about to spend enough money to float a Caribbean island, I wanted to know what kind of deal he would offer.

He's a good bloke is old Johnny Olive in many ways, but the speed at which he snapped '*Rien*' made me catch my breath. As I sat there thinking, perhaps I'll take my order somewhere else, he and I knew I wouldn't, couldn't. This was *the* olive man in the region. Nobody does it better. He knew it, and I knew it. He sells everything anyway. He doesn't need to seduce people like me into his lair with come on offers of 'buy ten – get one free'.

I left a deposit with him for two big ones, five smaller ones, a plane tree of two-metre girth – that's nearly a jumbo plane – and a ten five-metre cypress trees. As he would be delivering and planting the following spring, we made a date for him to visit the site and assess his access. I now needed to go and check out another olive grower, a bit further north and a bit less grand.

I rang and made an appointment. The only time Monsieur Vert could see me was 2.30 the following Tuesday. I motored up towards Mont de Ventoux, a journey that sees the landscape change quite dramatically. As you climb, the vines are left behind and the countryside becomes increasingly craggy. The fields are steeper and the roads less crowded. I found the Vert residence easily enough, and parked my car outside the house that looked a bit like a chalet. There was no sign of anybody, only a loud barking coming from some dogs that happily seemed to be tied up. A clutch of motorbikes were scattered around the place, mostly new and gleaming, apart from the off roaders, which were splattered with dried out mud and had harnesses thrown over their handlebars. These were to keep your body in one piece as you leapt around the escarpments. I walked round the house calling out names, went through a hole in the hedge to find some old lorries and an abandoned loading bay. I sauntered back to a terrace that looked out over the valley and saw the noisy dogs below. They were a couple of retired spaniels and a dozy half-breed. Between them they made an impressive racket, but I doubted they would have bitten anything much more than their tongues.

It was very hot, and the afternoon had taken on that mantle of stillness that is punctuated mostly by the buzz of various insects. A sort of throb that the open country gives when it gets into the high nineties pumped away all round the hills. I was about to abandon the mission when a teenager appeared. I explained that I was looking for Mr Vert, indeed had a meeting set for half an hour ago. He too hollered, and when this was ineffective, he went into the house.

He returned presently.

'*Il arrive,*' he said and disappeared.

Five minutes later Patrick Vert shambled out of his house. About thirty, fairly unshaven and unfairly good looking, he had loosened off the top half of his dungarees and they hung round his waist strip-style. His white vest was suitably covered in earthy smears and he looked like that poster of a James Dean clone working in a garage. He had been asleep, and still very nearly was. He asked me into his office at the back of the house. As we passed through the garage a brand new Porsche Boxster did its best to block the way. Behind it were a pair of vintage pick-up trucks and a beautiful restored little 40s Peugeot.

There's money in olives, I thought as I dribbled with desire. His office was lined with slick communication tools, digital video cameras, digital still cameras, portable phones, laptops and televisions, DVD players, and full-size games arcade. He also had a pretty young wife and a pretty young daughter of three. The pictures on the walls were of glorious moments in the superbike series, and I was hard pressed to find any reference to an olive tree, as hard as I might look. Seeing my surprise at the Porsche, he pulled out a scrapbook that had a picture of him on the front winning a soap box derby. Inside, it was him again posing proudly on the bonnet of his immaculate 356B 1962 cabriolet Porsche as driven by Paul Newman playing Lew Harper in the 1996 movie, *Moving Target*.

He lit a cigarette, left it in his mouth, and as the smoke twirled into his eyes causing them to half close, and water slightly waterly, he asked me what kind of olives I was looking for?

'Big.'

He told me the biggest ones he had were about ten minutes down the road, and that he would just go and get a vehicle. '*Ne quitter pas.*'

I waited in the shade for what I presumed would be a midnight-blue, six-wheeled Range Rover with black windows, to pitch up. When the little white Citroen Dyane limped into view, its bodywork needing bodywork, I just accepted this surreal experience as par for the course. We lurched and hopped around various dried-out fields looking at some fine, but smaller trees than I had been hoping for.

I photographed a few with my own digital camera – well, you have to keep up – and discussed prices and sizes, availability and numbers. He was very knowledgeable and clearly passionate about these extraordinary trees. I levelled with him about needing something bigger and he said that although that wasn't his bag, he'd check out a few fellow traders and see what could be found.

I left him heading back, I suspect, to his bunk. He had had a full afternoon after all.

A few days later I was sitting at the table on the terrace having a bad time. The night before, just before going to bed, I had blown hard on a stubborn candle that was refusing to die. I had blown again, even harder, only to have the hot wax spit back at me, leaving me covered in nasty little burns all over my mouth and chin. The blisters were making me look like a walking herpes. In the distance I could hear plodding footsteps on the gravel coming towards the house, and when I looked up, I saw the *gendarmerie* marching down the path.

What the hell do they want? I wondered. Of course I immediately started feeling guilty about something, although for the life of me I couldn't think what it might be. I live very honestly down here. I don't steal from anybody, although a couple of clients have thought my fee quote daylight robbery. I don't grab handbags from old ladies, I seldom cause a public disturbance and only very occasionally commit a traffic crime.

Ah. That might be it. One dry day in March, nearly eighteen months earlier, I had crept out of a side turning on to the National 100, the local main artery road, at close to a quarter of a kilometre an hour. There was no traffic coming or going, and I was turning right, that is, into my near side lane, so I didn't have to cross the road or anything daring like that, when out of nowhere jumped a van load of *gendarmes* and booked me for dangerous driving. It seemed there was no room on the form for mitigating circumstances, no corner for lenient understanding. It was quite uncomplicated really; black and white and read all over you. Trapped and guilty. After a year or so the fine came through and was duly paid, now nearly another six months later, here were the boys in blue. Somehow I just knew these guys weren't here to see if we were all OK, they weren't checking to see if we had peace of mind. 'Any complaints about the service monsieur?'

As the older *gendarme* stood with his arms crossed and his legs apart watching his younger colleague do the official bit, I was tempted to ask them what they thought about this:

A couple of months earlier one of my clients was lying awake in the middle of the night as one sometimes does. It was about 4 am, that time when your sugar levels are low and your worry grades are high, that he heard one of his cars being started. He had a couple of four-by-fours; one a creaking old mini jeep, the other an altogether more slick and modern off-roader. He hauled himself out of bed, looked through the window and saw the wee jeep disappearing off down the drive.

Quick as jack flash, he pulled on a set of clothes, shot downstairs and out to the remaining vehicle. Within minutes he was in hot pursuit, tailgating the unfortunate thief, and waiting for a chance to run him off the road. The moment came as the route widened out, about four kilometres south of their house. Accelerating up along side the little jeep, our hero gently started to push him off the tarmac. 'You want to do some cross country stuff? Then have it on me,' he growled, eyeballing the robber. The petrified crook tried in vain to keep himself in control but to no avail. He pulled the jeep up as quickly as he could, leapt out of the still moving car and started off across the fields. Meanwhile his wife had called the local police, had been diverted to a central control office in Avignon and was told to ring Cavaillon. This she did and was told to ring Bonnieux again, on a different number. After endless rings it was answered by a voice in pyjamas that took a bit of time to orientate itself, and find the forms that needed to be filled out. Eventually the drama was recorded but it had all taken nearly forty-five minutes, and still no lawman had turned up at the house. The shudder was, what would have happened if an aggressive intruder had been disturbed actually in the house, and had seemed like he wanted to shoot your face off?

Anyway, I didn't bother to discuss this little matter with the short arm of the law, after all they had, as I suspected, come to take my licence away. For fifteen days. I wasn't looking to make my life any more difficult. I was banned. An outcast from the highway. A non driver. Oh the shame…

It coincided with the week I was moving office, so not having a licence made things pretty hard. I had taken a small house in the village. It comprised three rooms on two floors and overlooked the valley below. I could look down on our property quite clearly and, with the help of binoculars was able to spy on the family most satisfactorily. I spent the next few days organising the rewiring, security, telephone lines, carpentry, plumbing and redecorating. It all involved a lot of walking, but the up side was how many lifts I was offered from local farmers whom I knew only vaguely. It gave me an opportunity to natter, which of course is missed if you drive everywhere. If I walked across the fields I took to carrying a small pouch of salt with me. Then if I met Georges or Joel, and they passed me some freshly picked vegetables, I was equipped for an instant banquet. Finding a cool, shady spot, I would sit down and take five minutes out. It was as happy a break off as you could wish for. Bobble would lie in a stream if she could find one and patiently wait to be tossed a tomato or an off cut of cucumber. Munching on those newly picked, ripe vegetables, sprinkled with gritty sea salt, was just as good as forty winks.

Masses of butterflies floated and fluttered everywhere. The Red Admirals lit on the forming blackberries, small Tortoiseshells

Fig 2

clouded round the wild buddleias and the Meadow Browns skittishly warmed themselves on the blades of dry grass. Painted Ladies were at their peak, shamelessly competing with the flowering thistles they like to rest on. Perhaps the most prolific big butterfly in our region is *le Flambé*. It has unusual zebra-type markings and can be seen from May to September, and always grabs attention. There is another funny fellow that works hard during the summer months and looks like a cross between a bee and a moth, with the capabilities of a humming bird: *le Sphinx* or hawkmoth. There are various strains, but it is the Vine Sphinx that gets my prize. Apart from being associated with the vines, he seems to have a predilection towards blue flowers. He zips around with the speed of a bee late for a party, then pulls up practically in his own length, and starts to hover just outside the trumpet of a flower. He closes one eye and inspects the insides for goodies, and either dives in or buzzes off again. He's not very beautiful compared to some of his more showy relations, but he remains, none the less, an original.

One morning, towards the end of August, I opened the kitchen door to find Joel Neighbour with his friends Yves and Christian busy picking figs for the market. The tree was drooping heavily under the weight of the ripening fruit and we were keen to try and get as many collected as possible before they rotted. Nicky had discovered how to make fig ice cream, she turned in a mean fig tart, the fig jam was damned good and fresh figs for breakfast were better for the constitution than any amount of prunes, but there was a limit. They also attracted hornets, which is why Joel & Co.

were out early, beating them to it. The cats were sitting on the terrace table watching the activity, waiting for breakfast. Posy, feigning little interest, looked up momentarily, then returned to her morning ablution, one leg stuck up in the air like a dislocated ham joint, whilst Billy meowed as if she hadn't seen anything worth eating for months. Her erect, bushy tail quivered like a rudder on a dinghy, whilst her big plated eyes brimmed over with cupboard love.

The bleached valley below shimmered in the fading dawn. Hands were shaken all round, then, quite unexpectedly Christian told me that the eighteen-year-old son of a mutual acquaintance had died in a road accident early the previous morning. He had been coming home from a party and had hit a wild boar on the N100. The animal, a big male, had seemingly trotted out of the hedgerow, onto the road just at the moment the boy was passing. It had killed both of them.

I sat down and reflected on the tragedy. It must be the very worst of all to lose your child. In the great circle of things you can expect your parents to die before you do, as indeed you would expect to die before your children. But to have an offspring's young life cut short like that must be unendurable. I went slowly upstairs and looked through the half-open bedroom door of at a still sleeping Theo. The shutters were letting in a pale shaft of sunlight that fell across his bed. I needed just to check up, to steal a moment of reassurance. He lay on his back with his legs slightly raised, an arm nonchalantly wrapped around Vanilla, his big white teddy bear. A handful of little fingers gripped randomly onto the soft toy's chest, as his head nestled down into the big soft pillow and he breathed gently into that good morning. I knew that in the bag of a million bubbles that made up my unadulterated adoration, not a single one had escaped or burst. But I felt the tears run down my cheeks and I sobbed quietly for the parents of the young motor cyclist.

Since we had lived here we had seen three children born, including our own, been to one wedding, and experienced two funerals. And here was another one. Apart from it sounding a bit like the name of a movie, it made me realise that we were now fully paid up members of the local life. The building blocks that make up our existence, the joins and rips in the fabric of our society were in place. We were not on holiday in the South of France, we were not playing at being here: it was very real.

Calling Bobble, I set off for a walk. Everywhere was now looking very arid and parched. Apart from 'that night of the terrible storm' it had been months since we had had any proper rain and the countryside was tired. The few remaining wild flowers were sagging and even the yarrow was finally beginning to look depleted. The flat white flower heads had started to curl up into light brown cups, ready to disperse its seeds. The water in the basin was flat and clear. The detailed reflection of the surrounding giant oaks and towering, hundred-foot poplars was broken by the gentlest hint of a ripple as it expanded out over the dark surface, a tiny clue that the flow continued. A rustle in the leaves produced a big green lizard. *Le Liézard Vert* is about 25–40cms long, and tries to avoid contact but if he's cornered, he will allegedly bite your finger and never let go, preferring to part company with his head rather than release his grip. His relative, *le*

Léizard Ocelle at 50–60cms long, is the biggest you'll find in France. He has distinctive, almost leopard-like markings and can be found hanging around dry stone walls. He is inoffensive to humans, but conducts violent attacks on other males.

As we turned and headed back for breakfast the flaxen sun cast a warm shadow over the ripening grapes, their purple hue deepening. The vine leaves showed their first tell-tale signs of an early autumn, as in places they began to crackle at the edges.

It would soon be harvest time.

CHAPTER NINE

Back to School

The first day back at work in The Owners' garden was rumbled by a heavy and continuous downpour. The hopelessly dressed workmen pulled up collars they hadn't got, huddled with hands in pockets, and pulled on soggy cigarettes. Their faces hung like dejected parents at a washed-out sports day, as they threw their eyes up to heaven and their shoulders into a resigned shrug. It looked set to last, and as the site turned from a dry, debilitated parch-land, into a muddy, sloppy quagmire, the whistle was blown and the crew slunk thankfully off to the café.

Meanwhile, in the garden almost before my eyes, the water from the skies seemed to work like a magic ointment. It healed the burns, revitalised the sprigs and woke up the weeds. As the earth absorbed the wetness, a green tinge crept out of the shadows and advanced slowly but confidently across the ground. It was as good as having a swim in the ocean after a few days spent in the desert.

I was glad to be back. I had been involved with this lovely, quaint little garden for a long time now, on and off, and had become peculiarly fond of it. We had shared some hairy experiences after all.

On top of which I had worked on lots of drawings and plans, made dozens of readjustments, and had even got to know The Owners quite well. I was looking forward to bringing it up to scratch, and I took it as a good sign that it had rained that first day: the garden had been given a thorough clean up and shaken back into life. There was also the fact that, having been held back by holidays and mishaps, planning delays and modifications, I wanted to get the project finished, and move on before it became stale. It would soon be a year since we had started discussing the project and, for a modestly sized garden, that was quite long enough.

Within a couple of days the wind had chased the rain away, shooing it off towards the Pyrenées. The sun swam lazily around in an azure sky, thrilled to be able to make warmth without war. The days were still hot, but at night the chill of autumn was mounting a slow offensive, edging its way around the houses, and the shutters were being closed ever earlier. Little lorries were busy rushing here and there delivering logs. Measured piles of wood, known locally as a *stère*, weighing approximately 1000 kilos, were dumped, waiting to be carefully stacked in sheds. The earlier the consignment, the more likely that the wood was old, and would therefore burn well. Late demands usually brought a hissing green cherry that wanted to perform about as much as a chorister with a cold.

Because events had dragged on so much at The Owners' garden, I had become used to little or nothing much happening, so it came as a bit of a shock when Mr Noir and Manuel announced one mid-September morning that the pool was ready to be filled. It was also the fact that the interior had been tiled in a dark colour so the hole was less noticeable, and had been drawing little attention to itself.

The water hoses were lowered into the deep end and the taps turned on. Two days later somebody would have to take the inaugural plunge.

There followed a mammoth clearing up operation. This involved getting all the builders' paraphernalia off site, cleaning up the debris, raking up the ground and generally getting ready to start gardening. Quite suddenly we were on the spot. The electricians and plumbers had finished putting in the basic wires and pipes for the garden lighting and irrigation, so we figured that we might as well start with that. We needed to fine-tune the points at which the services were required. It is always a bit of a chicken-and-egg thing when building in a watering system. On one hand you really need the plants dug in before you start laying the extraneous pipes; however, on the other hand, if you don't have the system there before the plants, you risk the newly installed roots drying out. Problems, problems.

Over at the Professor's property, the solution to the irrigation problem had been given to us on a plate. Running round the property were a series of ditches that during the spring, summer and autumn, carried the water drawn off the Alpilles, the mountain range that marches across the background. This could be directed through a series of gates and gullies to perform some water magic. After some diligent grading, the water would 'fall' naturally across the fields, keeping the grasses alive. This supply would also be used to feed the lake, and subsequently support the irrigation system. It was a realistic solution and reasonably economical.

Back at The Owners' garden, due to a small misunderstanding, the first lorry load of top-soil delivered was dropped off outside the front door, in the middle of the narrow street. Being well mixed with manure, it not only stank but also looked unsightly, prevented any passage, and gave palpitations to the gardening crew. The lorry driver, far from being apologetic about his idiotic action, was actually rather proud of his prowess at managing to squeeze a ten-ton lorry up the neck of a medieval village alley and dispense with his load in one go. Pedestrians, pinching their noses, side-stepped the heap of natural garden goody and dived into the chemist to pick up their prescriptions, shaking their heads with predictable disapproval. Ten tonnes felt like ten times that by the time it had been barrowed up at lightening speed, and shifted round the side and down into the garden.

Keen to avoid any more delivery hassles, I went to great lengths explaining to the nursery boys how to find a suitable spot to unload the plants. I sent faxes with cute little maps, I spoke to the driver on the day to confirm his early morning drop – always a mistake – and reserved a parking bay between eight and ten, the time I was promised I could expect them. It was a Friday and the one day you do everything that you can to avoid deliveries. The workforce knocks off at three, and should anything arrive after that it tends to be me who has to move the goods onto the site.

At eleven I rang the nursery office, who having put me on hold for so long I was becoming deranged, finally announced that Monsieur Chauffeur would be with us about four pm. I remonstrated in a low voice that was as full of menace as I could muster and reiterated the extreme difficulties this was going to cause. I also threw in a chain of four letter words that at least made me feel a bit better. The receptionist with the sing-song voice of the 'it's-got-nothing-to-do-with-me' type warbled, 'Merci monsieur, bonne journée.'

I was left to deal with it. My heart sank. I know only too well from past experience that these drivers definitely do not see it as part of their job to help with the unloading, especially if they are haulage contractors and not employed by the nursery.

I once had a local delivery of Italian trees and shrubs brought to us by a French freight company. It wasn't a very big order, nothing that wouldn't have fitted in a large box van. But when I got the call to say that the lorry was waiting for me in the town square as arranged, so that I could direct him to the site, I found a grumbling thirteen metre articulated truck, panting with exhaustion after a thirty-two point turn. I climbed up and knocked on the driver's door, the bottom of which was about a metre above my head. Inside sat Vanier, bolt upright. I had had the misfortune of meeting this chauffeur before. The last time it had been raining hard and he had managed to get his mammoth truck stuck in the mud. It had taken three tractors two hours to unplug him. The window slid down and the communist turned his head towards me. He had the practised look of an intolerant trouble-maker, backed by a black belt in client abuse. Because everybody shakes hands all the time in France, I offered mine only to have him look at it as if I was passing him some fresh dog droppings.

I have quite picked up the habit of hand shaking. I rather like it. It saves on small talk. It might just be a quick touching of palms as you enter a bar, passing round half a dozen acquaintances, with very little eye contact. It might be the warmer, lingering hand shake used when you meet up with a chum, even though you probably saw him or her a few hours earlier. Or, it might be the high-octane shake, helped by three kisses on the cheek whilst the other hand grips an elbow. You both look meaningfully into each other's eyes, then turn, still holding on, and smile to the camera. Or there is a special one invented by our neighbour, old Monsieur Voison. He proffers his shaking hand, dangling it at you like something he found in the off-cuts bin of the local morgue. You take hold of this limp fillet and it suddenly bursts into life. It tightens round your hand with a vice-like hold, locks into place and cannot be shaken off for love or money. You stand there for the next ten minutes cuffed to the conversation, being wielded about as Mr Voison expresses his views on the state of agriculture.

The lorry driver told me to lead on, which I did with mounting trepidation. How this mechanical monster of his was going to negotiate the narrow lanes, let alone the driveway down to the house, I couldn't think. The short answer was, it wasn't. As we pulled out of the town, taking a sharpish turn to the left, I could see we were already in trouble. The dinosaur gave a blood-curdling screech as the air brakes belched and hissed, whilst the whole rig rocked. I sat tight and let him snort and sort it out, which he did after making sure everybody within five kilometres heard his misery. Every few hundred yards I had to stop, get out of the car and with the aid of a rake I fortunately had with me, stand on the bonnet and push up an overhead telephone wire, so that the blasted artic. could pass underneath. We pulled up at the entrance to the property, one that happens to have about a mile of stone track leading down through lavender fields. The driver looked at the little road and said simply, almost politely: 'No-way,' and started to roll up the sides of

Heavy plant crossing

his trailer so that he could get unloaded, and away as soon as possible. Before I knew what had hit me I had eight mature *Pinus sylvestris* teetering on the edge of the flatbed, about to be rolled over and out, dumped without ceremony on the side of a road, miles from home. Their root balls weigh far more than two men could hope to lift, and would happily have crushed my legs if the ape had let go of them.

'Haven't you got a hydraulic lift at the back?' I asked.

'No,' and down came the first one. The delivery drivers employed by a nursery may not always be a huge amount of help, but at least they know that their cargo is a living thing, and as such should be treated with the respect it deserves, particularly if he wants to keep his job. But no such luck with this micro thug. When I had first met Vanier, perched up close to heaven in his pin-up-papered cab, I had imagined him to be enormous, a giant with muscles in places that I don't have. When the doors of his triple turbo-charged commercial chariot were flung open, I expected this shire horse of a man to leap down like the amazing hulk. In fact he was a jockey in stature. The only difference being that he had obviously trained in a truck without power steering, developing arms and shoulders that a swimmer would give up his feet for. Besides, he would have removed any race horse's head with one jerk on the bridle.

After an hour, with no thanks to the vertically challenged king of the road, the delivery sat on the grass verge. Apart from the Scots pines, there were some big green oaks, a few parasol pines and a clutch of assorted shrubs. It was five o'clock and nobody was about. Nobody was about to help either. It was another one of those awful bare-root tree jokes.

'Have you got a brush?' demanded the lorry driver

'A brush?' I asked, hauling myself back from trying to imagine what I was going to do with this lot.

'What do you want a brush for?'

'I don't, you do.'

'I do?' I was becoming acquiescent.

'Yeh, to clean my lorry out.'

At moments like this I long to able to articulate my feelings in perfect French to an inarticulated lorry driver. Sign language works pretty well, but I longed to be pithy and sarcastic, colloquial and trashy, and for him to be floored by my senior command of his beautiful language. As it was I managed to tell him that no, I didn't have a brush, and if I had, I would hammer it up his exhaust.

He looked at me with his turned-down mouth, his stumpy little legs spread apart and just fumed. I watched and wondered if he had a wife or partner, and what he, she or it thought of this disagreeable misfit. There are lorry strikes every year in France. The drivers demand more for less and are generally backed by the long-suffering public. When they don't get what they think they deserve immediately, they hold us all hostages by making road blocks and parking their trucks every which way they can along the main routes. I bet Vanier's first off the starting block.

I had a childish fizz of pleasure when he asked me if he could turn his truck round, further up the lane.

'Yes, yes, very easy, no problem.'

I knew it was a cul-de-sac, about two kilometres away, terminating in the driveway of an elderly couple's bungalow. There would be a small team of equally elderly vehicles, and absolutely no room to turn a wheelchair let alone a thirteen-metre trailer. Have I got a brush, indeed.

The big trees were too heavy for me, or anybody else to move. But I reckoned they would be safe enough on the side of the road, at least until tomorrow when I could coerce someone into helping move them. It was the shrubs that were the nuisance. Since I had slipped a disc a couple of years earlier I was very wary of lifting, or even trying to drag too heavy a load.

I had been raking the stones off a border one Saturday morning, trying to get the beds ready for planting the following week. I was on my own because my co-workers didn't want to know about weekend work, the client was in America and there was no one else in the house. I had made a completely innocuous pass with the rake, pulling some light stones towards me when suddenly, in a split second, the most massive stab of pain thrust right in to the core of my spine. It vibrated out in waves of shock, and the agony was unimaginable. A yell exploded out of my head and I sank to my knees, then fell over onto my side. My breathing was jagged and irregular, I couldn't persuade my lungs to move without the pain rushing at me with its head down and horns extended. I was perspiring like a greyhound after chase, and could no more move than fly. The very slightest action woke the beast who immediately stamped on the point of torment, adding a couple of well-aimed kicks for good measure. A terrible blanket of depression smothered me within minutes.

As I lay there I thought about the actor Christopher Reeves and his appalling riding accident, and wondered if I would be as brave as he seemed to have been. I thought about paralysis and shivered at the thought of not being able to lift Theo ever again. I couldn't think how I was going to get out of this one, there was no portable phone in my pocket, and Nicky wouldn't be expecting me back for hours. After an interminable half hour two little lads of about ten came round the corner in the road, about five hundred yards away. They were ragging each other, throwing stones into the trees and generally boying around. I thought God if they see me, an old man to them, lying still on the ground, on my side like this they will think I'm dead. It will scare the daylights out of the poor little souls. With this in mind and the fact that the gnashing teeth of hell had subsided a fraction, I flung myself at the pain barrier and slid through with flying colours. It was so extraordinarily dreadful that a kind of martyrdom encompassed me. I managed to muffle my mouth, and staggered to my feet using a helpful young cypress tree as a prop. The kids arrived at about the same time as I did, we exchanged weak little hellos, I contained myself until they had passed, and then fell into the tree. I tell you it couldn't have been much worse at the front line. At least there you had some sick camaraderie with like-inflicted fellows.

I was just about to try and stand and walk when the housekeeper arrived in her ancient little Citroen. She jauntily got out the car and waved to me as she rushed into the house. I had tried to call out, but the effort of summing up the breath to put some speech onto, had shat out the fearful pain once more, causing me to freeze mid endeavour.

Twenty minutes later I had managed to manoeuvre myself along the border and was eyeing up a pomegranate as my next unsuspecting companion, when out of the house came the *femme de ménage* again, still rushing like mad.

'*Ça va?*' she called out.

I couldn't think where to begin, but I started to explain the best I could using little words that fell out of my mouth like sharp stones. I thought I was doing rather well, as she appeared to be making sympathetic noises and gestures. I was gaining confidence by the sentence, and was about to ask her if I could possibly lean on her and perhaps together, we might make it to my car, thus opening up the possibilities of me getting myself home. Evidently she mistook my guttural groans of throbbing discomfort for some kind of perverse sexual awakening. She took a couple of brisk steps back, distancing herself. She looked at me with a mixture of suspicion and quizzical curiosity. We had passed the time of day before, but had never engaged in conversation deeper than that. I stood motionless as she presumably thought it best to leave. She climbed into her car and turned on the ignition. I stood motionless as I listened to a flat battery refusing to fire up her transport. I stood equally motionless as she climbed out again and came over and asked me if I would be kind enough to give her dud car a push. With what felt like a broken back, I replied with a broken voice in broken French that I didn't feel that that was on the agenda. I was about to explain my plight again, when she turned, and in her usual rushing gait, set off down the drive, evidently looking for a better class of help.

That evening I had lain in bed with morphine canoodling my corpuscles. It soothed me so much that a dumb grin had flanneled my face and I had felt cocooned in a corner of paradise. The young doctor had taken one look at me and conceded that the drug would probably be the best thing. Against the odds I slept until six when I awoke needing to have a Jimmy Riddle. I'll pass on all that but it was no bowl of cherries I can promise you. The next morning the district nurse arrived. She had been booked by the surgery to come twice a day for a week to give me injections. Madame Piqûre, a smart middle-aged lady, tooled in before breakfast dressed from top to toe in Dior. She looked as if she was off to a rather smart drinks party, clanking with gold earrings, belts and buckles. Her medical bag sadly wasn't Louis Vuitton, nor her needles Tiffany's. Following a week of jabbing me, I am sure she would have been able to recognise my bottom anywhere. Having seen me up and heard me showering, she was happy to sign off, and so was I.

Meanwhile back at The Owners' garden in Ménerbes, Mr Chauffeur had duly arrived at about half past four with the consignment of plants, thankfully, in a fixed-chassis van. Quite big enough to be a nuisance, but at least we would be able to find somewhere close to the garden to park. I explained to him that he really did have to help me unload and get the plants into the garden, and that it would definitely take an hour or so, and that I would unquestionably be bunging him a handsome tip for his effort. He was only a young chap, strong and probably doing very well on four or five hours' sleep a week. I held my roll of notes clearly in his line of vision, peeling them back with an Arthur Daly swagger. About three and a half minutes later, or what felt like it, we had unloaded, moved, and stashed all the plants, long, tall and short, big, fat and thin, into the holding bay in the garden. The boy took his tip graciously and I went off to water the plants before going home. I was looking forward to spending a bit of time in our own garden for a change.

It was late September but there was still plenty of colour. Most of the roses were holding centre stage and the *Ceanothus arboreus* 'Trewithen Blue' and 'Concha' had made a welcome autumn comeback. The *Aster novae-belgii* better known as Michaelmas daisies, and a leftover from Mr Vendor, were flowering strongly under the *Albizia julibrissin, the* Constantinople acacia, but needed a bit of support whilst their deep blue heads lent a penetrating wave of colour. The tall spiky blue *Perovskia atriplicifolia* and free-form pale pink *Gaura lindheimeri* were still going strong and competed with some surprisingly long-flowering blue *Agapanthus praecox* subsp. *minimus* 'Adelaide'. Behind the silvery *Artemisia* 'Powis Castle', the *Viburnum tinus* hedge was looking a bit confused as it started to push out its big white clusters of flowers again. I would rather it saved its energy for the winter.

Along the edges, that old favourite of Gertrude Jekyll, *Erigeron karvinskianus* with its long-lasting daisy flowers, tried to elbow out the low-growing *Convolvulus sabatius* (syn. *C. mauritanicus*), whose simple dark blue little flowers had been showing off all summer. A large group of *Ceratostigma plumbaginoides*, with yet more blue flowers, was holding court in front of a deaf and fading *Cotinus coggygria* 'Royal Purple'. You can see we are suckers for blue around here. In the middle of the border the long reaching panicles of *Salvia uliginosa* nodded in the breeze with a band of white Japanese anemones. Just round the corner there was a second, albeit slightly weak, showing of *Geranium* 'Johnson's Blue' mingling with a fast-fading collection of *Caryopteris* x *clandonensis* 'Heavenly Blue' mixed with *'inoveris'* and tall *Verbena bonariensis* and small *Verbena venosa*. The decorative grasses, *Miscanthus sinensis* 'Yakushima Dwarf', with its long, thin, brown panicles and silvery plumes, and the tufts of *Carex buchananii* backed by *Ampelodesmos mauritanicus*, all looked magnificent, especially with the dipping sun behind them. Our garden has plenty of *Centranthus ruber* 'Albus', slightly more than intended, but it was still as full of life as it was way back at the beginning of the season. It had arranged itself behind a mass of *Oenothera speciosa*, a fast spreading, pale pink, mid-sized chap that loves the sun. The tall pink *Lavatera olbia* was looking a bit tired by it all, and lent against the pale green leaves of the *Lobelia syphilitica*, which despite its unfortunate name, seemed in the best of perky health and quite happy to prop up its neighbours.

The annuals were still blowing their bugles and would continue to do so for at least another eight to ten weeks. I treat the *Lantana camara* and *Lantana sellowiana* as annuals here, as I do the *Plumbago auriculata* (syn. *capensis*). It gets far too cold in the winter for them to survive. We filled up huge terracotta pots full of white busy lizzies or *impatiens* letting them spill over in a dense mass of low, white flowers, drawing the eye to certain corners of the terraces. But my star prize went to the *Mandevilla* x *amabilis* (syn. *Dipladenia amabilis*). It grew on the south-eastern corner of the kitchen terrace, out of a big pot and was trained onto a simple frame. It had been covered in big, waxy white trumpets with yellow centres since I planted it in April. Before that it had been flowering in the dining room since just after Christmas. Unless it is brought back indoors before first frost, it won't make the winter, but with a performance like that it's worth building a greenhouse just for him alone. The English lavender, *Lavandula angustifolia* had started to put on a little fresh leaf growth, and *Lavandula dentata* with its purple tufted flower spikes, was still in bloom, growing next door to some purple berberis with a long-flowering white ground cover rose, *Rosa 'ice' meillandecor* spreading around their feet.

I made a note to remind myself to remove the *Yucca aloifolia plants* I have on either side of gran alley we use for playing skittles. Despite its beautiful flowers shining at night like candles, waiting to be pollinated by moths in the moonlight, those hard, sharp points at the end of their leaves make it too dangerous to have around children's play areas.

Theo and I went over the way to inspect some pumpkins. There were field upon field of these strange vegetables. Sometimes they looked like a well-organised harvest, neatly stacked and ready to go, other times they looked as if they had been laid randomly by a very tall bird from another planet. These were not just the orange variety that everybody uses for Halloween, but also the squatter, more ridged breed that are greener in colour and sit looking like they have been dropped from a considerable height. The first time I saw this crop I couldn't believe that so many people would be eating it, that it was so popular, that it could be turned into a dish to order in preference to anything else. I knew the Roux brothers rather enjoyed an *omelette sucrée au potiron*, or sweet pumpkin omelette, during the depression after the war, since both pumpkins and eggs were readily available even during those lean times. I also knew that pumpkins and almonds joined forces for a traditional Provençal Christmas pudding. I even knew it made a passable soup. But to look at the

Mini Courges
5^{Frs} pièce
60^{Frs} le plateau

Pumpkins

stockpiles in the fields, to see the loaded lorries bowing under the weight of these Cinderella Charabancs, was to realise that this must be a major local fodder.

Theo was more interested in going to find the Gobbos' house. Ever since Noddy had had his little yellow car stolen by Goblins, we had been looking out for a place that they might have hidden it. We had found just the spot one day when walking along the edge of The Old Oak Wood. An abandoned stone shelter built into the bank had presented itself, and we both knew without doubt that this was where the Gobbos' lived. The roots of one of the regal trees had permeated through the decaying pointing, and the roof was a mixture of stone, tubers and damp soil. Inside, there were a few large old rocks and a scrap book of shoe prints.

'Here's a clue,' said the explorer, taking a magnifying glass out of his adventure bag. 'Pass the torch.'

Like Watson to his master I handed the device over.

'Bimbtoculators,' he continued.

Now the nurse to the surgeon.

'There's definitely been Gobbos staying here, they've had a wee.'

In the excitement of his discovery he had been holding his flask of water upside down, but I wasn't the man to tell him.

We took a rest under a fine spreading walnut tree, and the sun dappled through the leaves lighting the pale blue autumn crocus that carpeted the ground underneath. A few were picked as a bouquet for Mum, but the little hand had practically throttled them by the time they were presented.

The following day The Musicians asked us out to lunch. In the big rambling sitting room on the first floor of their converted barn,

I stood at the window looking down over the ripening vine. The September sun shone out of a near-perfect blue sky. A scribble of cloud, hardly noticeable, drifted gently in from the south. Mr Musician sat in the shade of the shuttered window playing a cello. Theo watched entranced, as the cellist's fingers moved up and down the fretless neck, and occasionally offered to help. The notes, both rich and deep, and sometimes almost as light as a violin, occupied the space with an eminently respectable noise. Everything knitted together most satisfactorily, and as we were called to lunch, already laid out on the big stone table under the weeping ash, I felt precious close to Pseuds' Corner.

Mrs Musician had made some bread, and it was still warm and soft. Apple olives and goat's cheese, slices of cucumber with dots of chilli, late tomatoes plus a little caviar that a friend had brought. A couple of bottles of Champagne were produced, glasses filled and chinked whilst the children dived in and out of the hanging branches, giggling and squeaking as if they had downed a bottle of their own. The dogs failed miserably at pretending not to look interested in the proceedings. A spaniel had presented herself apologetically from next door. A submissive grin on her bowed face, she had advanced with her little body virtually bent in half, almost walking sideways. Her cropped tail did its absolute best to wag with deferential friendliness as she introduced herself to the party. Bobble welcomed her with a tractable tolerance, but made it quite clear who had first call on any hand-outs. Chicken cooked in lemon and orange, with cous cous, and broccoli followed, then more cheese and salad all bossed around by a white Chateau-Neuf.

I bought the wine when Monsieur Marcheur had taken me to the

A la main

festival in Chateau-Neuf at the end of August. He had been a little reluctant on account of the tourist interest, but being an old hand at the ropes, he agreed to show me this once, thereafter I would be on my own. Chateau-Neuf is an attractive small town dominated by the castle. It sits high up with a commanding view over thousands of hectares of vineyards and the Rhône valley – from Avignon in the west, up to Mont de Ventoux in the north. We arrived and bought the little tasting glass they suggest you should have, and start seeking out the temperature-controlled *caves* to throw ourselves into with unashamed abandon. We smirked like adolescents at the fully rounded, voluptuous big-bosomed blancs of '95, and giggled childishly at the grievances of the gale-blown '94, so anorexic and flat-chested by comparison.

In the main square, a big circular pond and fountain gushed water from three of its sides. It was dappled and shaded by a big, proud plane in whose arms, a full three metres up, was cradled a keg of fine Côtes du Rhône. An umbilical chord ran down the trunk to take up position on the fourth and remaining side of the fountain, from which ran an endless stream of the fine red ruin for everyone to help themselves for free. There was a non-stop scrum of pushing and shoving, pulling and kicking drinkers doing their best to get in and get more than anyone else. Any kind of retiring attitude would leave you with an empty glass, mug, bucket, cement lorry or whatever else you happened to be holding. So, using my height and weight I was in there like I was hooking for the big win in the Five Nations, filling my glass and toasting the charity of the town. Very good it was too. After a few more tastings, and one or two purchases, Mr Marcheur suggested we visited a little hotel he knew whose terrace overlooked the town, and where we could wash out the palate with some local fizzy water. We would then be ready to introduce ourselves to some of Chateau-Neuf's unusually deep coloured, strong tasting and arrestingly seductive rosé. He left me to order and went to buy some freshly baked olive bread, *saucisson* and regional goat's cheese. As the sun sank drunkenly behind the Roman church, the conjurers, medieval jugglers and dancers emerged from the shadows. The festival lights came on and we became so mellow I feared we might be picked up, dusted with ginger, laid on a slice of *jambon sec* and eaten.

As September wound down, the wine harvest, or *vendange*, started up. Everywhere little tractors and trailers, small enough to fit between the rows of grapes, trundled down towards the Co-op *vinicole*, to deposit their loads. The co-operative is made up from the contributing farmers who pool their pickings and share out the profits made from the yield. Most of the vines grown around here are treated as a crop, and not given any particular special treatment. The grapes are still gathered chiefly by hand, but increasingly a mechanised harvester is becoming an everyday sight as it works its way methodically down the lines of burgeoning vine. It is an odd-looking device: tall and gangly, it fits over the grapes keeping its spindly wheels on either side of the bushes, whilst big rubber belts worry the bunches free from their branches. It is quick and efficient and will no doubt rub out the camaraderie that comes each year when the pickers arrive.

Once collected, the grapes are weighed in, passed up an elevator, cleaned and then pressed. It makes a completely useful, drinkable wine that expects no postcards. It is cheap and friendly, and

Pas à la main

although it varies from commune to commune, it is nearly always consistent and companionable. It is unlikely to find itself on the shelves of foreign supermarkets, and will never grace the wine lists of the smarter restaurants. There are however, some relatively grown-up vineyards in Provence. There are chateaux that produce the best in the region, and given time to mature can hold their necks up with the big boys. Often *biologique* or organic and more carefully nurtured, thousands of these bottles will sell both here and abroad. Who, for example, doesn't recognise the embossed shield on the chest of a bottle of Chateau-Neuf?

They were also harvesting the grapes at Chateau Vignelaure and it is a strange coincidence but every time our stock of '97 Vignelaure is running low in the *cave*, or the cheery bottles of rosé seemed to have escaped the fridge, it coincides with the need to go and talk plants, or maintenance or future plans with Mr & Mrs O'Irish. Having completed the formal gardens, it was time to move on down to the lower fields. In the last year, four children had been born in their immediate circle. One to the O'Irishes themselves, and three others to close friends and colleagues, and Catherine wanted to plant four olive trees to commemorate the occasion. She also wanted a 'cutting garden' mostly made up of shrubs that would produce some colour year round for the house. Further, it was agreed that the screening hedge at the bottom of the drive needed thickening up to block the lower road that led off to the vine fields. We discussed the idea of the new hedge having a two-metre wine bottle cut into it, carefully lit, and to act as a folliesque homage to their industry.

We Range Rovered up to the top of the hill behind the chateau, and looked down over the rolling vineyard. Men were busy picking the ripe fruit, loading it gently into buckets before transporting it by trailer back to the processing yard. It was a fine sight and gratifying to know that all this hard work goes into making some increasingly good wine. We had a look at the grapes being fed up rubber escalators and onto their destiny. We chatted with the man responsible for controlling the huge aluminium vats, and generally got in the way. We talked of how technology has changed and how the beautiful old oak vats given a set of wheels and a window would make very good gypsy caravans.

It had been, as always, a congenial meeting, and was adjourned only after the car boot had been loaded.

In Provence the farmers plant by the lunar cycle. They watch the weather as a new moon dawns, and read by experience the best days to sow the seed. Very often the weather on a new moon will dictate the pattern for the next twenty or thirty days, and this will warn them to move quickly or hold back. To pause when a certain pattern is played out while the moon waxes, or to capitalise on the conditions as it wanes and move accordingly. There is nothing particularly mystical about it as far as the farmers are concerned, just the lore of the countryside that has passed down through the generations. I have tried to find the rhythms, but being unpractised find myself wandering off course. A few years back, my mother-in-law was experiencing considerable success treating people with a variety of complaints through Radionics. Perhaps best known as the 'Black Box', this supplementary form of medicine is difficult to explain, but when I asked my then doctor, a smart fellow who has his practice in Knightsbridge, what he thought of Radionics, he was cautiously complimentary about it. He knew little, but had heard that it had been very successful in the veterinary profession. The Queen's racehorse trainers for example, had been working with it for years.

Interestingly Radionics applies itself to agriculture, and in turn horticulture as well. In treating humans and animals, dowsing identifies the treatment. That is to say, a pendulum is suspended on a thread and held over a V-shaped bay showing the positive and negative signs at its points. Simply by a process of elimination through straightforward questions, the practitioner can start to assess the symptoms and decide on the patient's treatment, the ball having swung towards the 'yes' or 'no' tips. When a suggested treatment has been determined, it is related to a numerical code. Armed with this information, the instrument is then programmed to complement the condition of the patient. An electrical current is passed through a copper plate on which a strand of the sufferer's hair lies. The treatment then begins. Incredibly, and perhaps with a drop of celestial approval, the patient more often than not begins to heal. This is not some quixotic device dreamt up by a witch on a vacuum cleaner, but an auxiliary medicine that undoubtedly works. The proof is overwhelming, and because of that is often seen by the traditional medical profession as something of a threat. But then so was homeopathy only a few years ago. Funnily enough it was the Royal Family who lent credence to that as well.

Exactly the same principles apply in agriculture, too: dowsing followed by treatment. Mrs Mum-in-law easily persuaded me to meet a lady who was, if you will, head doctor. A small unassuming lady in her sixties, she kindly explained the principle of how Radionics helped farmers and gardeners alike. She told of how a sample of soil was taken from the land, and like the hair, was placed on the copper plate. She showed me photographs of wheat fields before and after treatment, of plant borders that had been moved because of bad energy. It was all deeply impressive, and because I found no obstacles when I worked the pendulum, I was aware that I was potentially a sound student of the phenomenon. However I felt that it would require a degree of commitment that I just wasn't ready to hand over.

In the late sixties I had been affected by a story of an American professor, who having read about Eastern philosophies, and been inspired by the outrageous indoctrination of Timothy Leary's 'Turn on, tune in and drop out' theory, gave up his lucrative teaching post at Harvard. He turned in his middle-class respectability and headed out to Guru land. His book *Be Here Now* has the stain of hippiedom about it nowadays, I suppose, but it taught me two worthwhile things. Firstly, that to truly appreciate the wonderment of a moment, you didn't need someone else to share it with you – although that was a bonus – nor the exaggeration of memory to make it live up to its initial impact. Secondly, that whilst he didn't achieve enlightenment himself, he knew from his experiences in the spiritual landscape that it was possible. In a smaller way, I felt the same about horticultural Radionics. It existed, it worked, but I didn't feel it necessary to commit myself to convince myself. Beyond which I couldn't see how I was going to have the time to spend on the learning process. It required a pledge that I was unable to offer at that time.

Getting back to the earth, the month was running out and it was very nearly time to have a small panic attack about planting at The Owners' garden. I had to quickly galvanise everybody into a final push and get everything completed without delay. We had a serious stack of plants that had been delivered to the garden, and they were waiting in the wings, ready for us to action up and get them into place.

Monsieur LaBour had finished rebuilding the steps, the paving stones were down, the walls finished, and the top soil and fertilisers in place. The irrigation had been virtually installed, just a few finishing touches would be required after everything was dug in. The lighting had been wired in, or at least it had started to be wired in. Unfortunately a bit of a huff had blown up between the Mr Electrician and Mr LaBour. An awful lot of macho manoeuvring had been going on, and the net result was: no more electrician. So the lamps and their positioning would have to wait.

The garden looked clean and tidy and ready to do business with some trees and plants.

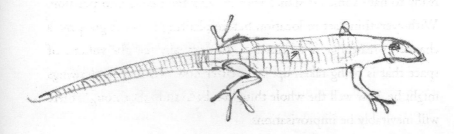

CHAPTER TEN

The Home Run

M arking out for what plant goes where is a slow process and is best done on one's own. I don't like to feel the presence of workmen looking over my shoulder, and if possible I prefer not to have the clients there either. The plant lists and planting plans are pinned to the ground with stones, and probably four sets will be set up all over the garden. Using white sand or marker paint, I trace out the design onto the soil, in scale to the plan and start transferring the whole thing from paper to ground. When I have finished and made adjustments and am satisfied I have done it properly, I am ready to have some assistance with moving the plants into position. With everything set in location before planting starts, it gives me a chance to rearrange if required, and to actually feel the volume of space that is being taken up. No matter how detailed the drawings might be, how well the whole thing has been thought through, there will inevitably be improvisations.

I spent a contented Sunday preparing The Owner's garden for the next day's planting shindig. It coincided with the start of the bonfire season, and having not been allowed to burn anything since

March, bonfires were starting up all over the valley. Plumes of grey smoke curled themselves slowly up into the still atmosphere, and the scent of burning leaves wafted over the countryside A more evocative smell of autumn would be hard to imagine. A large red-and-orange balloon dawned up over the hill tops and hung in the still air like an escaped full stop. By late afternoon I was happy that we were ready to start.

Three days later all the trees, shrubs and plants were dug in. It had been hard work, but with well-prepared soil it went quite quickly. It reminded me of setting up a garden at the Chelsea Flower Show. Everything was all so new, weed and bug free, and slightly theatrical. The Owners' garden, whilst it had always been there as a bit of land, now looked as if a magic wand had been waved over it. It looked a bit coy at its sudden arrival, nobody had really got to know each other yet, or made friends and settled down to make it all work.

I have mixed feelings about the famous flower show in the grounds of the Royal Hospital. It is unquestionably a formidable exhibition on lots of levels. From the people behind the scenes who so beautifully organise the whole production, seamlessly bringing it together year after year, to the people who put up some four acres of tenting with military precision, to the staff who cater and clean, on to the overwhelming dedication and effort of the growers themselves. These are the professionals who cajole, nurture and tenderly raise the stars of the horticultural hotbeds, who carve their names with pride onto the embossed badges of accomplishment, proudly holding gold, silver and silver-gilt medals high above their heads like athletes. Well, they are athletes of a kind. They are the long-distance runners whose attenuated hours of botanical prowess shine for a few moments in front of the bright lights of television cameras and applauding judges. I particularly like the silver gilt for third place. It has a kind, consolatory ring about it, sort of second second, rather than third, and more glamorous than bronze. A metal that patinates but never shines like its posher cousins.

Garden design is very much a support activity, but a popular and important ingredient none-the-less. The designers manage to build the most incredible 'sets' to show off their abilities, their flowery imaginations and, occasionally, talent. Extraordinary little vignettes appear, blossom briefly and are struck off unceremoniously after five days. Wisps of ephemeral fantasy blown in on the wind and carried out in black plastic bags. The down side to the whole spectacular event, apart from the rain that invariably wrings itself out over the grounds during the third week of May, is the hopeless amount of people that pitch up. Despite encouraging a second members' day, selling tickets in advance only, and the impossible mission that is parking, the attendance figures are so high that it denies anybody a comfortable, relaxed day out. Instead you have a scrum of battling old ladies, ill-mannered men, and the moody members of various suburban gardening clubs, all doing battle way outside of the Queensberry rules. The photographs taken on press day, or those happy shots of a Royal being walked round the empty show ground belie the physical nightmare that is the reality. It is bad enough on a sunny day when bus loads of ice-cream-licking amateur gardeners are spewed out onto the lawn banks, but throw in a storm and suddenly the tents become like overstuffed rush-hour tube trains. You shuffle round supposedly in a one-way system that is about as effective as a set of traffic lights in the Sahara, and if you're lucky you get to see a

Le jardin secret

few unnaturally perfect delphiniums, hollyhocks and lupins just because they are so tall. All the time it sort of thinks of itself as the Royal Enclosure at Ascot, when in fact it feels more like the exercise yard at Wormwood Scrubs Prison. Not that I know what the exercise yard at the Scrubs is like, you understand.

Back at the garden I watched as the little metal gate and arch that had been made to seclude the swimming pool from the rest of the garden was fixed into place. You know the thing should fit because you have drawn it carefully, but it is always a relief when it slots into place as intended. Mrs Owner had asked for a 'Kiftsgate' rose to scramble over the arch and along the walls that flanked the tiny entrance. She wanted to swamp it, and encourage a feeling of Frances Hodgson Burnett's *The Secret Garden*.

The pots had been delivered and filled, the *Clematis armandii* was trained to scramble up and into the hedges, little thyme plants had been put into the cracks between the old paving stones, and a few bits of garden *brocante* or snazzy junk, had been integrated into the layout. The furniture was bought second hand and looked all the better for it. Mostly metal frame with new cushions covered in old fabric. The little shed had been requisitioned for the filtration equipment, but it still had enough room for the seats, pool chairs and cushions to be kept in when not needed. It had been painted with a pale green wash, and planted with that delicate pale pink flowering climber, *Solanum jasminoides*, delicate like its sister, but worth trying

On the upper levels, the decision to plant mature shrubs and trees was paying off. The instant-garden philosophy made sense in this relatively small garden that had been stripped right back to its bare frame and rebuilt.

It was a bright clear morning with some cold bits at the corners, as I stood once more on the terrace looking down into the garden. In my hands I had the photographs that I had taken about a year previously, and the difference was formidable. The 'before garden' showed a rundown, over-grown space wherein it was practically impossible to define the shape or size of the plot. A few old roses struggled to find space to show off in, and the weeds were beating each other up like the back-street kids they were. And yet for all that there was something romantic about the place. Perhaps it was the secrets it hid, the hints of what might be unfurled, and the general anticipation of what would be. It had been neglected for a long time, during which a natural army of flora and fauna had crept in. Looking at the 'after' shots you saw an organised and well-laid-out garden that was already beginning to knit together, but it needed time to fully expand into itself, to blow out the corners, and to fill in the cracks. No matter how grown-up the plant stock we had installed might have been, it required a season or two to fully synthesise and settle down. The swimming pool glistened with the reflection of the sky, and the undressing branches of the cherry trees were mirrored in the water. A tranquillity hung on the late October air. All the noises of construction and installation had receded to a distant whisper, a fading memory, soon to be blown away altogether.

I went down the steps to the first level and picked half a dozen quinces before they rotted, and sat down on the edge of the wall to breath it all in. We had done it.

A small corner of the Luberon had been tamed and transformed into a well concealed little garden treasure. But much more than this, it brought together the characteristics of the local Provencal landscape with an abundance of imported ideas and stirred in an unexpected variety of flora. This would not only please the inhabitants of the building, but also send out encouraging signals to the indigenous wildlife. It stood shoulder to shoulder with the newly restored house, bringing, as only a garden can, that extraordinary mixture of homeliness and enchantment.

The Owners arrived a few days later to sign the project off. A maintenance programme was discussed, some trivial points covered, and generally there was a good feeling between us all as we repaired to the house to name the ship.

As I left it felt like the end of an affair. It had been mostly good, a few hiccups, but we hadn't had to go to a counsellor or fight in public. It had been long lasting, and rewarding, but sadly it was over now, and I had to walk and not look back.

A few days later it was Theo's fourth birthday party and I found myself rushing round the maze chasing about twenty happy children in and out of the labyrinth. The walls were now the height of the kids and it was the first time that we had actually seen it working properly. After all the kids had gone home laden with little toys, balloons and full tummies, Theo and I lay in a pile on the grass, exhausted but happy. The early evening dusk gathered around our shoulders, it was the eve of the wintry months and it would soon be Halloween. It is one of the oldest of holidays, with origins going back thousands of years, and the festival has had many influences from many cultures. The Romans, the Celts and the Christians have all contributed.

The Halloween we celebrate today takes bits from each festival; Pomona Days' apples, nuts and harvest, Samhain's black cats, evil spirits and death, with the ghosts, skeletons and skulls from All Saints and All Souls.

Nowadays, in Provence it's a time when absolutely everything closes, stops or grinds to a standstill. There is no shopping, banking or public transport. Even if you wanted to work, it would be pointless, so you might as well join in and buy a ghastly chrysanthemum. You know it's coming when suddenly these huge great pots of forced flowers, in a multitude of garish colours, carpet the pavements. They suddenly appear by the million, everywhere. Seas of funereal blossoms bury every square centimetre of available space, in every market town and village. People clutch them as they stagger home with their provisions for the long weekend, ready to grieve for the dead. They are as symbolic of All Saints as a poppy is of Remembrance Day. It is a melancholy break, and one that causes reflection as well as celebration.

I was just explaining all this to Theo when he interrupted and said, 'Dad?'

'Mmm?'

'You know somethin'? Dad, I've got a *really* good idea.'

'What, something to do with Halloween?'

'If you stop writing on your 'puter, then we can do more playing together.'

'Oh, OK. That really *is* a good idea.'

Plant Lists

Chapter one

lavender	Lavandula	francoise (blue)
	Lavandula	angustifolia edelweiss (white)
santolina	Santolina	chamaecyparissus (grey)
santoliona	Santolina	viridis (green)
salvia	Salvia	uliginosa
	Salvia	chamalaeagna
	Salvia	lavandulifolia
	Salvia	coccinea alba
artemisia	Artemisia	arborescens
	Artimisia	camphorata
	Artimisia	absinthium
	Artimisia	lanata
box	Buxus	sempervirens
teucrium	Teucrium	fruticans
photinia	Photinia	fraseri red robin
dorycnium	Dorycnium	hirsutum 'frejorgues'

Chapter three

iberis	Iberis	sempervirens
alyssum	Alyssum	maritimum
convolvulus	Convolvulus	cneorum

philadelphus	Philadelphus	coronarius minnesota snowflake
ipomea	Ipomea	learii
artimisia	Artimisia	arborescens

Chapter four

osteospermum	Osteospermum	caulescens
florence cypress	Cupressus	sempervirens stricta
anise	Aniseed	
basil	Basilica	
coriander	Coriander	
oregano	Oregon	
marjoram	Marjoram	
box	Buxus	
lavender	Lavandula	
fig	Ficus	carica
buddleia	Buddleia	davidii blue
honeysuckle	Lonicera	japonica
clematis	Clematis	flammula
rhyncospermum	Rhyncospermum	jasminoides
ALSO KNOWN AS	Trachelospermum	jasminoides
lavender	lavandula	angustifolioa nikita

Chapter five

campanula	Campanula	portenschlagiana
olive frangivento	Olea	europaea pyramidalis
elaeagnus	Elaeagnus	ebbingei
florence cypress	Cupressus	sempervirens stricta
aralia	Aralia	sieboldii
OR	Fatsia	jaonica
acacia	Acacia	bon accueil (french)
pinus	Piinus	picea
thuya	Thuya	occidentalis rheyngold

acers	Acer	palmatum dissectum
	Acer	palmatum atropurpureum
azalea	Azalea	japonica
lagerstroemia	Lagerstroemia	indica 'nivea'
chamaerops	Chamaerops	humilis
paulownia	Paulownia	tomentosa
plane tree	Platanus	acerifolia

Chapter six

ceanothus hearstorium	Ceanothus	honsturium
florence cypress	Cupressus	sempervirens stricta

Chapter nine

inoveris	Caryopteris	grand bleu inoveris
rosa ice meillandecor	Rose	white ground cover (french)